WINSTON SALEM CAMPUS

A Call to Greatness

The Story of the Founding of the Progressive National Baptist Convention

A Call to

Greatness

The Story of the Founding of the Progressive
National Baptist Convention

William D. Booth

Foreword by Dr. Bill J. Leonard

Brunswick

Library of Congress Cataloging-in-Publication Data

Booth, William D. (William Douglas), 1944–
    A call to greatness : the story of the founding of the Progressive National Baptist Convention / William D. Booth ; foreword by Bill J. Leonard.
      p. c.m.
    Includes bibliographical references (p.) and index.
    ISBN 1-55618-196-5 (alk. paper)
    1. Progressive National Baptist Convention--History--Sources. 2. Booth, L. Venchael, 1919---Correspondence. 3. Baptists--United States--Clergy--Correspondence. I. Title.

BX6460.9.P77 B66 2001
286'.135--dc21   2001037391

Reprinted (with the exception of preface, foreword, appendices, bibliography, and index) from *American Baptist Quarterly,* Volume XX, March, 2001, with permission of American Baptist Historical Society, Valley Forge, PA 19482.

First Edition
Published in the United States of America
by

Brunswick Publishing Corporation

1386 Lawrenceville Plank Road
Lawrenceville, Virginia 23868
434-848-3865
www.brunswickbooks.com

Dedicated

to

The Rev. Dr. L. Venchael Booth

who as Founder of the Progressive

National Baptist Convention, Inc.

dared courageously

sacrificed greatly

labored faithfully

and

who as my father

loved me unconditionally

encouraged me unstintingly

supported me unfailingly.

May his legacy

ever live

to the glory

of God.

TABLE OF CONTENTS

PREFACE

This preface is written at the request of the author and compiler of this wonderful story of the founding of The Progressive National Baptist Convention, Inc. It will probably prove to be just as controversial as the organization of this great movement turned out to be.

Once the organization was formed and prominent pastors had joined, the fight began on how to obscure and ignore the founder. Some have tried to make the 1962 Convention in Philadelphia the founding session. Still others have tried to highlight certain outstanding leaders as founders.

The founder has traveled a rocky road from the "Call Meeting" forward. As he journeys toward the end, it is possible that the road may get more "rocky." A noted writer asked, "Why is it necessary to clear up the matter of who founded the Convention?"

It is necessary:

> To redeem the soul of the Convention and lift it to the high ground that was intended.
>
> To build the Convention on solid ground—the truth.
>
> To give "God the glory," for rewarding a very costly sacrifice.

The founder is greatly indebted to his son, Dr. William D. Booth, who has recorded this history with integrity and passion. He also acknowledges his indebtedness to a host of saints who still travel with us and especially those who have gone before us and await our coming.

It is our prayer that no one will be hurt or insulted for our keeping a faithful record, nor for our passing it on to oncoming generations.

May our Convention prosper and continue to do a great work in Kingdom building.

L. VENCHAEL BOOTH
May 2001

FOREWORD

"Baptists multiply by dividing," we sometimes say in an ironic attempt to explain why there are so many divisions among Baptist churches, denominations and individuals. Truth is, Baptists began that way. The Baptist movement began in Amsterdam in 1609 when a group of Puritan Separatists, exiled from their native England, constituted a church on the basis of their common faith in Christ, followed by "believer's baptism." John Smyth, a leader of the little band, baptized himself by trine affusion, pouring water on his head three times in the name of the Father, the Son and the Holy Spirit. He then baptized the group's other leader, Thomas Helwys, and a few others. Shortly thereafter the congregation split over the authority to perform baptism with Smyth and some of the others leaving the new sect and seeking membership with the Mennonites. By the mid-seventeenth century Baptists in England were divided into General (Arminian) Baptist, Particular (Calvinist) Baptist, and Seventh Day Baptist communions. These were but the first of what often seems an unending collection of Baptist groups worldwide, extending across a wide theological, racial and regional spectrum.

In fact, Baptist polity seems to make division not simply possible, but probable. Consider the characteristics of Baptist identity. They affirm the centrality of Scripture while acknowledging the importance of conscience, individual and communal in interpreting Scripture aright. They promote the autonomy of the local congregation while forming associational and denominational alliances freely. They assert the priesthood of the laity while ordaining and investing ministers with significant authority for the work of the congregation. They stress the pervasive power of the Holy Spirit while providing for a congregational polity that determines the will of the Spirit by majority vote. They promote confessions of faith as guides to doctrine, while often insisting that individuals may accept or reject such extra-biblical documents as conscience may dictate.

All Baptist groups illustrate and experience the tensions inherent in Baptist polity, theology, and practice. This volume illustrates that African American Baptists are no exception. Indeed, their own "roots" are anchored to splits in the fabric of American and Baptist life. African American Baptists trace many their roots to the slave culture of American society in general and Southern society in particular. Slaves were brought to the camp meetings and revival services of eighteenth and nineteenth century American religious life, experience conversion amid the harshness and depravity of the South's "Peculiar Institution." Many of these converts were admitted to membership in Baptist churches, worshiping in the "galleries" of churches with, but not alongside, white members. Many of the early slave preachers such as Nat Turner, were nurtured in the Baptist community, but heard a different drummer calling them to address the enslavement of a people. The Triennial Convention (1814), one of the earliest missionary organizations founded by Baptists in North America, divided in 1845 over the appointment of a known slaveholder to missionary service. When Northerners refused to approve such an arrangement, rejecting any action that would imply "approbation" of human slavery, white Southerners broke away to found the Southern Baptist Convention.

African Americans also founded their own churches. The Silver Bluff Baptist Church in South Carolina was probably (there is some debate here) the first African American Baptist church in the South, founded in the late eighteenth century. Black churches appeared throughout the North, and, after emancipation, and in response to their second class status in white churches, blacks moved to establish their own congregations and, soon after, there own denominations. Our family worships at First Baptist Church, Highland Avenue in Winston-Salem, North Carolina. It is a predominately African American church founded in the 1880s when blacks left First Baptist Church on Fifth Street to found their own congregation. Thus, Winston-Salem, like many North Carolina towns, has two first Baptist churches, divisions that reflect racial and congregational differences to this day.

Associational and denominational connections among African American Baptists were often born of missionary concerns and efforts to provide funding for persons such as George Liele, Lott Carey and other blacks sent to Africa or the Caribbean to evangelize and establish churches. Missionary societies and boards many founded or funded by black women were the foundation of denominational organizations. Almost immediately these organizations divided over strategy, leadership or other differences. African American denominationalism took many forms and experienced many schisms. In the early 1900s the National Baptist Convention, a major organ of black Baptist life, divided into two denominations, largely due to divisions over control of the denomination's publishing house. This schism produced two new denominations, the National Baptist Convention, Incorporated, and the National Baptist Convention, Unincorporated.

This volume, *A Call to Greatness: The Story of the Founding of the Progressive National Baptist Convention*, details yet another schism among African American Baptists. This controversy, born of divisions in the National Baptist Convention, Incorporated, produced a new denomination known as the Progressive National Baptist Convention. This book is important for several reasons. First, it provides a survey of the divisions that produced the Progressive National Baptist Convention, a significant denominational configuration among African American Baptists. Second, it illustrates again that Baptist polity is geared toward a tradition in which "peoples' movements" may arise to challenge existing authority and organization at any time. The divisions evident in this volume are not unique to this particular group of Baptists; indeed, they are present in some form in most Baptist churches and denominations. Third, Booth's account illustrates that the 1960s were a turbulent time for African American Baptists in both the society and in their own churches. Amid the terrible upheavals that resulted from the civil rights struggles, amid the courage and valor of African American Baptist leaders, there was also another battle occurring, the struggle for the mind and heart of a particular Baptist denomination. Fourth, Reverend Booth's approach to and understanding of the controversy is itself potentially controversial since he presents materials that reexamine the earliest leadership of the new denomination, affirming the work of his own father, the Reverend L. Venchael Booth, in shaping the Progressive National Baptist Convention. Not everyone will agree with some of his assertions, and that is part of the debate that continues. Finally, this book is a valiant tribute of a son to a father, an acknowledgment that amid the divisions that separate Christian brothers and sisters, amid the pain and brokenness of schism and separation, one truth remains: "the greatest of these is love."

BILL J. LEONARD, Ph.D., Dean and
Professor of Church History
Wake Forest Divinity School
Wake Forest University

Dr. L. Venchael Booth and the Origin of the Progressive National Baptist Convention, Inc.

The Progressive National Baptist Convention, Inc. (PNBC) was founded in 1961.[1] To understand its history is to discover why a cloud of inaccuracies hovers over its origins and to explain why its organization was necessary in the first place.[2] The story of the PNBC is also a story about the National Baptist Convention, U.S.A., Inc. (NBC), the largest African-American denominational body in the United States.[3] As organizations sometimes do, the National Baptist Convention developed an internal battle that would pit men of the cloth against one another. Tenure would emerge as the primary issue and the office of Executive Secretary would be the secondary one.

Concisely stated, efforts under the NBC administration of Rev. D. V. Jemison to establish tenure as a safeguard against the emergence of dynasties would be thwarted under the new leadership of Rev. J. H. Jackson of Chicago, Illinois. The tenure policy, finally adopted in a revised constitution under the presidency of Rev. D. V. Jemison, would be later lifted and rejected under Dr. Jackson and his supporters. Not surprising, two camps developed within the NBC body—those persons who supported Dr. Jackson and his mindset, and those who opposed an administration that sought to remove the organization's revised constitutional provision limiting tenure of the office of president to four consecutive terms.[4] Surprising was the chaos, guile, and heavy handedness that would surface in an organization of Baptist ministers.

Not everyone was taken by surprise regarding the direction of the NBC. Sensing the implications of the ill winds of change even before Dr. Jackson successfully assumed the mantle of the presidency from Dr. Jemison in 1953, Rev. L. V. Booth, one of the NBC's younger members, forwarded the following letter to Dr. Jemison in the late spring of that year.

> Dear President Jemison:
>
> This is an individual and personal appeal from one of the younger members of the National Baptist Convention, Inc., addressed to you, our worthy leader and retiring president for your prayerful consideration.
>
> Will you consider setting a *Day of Prayer* for the guidance of Almighty God in the selection of your successor? It has occurred to me that amid all the campaigning and collective bargaining for the presidency (some of which has been going on for a number of years) a sober thought should be injected into this campaign. Perhaps we should make an appeal to God for guidance as we assemble in Miami. Permit me to set forth my suggestion:
>
> Whereas the presidency of the National Baptist Convention represents one of the most powerful offices within the gist of our race; and whereas the wisest choice is necessary for the continued unity and advancement of our people; and whereas the clergy is indebted to the laity to set forth a good example; Be it therefore resolved that the Fifth Sunday in August (August 30, 1953) be designated by the President and his Executive Board as National Prayer Day in our member churches that prayer be offered for guidance and the execution of God's will to the end that our choice will bring unity, peace and

brotherhood. Our theme for this Day should be: "Let God Lead in Miami."

1. It should be recommended therefore, that all commitments, pledges and collective bargaining[s] be set aside and the guidance of God sought by everyone. (We should all concede that the man God wants [might] not even be running.)

2. It should be recommended that candidates for this high office refrain from further campaigning after a National Day of Prayer is agreed upon.

3. It should be recommended that present hurts and animosities created be forgiven and a pledge of non-vengeance be made by all announced candidates. It might be helpful if every pastor is asked to read Psalm I, in the Old Testament and the entire Epistle of Jude in the New Testament and lead his congregation in prayer in both the morning and evening worship.

Kindly consider this proposal Mr. President, and if it strikes you as having merit, present it to the Board in Brooklyn. There need not be any mention of my name.

Yours in His Service.

L. Venchael Booth

Dr. Jemison responded to Rev. Booth with very candid observations.

June 16, 1953

My Dear Dr. Booth:

I think that your letter of recent date is indeed a good one, and I do wish that this plan of operation could be put into effect, as it relates to the election of officers in the coming session of the National Baptist Convention.

Brother Booth, I have discovered when people want to

make a big display and have a big fuss, that it will take God himself to pave the way for peace. I have prayed and am continuing to pray for a peaceful meeting in Miami, but regardless of what procedure we would take, we would not be able to succeed in getting all of the men to consider prayer first.

I know that the wrong method is being used, and that much trickery and campaigning is being done, but what can we do?

My only suggestion is that Christians like you will consecrate ourselves in asking God to bring peace out of confusion. I don't know, but I have a feeling that the Lord is going to come into this election, I don't know how at this time, but I have a deep feeling within, that things will not be as bad at Miami as they seem at this time.

Join me in Prayer for the contents of your letter to become a reality, and please be assured that I appreciate every word that you said, because I feel that they were words from a consecrated heart.

May God bless you and your dear family is my prayer.

Very truly yours,

D.V. Jemison, President
National Baptist Convention, U.S.A., Inc.

Dr. Jackson's successful bid for leadership came after a grueling, and hotly contested campaign in Miami, Florida, in 1953. With the resignation of D. V. Jemison there had been no dearth of aspirants for the prize of the presidency. After the elimination of Marshall Shephard, Sandy F. Ray, H. B. Hawkins, and of J. Raymond Henderson, the two left standing to oppose each other were the vice-president-at-large, Reverend Dr. E. W. Perry, and the second vice-president, Dr. J. H. Jackson. The balloting and voting concluded in the wee hours of the morning at 3:30 a.m. with Dr. Joseph Harrison Jackson emerging as the thirtheenth president.

The debate over tenure gave Rev. Jackson and his supporters yet another opportunity to become victorious, even if it meant undermining the integrity of the organization's mandate as represented by its revised constitution. Victory, however, came at a high price to the reputation and solvency of the organization itself. A fifth term for Rev. Jackson (as opposed to the legislated four terms) was the election that broke the NBC's back. Several of those dissatisfied with Rev. Jackson's brand of leadership would become the nucleus for the "Taylor Team" and the Progressive National Baptist Convention.[5] On the other hand, records show that the split within the NBC had already preceded Rev. Jackson's election to a fifth term. Dr. J. Pius Barbour, said in an interview with the author, that "the real split of the convention was at Louisville in 1957."[6] Significantly, Dr. Barbour also recalled at that time that the Rev. L. Venchael Booth had contended that, "the only thing to do is to organize another convention."[7]

The Seeds Of Dissent

In 1959, an underground movement began with "a few like-minded" men who were concerned about the integrity of the NBC as well as its failure to embrace a position strongly advocating the Civil Rights Movement, particularly with reference to the leadership of the Reverend Dr. Martin Luther King, Jr. A letter[8] under the signature of Rev. Cornell E. Talley circulated among the small group regarding a consultation. Rev. L. Venchael Booth[9] was identified by Talley as the host responsible for the arrangements and accommodations for the meeting to be held at his church, the historic Zion Baptist Church of Cincinnati, Ohio.[10] Needing a personality of sterling leadership, stewardship, and integrity, the "underground movement" laid a foundation for the change resulting in *A Call for Leadership* from 293 NBC ministers to Dr. Gardner C. Taylor in June 1, 1960. When he answered the call affirmatively, the "Taylor Team" was ready to start planning for action.

The disenchanted group made an excellent choice in electing to support the Reverend Dr. Gardner C. Taylor for the presidency of the NBC against Rev. Jackson. First, Taylor, the son of a former NBC vice-president, was a man of integrity with impeccable national and international credentials. As the author stated in *The Progressive Story*:

> On the international scene, in the Baptist World, his stature as a pulpiteer was peerless. On three occasions he preached before the Baptist World Alliance, Copenhagen, Denmark, 1947; Cleveland Ohio, 1950; and London, England, 1955. During the summer of 1959, he spent six weeks as guest preacher for the Baptists of Australia. He was the first Negro guest preacher on NBC's National Radio Pulpit.[11]

Second, Dr. Taylor was a champion for the weak and the oppressed. As one who had fought for integration of the public schools, he would be in a natural habitat in a continued struggle for the freedom of his people. Third, Dr. Gardner C. Taylor was already dissatisfied with the leadership of Dr. Jackson. And fourth, he had the recognition and attraction that would garner support from others in the convention seeking growth and viability.

The fallout of the so-called election in Philadelphia in 1960 sent shock waves through the Baptist world and beyond. The session ended with both ministers claiming to be president.[12] Looking chaos in the eye, Taylor agreed to step aside and let the convention members recast their votes; Jackson would not. The matter was fought out in the courts, though the presiding judge felt that the two contending groups, not the courts, should resolve the problem. But it was not to be. A court prescribed voting process at the Kansas City, Missouri session in 1961, suspiciously favoring the Jackson forces,[13] resulted in Dr. Jackson emerging as victor for his third four-year term as president of the NBC. Not only had he vanquished the ascendancy of the "Taylor Team," but it was also alleged that Jackson had cast aspersions upon the name of Dr. Martin Luther King, Jr. whom he ousted from the office of Vice-President of the Sunday School and Baptist Training Union Congress along with Dr. Martin Luther King,

Sr., Dr. D. E. King, Dr. Marshall L. Shepard, and Dr. C. C. Adams to name the more prominent ones.[14]

Responding to a press release that purportedly could be traced to Rev. Jackson for its accusations, Dr. King sent the following telegram to Dr. Jackson:

> I am deeply distressed about the statement, which appeared in headline coverage in several leading newspapers across the country in which you are quoted as saying that I masterminded an invasion of the National Baptist Convention, which resulted in the death of Rev. Mr. Wright.[15] In substance, the statement accuses me of giving impetus to a conspiracy, which had as its goal a homicide. Such an unwarranted, untrue and unethical statement is libelous to the core and can do irreparable harm to the freedom movement in which I am involved.[16]

Dr. King did not sue. Reticent to undermine his moral integrity, King said, "as it stands I am not now inclined to sue. My non-violent philosophy causes me to temporarily hold at this point."[17]

In contrast to Dr. King who was denied his post by Jacksonian maneuvering, Dr. Taylor was denied the post he sought by the Jacksonian machine. Accepting his defeat, Taylor chose to remain within the NBC. In Taylor's words, "The supreme court of the National Baptist Convention has spoken...Let us all close our ranks behind the leadership of Dr. Jackson. I will fall in behind Dr. Jackson."[18] The Associated Press reported its version of Taylor's armistice with Jackson this way: "He [J. H. Jackson] immediately received a pledge of support from his opponent, Dr. Gardner C. Taylor of Brooklyn."[19] Not only did Taylor support Jackson, but an interview with Alfredo Graham of The Pittsburgh Courier also quoted Taylor as saying that he "was completely satisfied with the results of the last election."[20] Furthermore, Dr. Taylor went on record as saying, "I have no personal following now that the election is over and I am not the leader of any 'opposition party' within the ranks of the convention."[21] Subsequently, articles published following the election also portrayed Taylor as one rallying to unite the NBC and opposing any ideas about splitting the ranks.

Dr. Taylor's acquiescence as well as that of the "Taylor Team" did not include Rev. L. Venchael Booth. He wrote about the Kansas City proceedings in an article entitled "*A High Call to Greatness*," making clear his position about a schism. He reflected upon why men would forsake their principles and remain silent. Booth questioned the position of maintaining unity in the NBC at any cost.

It was not that L. Venchael Booth had an aversion to reconciliation or relished separation for the sake of it. However, Booth had been down that road before with the NBC and discovered that it led to a dead-end.[22] The time had simply come " to part"[23] as the writer of Ecclesiastes pragmatically announced.

That publication did more than clarify Booth's stand; it also foreshadowed his willingness to lead in the absence of those who would not. The closing paragraph reads:

> The record should be set straight about who is splitting the Convention. We who separate at this time are not. We are simply trying to make the most of a tragic condition. The leader who creates disunity, expels members, throws out officers and banishes opponents is the real Convention splitter. We who separate are simply trying to salvage the dignity of a lifetime struggle, preserve the contributions of our Fathers and bequeath to our children the best of our heritage. Our separation is for the purpose of restoring men to a sense of responsibility, spirituality, and service. Ours is a high call to greatness.[24]

Some of the qualities and events that catapulted Dr. Gardner Taylor into the NBC limelight are the same ones contributing to misinformation about the actual founder of the Progressive National Baptist Convention. Because Gardner Taylor ran against Jackson, the uninformed mistakenly concluded that it was his action that led to the formation of the PNBC. Edward Gilbreath in an otherwise superb article in *Christianity Today* erred in attributing the PNBC's formation to Taylor and to King as well. Says Gilbreath:

> During that chaotic time 35 years ago, Taylor, King, and other ministers were involved in a controversial split from the National Baptist Convention, U.S.A. (NBC, currently the largest black denomination in the U.S.) after a fierce debate over King's civil-rights agenda.... *As a result, Taylor and others went on to form the Progressive National Baptist Convention* [italics mine] which today has a membership of 2.5 million."[25]

Taylor Branch in the second volume of his monumental work on the era of Dr. King, *Pillar and Fire: America in the King Years of 1963-1965*, missed the mark by leaving his readers in the position of drawing an incorrect implication from one of his inferences regarding Taylor's role in the split. Unlike Gilbreath, Taylor Branch's statement is not as direct. The error hinges on the interpretation of the phrase "a major schism." Branch asserts that, "In what amounted to a major schism, some two thousand pastors including Rev. Gardner C. Taylor and Benjamin Mays, president of Morehouse College, resigned with King...."[26]

Taylor Branch's phrase "a major schism" could be inferred to be a veiled reference to the split of PNBC from the NBC, given the fact that no other major schism within the NBC occurred during this time period. This being the case, Branch could potentially be used as a source to credit Taylor and others with the birthing of the PNBC.

Countering both Gilbreath's and Branch's assertions about Taylor's leadership in the formation of the PNBC was Lewis V. Baldwin, another biographer of King. Baldwin characterized the response to King's excommunication by Taylor in an entirely different way. Only thirty Black Baptist preachers—Ralph D. Abernathy, William Holmes Borders, Benjamin E. Mays, Sandy Ray, Fred L. Shuttlesworth, Kelly Miller Smith, and Gardner Taylor to name a few—denounced Jackson's actions as "vicious and un-Christian."[27] Baldwin made no mention of a major schism or of two thousand pastors tendering mass resignations from the NBC along with King, Taylor, and Mays.

The stinging news release issued by the thirty Black Baptists against Jackson (resulting from Jackson's ousting of Dr. King and his unleashing scurrilous innuendoes against King) on September 12, 1961, while constituting a rift with Dr. Jackson, did not even remotely lead to the formation of a new convention.[28] In spite of that rift whose wounds had not yet healed, Gardner C. Taylor was reported in the September 28, 1961 issue of *JET*, little more than two weeks later, to have become resigned to his defeat at Jackson's hands. In fact, Taylor became the drum major for unity within the NBC, though perhaps reluctant in doing so.

Later Dr. Taylor disavowed any connection with the new movement that was to become the Progressive National Baptist Convention. An article entitled "New Split Threatens Baptists; Jackson Denies Rapping Dr. King," appearing in the September 28, 1961 issue of *JET* spells out in no uncertain terms Taylor's stance. "The defeated Rev. Gardner C. Taylor," the article noted, "declared he would not condone such a split."[29] Moreover, in another interview, Trezzvant W. Anderson of *The Courier* reported that, "...Dr. Gardner C. Taylor of Brooklyn, N.Y., defeated presidential candidate of the Jackson opponents does not want the split."[30]

An even more telling testament to Taylor's position on the new movement came from a close personal friend and mentor,[31] Dr. J. A. Bacoats, President of Benedict College, Columbia, SC. Bacoats echoed Taylor's opposition to a split in a letter to the editor of the *Journal and Guide*. In making his own case for unity, Bacoats passionately pointed out that Taylor was absent from the leadership team of those advocating the formation of a new Baptist body and implied others should do likewise. Bacoats wrote apparently without fear of contradiction that "Dr. Gardner Taylor has already announced his withdrawal from any leadership or participation with forces that would divide. Often the defeated aspirant for an office becomes the leader of divisive forces."[32]

In a scholarly article appearing in the *Review and Expositor*, Dr. Edward Wheeler, writing a decade after the PNBC took its fledgling steps as a denominational body, concurred that Taylor had distanced himself and the "Taylor Team" from the new movement, while Booth had distanced himself from the "Taylor Team". "Both took care," Wheeler concluded, "to separate this call from the defunct 'Taylor Movement.' ...Neither Taylor nor the Reverend M. L. King, Jr., favored Booth's suggestion; both again called for unity."[33]

The venerable repository of the Black religious experience, C. Eric Lincoln, along with Lawrence H. Mamiya echoed in their findings the call of Taylor and King for unity. In their work, *The Black Church in the African American Experience*, praised by Dr. Peter J. Paris as standing alone in breadth and depth of analysis, Lincoln and Mamiya observed "Taylor...and King both called for unity."[34]

Another inescapable fact is that the *Minutes of the First Annual Meeting of the PNBC, Inc.* revealed that Taylor was not in attendance at any of the formative meetings in Cincinnati, Ohio, or in Chicago, Illinois, or in Richmond, Virginia. Absence from these meetings renders bankrupt any inference rooted in any data of history that Taylor was or could have been the Convention's founder.

What was not well known at the time was that Booth repeatedly made overtures to Taylor to join hands with the Progressives. In a letter dated November 21, 1961 from Booth to Taylor, Booth quotes Taylor as saying that he would be "coming to help us...in due course."[35] Though admitting that Taylor's presence would give momentum to the movement it otherwise would not have, Booth went on to say that he would forge ahead without Taylor. It may beg the question but it must be asked, does a founder require an invitation to the organization he had birthed?

Correspondence dated that same day from Mrs. Uvee Mdodana-Arbouin, President of the Corona Council of Church Women, an avid supporter of Booth's efforts, who later became President of the Women's Department of the PNBC, gave a rare inside view of why many of Taylor supporters, and perhaps even Taylor himself, were hesitant about getting on board. She noted (as reported to her by Dr. A. Ross Brent who was in attendance at the meeting) that while the new Ministers

Conference formed in New York following the Philadelphia convention gave a "thunderous applause" with the report of the formation of the United Baptist Convention of America, Inc., (The name would later be changed.), "there are not many souls who will greatly dare."[36]

Dr. Marvin T. Robinson, pastor of the Friendship Baptist Church of Pasadena, California, shared Dr. Arbouin's assessment. Though later to become the spokesperson at the Cincinnati Call Meeting against the formation of a new convention, Robinson, having failed in his summons for a top strategy meeting shared with L. V. Booth that he knew "how vacillation and how pastors will leave you holding the bag until it looks like victory and they pop out of no where...I don't plan to get out on a limb, as I can do nothing."[37]

Dr. A. Ross Brent, pastor of The Shiloh Baptist Church of Plainfield, New Jersey, offered another reason for the nonsupport of Booth and the new convention effort by those in the East:

> Many of the men here in the east who are in favor of the New Convention do not quite understand your avowed detachment from the (Taylor Team). Do we not need their strength? We will talk it over upon my arrival."[38]

It would not be until the first annual session in Philadelphia in 1962 that Taylor would step on to the Progressive stage. Warmly received with a standing ovation, Taylor "remarked that he saw many of his friends and had come to support Dr. Chambers and the Convention. He characterized the Progressive Baptist Convention as a 'rising sun'."[39]

Later in the PNBC's second annual session in Detroit, Michigan, Taylor emerged in the leadership cadre of the new movement he had formerly rejected. That emergence would be aided and abetted by Booth's invitation to Taylor to attend the session,[40] the relinquishing of his claim to the post of Vice-President-at-large in favor of Taylor, and the assuming of the newly created position of Executive Secretary. The Convention's reaction to Booth's magnanimous gesture, so rare in national Baptist circles, was succinctly recorded in its Minutes.

> There was great rejoicing at the manner the election was carried out. Rev. I. B. Lavinge moved and many brethren seconded the motion that a standing ovation be given to Rev. L. V. Booth for his big heartedness.[41]

In a handwritten note on hotel stationery later that day, Taylor expressed his gratitude and acknowledged that Booth was "the seer of a new convention."[42] Once back in New York, Taylor wrote again offering plaudits and his post-convention assessment of Booth's decision to step aside for him and to become Executive Secretary. "You were magnificent," Taylor wrote of Booth, "and I think in the long run you will find that you can do a more lasting job in your new post."[43]

Now in the groundbreaking, but lesser role as Executive Secretary, Booth seized the opportunity to serve the convention. His labors did not go unnoticed. Early on he elicited Taylor's praise. In correspondence shortly after the Detroit meeting, Taylor in a handwritten postscript commented that he was "confused at the speed with which you [Booth] got this to [him] and which led [him] to wonder if this is The Detroit... or Philadelphia...."[44] At another time Taylor referred to the synergistic effect their communications with each other had writing, "I think you and I must be communicating strength, one to the other, since I felt a surge of confidence after our meeting."[45] Still later he wrote of Booth, "You have a genius for organized, sustained promotion."[46] Added to these previous encomiums was Taylor's reference to having shared his assessment of Booth's work with others in this excerpt:

> Thank you for keeping me abreast of things. I am elated at the vigorous and enlightened way you are pressing the cause of Progressive Baptists at the World's Fair and generally among American Baptists and the National Council. I was commenting to Earl Harrison and others in Washington of what inspired service you are rendering to all of us.[47]

Taylor would later use the public forum of the presidential addresses to underscore the pivotal place Booth occupied in

PNBC history. These key excerpts from Taylor's addresses in Memphis in 1966 and in Cincinnati in 1967 respectively make the point.

> God willed this Convention to be! Some of us scorned the idea, but God willed it to be. It fell my lot to be the test of whether in a time of ferment, new wine could be put in old wineskins. To change the figure, it fell the lot of L. V. Booth to trumpet the call for a New Order and a New Instrument, the Progressive National Baptist Convention.[48]

> L.V. Booth envisioned a new mandate of Heaven, a new instrumentality of the Kingdom of Jesus Christ. All honor and credit are due [him]...for his vision and courage in the face of overwhelming odds for issuing a call to a heartsick, rejected remnant of God's true Israel who were deprived of a true denominational home in which their worthiest Baptist instincts of freedom could be exercised and honored.[49]

The comment from Memphis is singularly significant since Taylor, himself, defined his role as the one who sought to pour new wine into old wineskins—a change-agent within the existing structure of the NBC while implying that Booth's role was to pour new wine into new wineskins—a change-agent outside the existing structure of the NBC. While Taylor's laudatory comments fell short of calling Booth the founder, they eloquently and powerfully described Booth's unique and primal place in the formation of the PNBC as well as Booth's willingness to honor the cause-centered rather than personality-centered principle that he had espoused.

Sadly, Booth's self-sacrifice would not be enough for those in the PNBC ranks who wanted to write him out of the Progressive Story. Later, pressures would be placed upon him to choose between becoming a full-time Executive Secretary and leaving the pastorate of Zion in Cincinnati. Booth tendered his resignation to the convention. In 1970 the PNBC Annual Session, meeting in Kansas City nearly ten years after the NBC debacle in the same city, held a new challenge for L. Venchael Booth. This time the convention he had founded rejected, through its Nominating Committee, placing his name on the slate of proposed convention officers as 1st Vice-President. Left with no choice, Booth pressed his candidacy from the floor of the convention—none has successfully done it since—and came out victorious to the chagrin of those who wanted to archive his memory prematurely.

The elected president, Dr. Earl L. Harrison, known for his reserve, uncharacteristically expressed his elation in a hand-written letter to Booth. "I was overwhelmingly pleased," Harrison wrote, "at your complete and unquestionable victory in the race for Vice President in K. C. [Kansas City, Missouri] last week."[50]

The tracks of history have led us inevitably to conclude that Gardner C. Taylor embraced J. H. Jackson's leadership following the Kansas City defeat. That Taylor advocated unity within the NBC, that Taylor disavowed the new movement that would become the PNBC, and that Taylor acknowledged Booth's primal role in the PNBC's formation, rules out the ascription of founder of the PNBC to Taylor.

Other Theories of PNBC Origins

Another assertion about the PNBC's origin evolves around the "Taylor Team." The *Encyclopedia of African American Religions* gives credence to this mistaken notion that the convention formation was an outgrowth of the "Taylor Team." "On September 11, 1961, a national news release was issued which made concrete the determination of the Taylor Team to change the direction of African American Baptist denominational leadership to reflect the contemporary needs of the age,"[51] according to this resource. The phrase "made concrete the determination of the Taylor Team" clearly implied that the News Release issued on September 11, 1961, calling for the formation of a new national convention was a "Taylor Team" initiative when in fact the release represented solely the initiative of Booth.

With less subtlety, but just as inaccurately, David J. Garrow in his book entitled, *Bearing the Cross: Martin Luther King, Jr., and the Southern Christian Leadership Conference*, wrote, "...Taylor's supporters split from the Jackson group and set up their own organization, the Progressive National Baptist Convention."[52]

In a position paper, "Progressive National Baptist Convention: The Roots of the Black Church," appearing in the September 2000 *American Baptist Quarterly*, Dr. Wallace C. Smith committed a similar error in his inference that, "The defeat of Gardner Taylor and the reprisals meted out against Martin Luther King, Jr., and other Taylor supporters led a group of pastors to determine that it was time for complete severance from the National Convention...."[53]

None of the above interpreters of PNBC history provided any objective substantiation from extant sources to verify their conclusions. Thus, while their opinions are worthy of being considered, unless corroborating data are forthcoming, they must be viewed as unsupported subjective analysis.

A survey of the names of the 23 registered delegates gathered in Cincinnati, November 14-16, 1961 (the names of the other ten messengers, who did not register but participated in the deliberations, were not available) revealed that only L.V. Booth was among the "Taylor Team" supporters.[54] Even so, Booth was not a major player on the "Taylor Team." According to C. Eric Lincoln and Lawrence H. Mamiya, "The Taylor Team" as it was called, included Martin Luther King, Sr., Martin Luther King, Jr.,[55] Ralph David Abernathy, Benjamin Mays, and a number of other clergy committed to King's social change strategies which Jackson condemned as inadvisable and injurious to the cause of racial advance and harmony."[56]

Moreover, Booth took pains to establish the new movement's independence from the "Taylor Team." Those gathered never referred to themselves as the "Taylor Team." Little if any documentation is cited or summoned to support the assertion that the "Taylor Team"—defeated, disbanded, and defunct—had sufficient strength to launch the PNBC. In point of fact, the

September 11, 1961 news release unequivocally separated the summons for a new convention from the "Taylor Team." The announcement could not have been any clearer—this new instrumentality of the Kingdom among Black Baptists was separate from and disassociated with the "Taylor Team." Here is how Booth penned it:

> This movement is in no way connected with the past effort of 'The Taylor Team.' No officer of the former movement is either directly or indirectly involved. It is an entirely new movement under new leadership.[57]

Thus, not only was the "Taylor Team" not the author of the news release, but it was completely and unequivocally disavowed as the "former movement" and one with which the new movement under new leadership had nothing to do.

There is a haunting absence from the periodicals before and after this news release of any rebuttal to the contrary. Admittedly, Murphy, Melton, and Ward do indicate that "Rev. LeVaughn [Lavaughn] Booth" issued "the official call to organize a new convention."[58] However, that admission treats Booth's pioneering mission as if he was a tool of the "Taylor Team." In short, Booth is relegated by such revisionists to the backstage in the drama of the emergence of PNBC. Inaccurately, "the Taylor Team" is given center stage in spite of the historical data's demand that the reverse be the case.

PNBC records belie the verdict that the "Taylor Team" was the progenitor of the PNBC. Mortally wounded, painfully humiliated, and soundly defeated, albeit by the nefarious tactics of the Jackson forces, the Taylor Team with banners tattered, standards shattered, and the ranks depleted, retreated from the field of battle. Its captain, Dr. Taylor, acknowledged defeat and affected the surrender. This alone could explain the absence of any summons thereafter to fight on. Rather, the plea given was tantamount to asking battle weary soldiers to fold their tents and to follow in the footsteps of the vanquishing foe.

That's how Booth heard it. He said so in issuing "A High Call to Greatness!"

> Why do men begin crusades without any alternatives
> other than surrender? Are we so poverty stricken in
> wisdom that we are bound to the weak walls of tradition?
> Is our mental telescope so short that we cannot see beyond
> the bridge? Is it really true that we have only one leader
> today who is certain about something and really going
> somewhere? Are we over-run by philosophers who cannot
> bear a rugged cross?
>
> Is it true that we comprise a group that issued a call when
> there was no battle? Challenged the innocent when there
> was no war? Championed freedom while committed to
> slavery? What is the great crime of coming apart from
> those who defile us? Or what is the crime of separating
> from those who deny us our freedom? Or parting from
> those who would crush our initiative? What is the crime?
> Shall we have unity at any cost?[59]

To contend that the "Taylor Team" officially or unofficially
had the stomach to wage another battle for freedom from the
inside or outside of the National Baptist Convention is foolhardy
and absurd.

In disarray, the "Taylor Team" watched and waited on the
sidelines to see if Booth's movement would capture the
imagination of the Nation. None of the "Taylor Team" was
anxious to exacerbate the national shame already experienced
in the wake of Jackson's victory.

The progressive ship of state set sail and began successfully
navigating the uncharted seas for freedom among national
Baptists. Out of favor forever with the Jackson supporters, the
Taylor Team sought a safe haven among progressive Baptists.
The depth of the fissure in the NBC fellowship between Taylor
and Jackson forces was made painful clear in correspondence
written shortly after Kansas City by Dr. C. T. Murray, pastor of
the Vermont Avenue Baptist Church in Washington, D. C., to
Booth suggesting just how deep the rift had become.

> Many of the churches are divided on the issues. When
> ministers are invited for special occasions, a question is

asked in some of the churches, "Is he a Taylor team man
of a Jack man?"[60]

The PNBC afforded the dispirited members of the Taylor Team
the chance to achieve what wasn't achievable within the NBC—
the opportunity to exercise leadership gifts and the opportunity
to marshal Black Baptist behind the Civil Rights Movement.
Consequently, their first order of business was the crowning of
their fallen prince, Dr. Taylor. Detroit was the place they seized
the moment to position Taylor for his ascendancy to the
presidency of the PNBC. Something like that could never have
happened within the NBC under the Jackson regime.

Credit is due the Taylor Team, who by their defeat, made
obvious to the doubters that there was a crucial need for new
instrumentality among Black Baptists like the PNBC. However,
the Taylor Team did not shoulder the burden to usher into being
the PNBC. Yes, the Taylor Team bore the marks of their
engagement with the Jackson forces, but the bearer of the marks
for the emergence of the PNBC was principally one man, L.
Venchael Booth.

Another factual error put forth regarding the origin of the
Progressive National Baptist Convention is that Dr. Martin Luther
King, Jr. was the prime mover or that the Civil Rights Movement
spawned the PNBC. At the outset it must be affirmed that there
is nothing on record indicating that Dr. King claimed any role
in the formation or leadership of the PNBC. On the occasions
when he spoke before the PNBC, he simply referred to himself
as a member[61] and nothing more.

William Robert Miller penned a biography of Dr. M. L. King,
Jr. in 1968. Miller incorrectly identified the organizational date
of the PNBC as January 1962 instead of November 1961. Then,
he made the factual error of concluding that after the
unsuccessful attempts to unseat Dr. J. H. Jackson, NBC president
in 1960 and 1961, the "strong backing by Martin Luther King"[62]
led to the formation of Progressive Baptists.

Anne Devereaux Jordan and J. M. Stifle in a volume entitled,
The Baptists, committed the same faux pas. In their version,

the PNBC was "founded with the help of Martin Luther King, Jr. as a reform group within the National Baptist Convention in the U.S.A."[63] The *JET* article referred to earlier, however, unequivocally reported that Dr. King was neither a strong backer of nor a facilitator in the founding of the PNBC, but was as adamant as Dr. Taylor in refusing to condone the split. Lewis V. Baldwin's astute analysis decisively put to rest any notion that King should be credited with a hand in the PNBC's formation.

> The nature and extent of King's role in the founding of the Progressive National Baptist Convention has been the subject of much debate. William R. Miller claims that King was a founder of this convention. Edward L. Wheeler notes that King, in the interest of black church unity, actually opposed L. Venchael Booth's call for a new convention. David L. Lewis contends that King actively supported the organization. It is more correct to say that King, while siding with the progressives, had no active role in the organization of the Progressive National Baptist Convention. Its founders, for the most part, were his followers.[64]

During the PNBC meeting in Cincinnati in 1967, the last time King would meet with Progressive Baptists, he emphasized, "that he is a member of the Progressive National Baptist Convention. He has come to speak not as a civil rights leader, but as a minister of the gospel."[65]

Without question, Dr. M. L. King, Jr. was the martyred hero of the Progressive National Baptist Convention, but he was not its founder. There is no doubt that the relationship of Dr. King to the Convention was important to King and his movement. Baldwin offered this summary judgment: "King supported that body because it provided him with the strong support base and the reform vehicle he has long struggled to establish among black Baptists."[66]

Tangentially related to the issue of Dr. King's assumed role in starting the PNBC was the matter of whether or not civil rights provided the impetus for the Convention's formation. Gilbreath again posits this factual blunder in his comment that the split was "after a fierce debate over King's civil-rights agenda."[667] In addition, the *Handbook of Denominations* implied that the civil rights issue was as significant as the issue of tenure. Mead and Hill, the collaborators on this volume, frame it this way:

> Two issues loomed quite large. First the absence of term limits for that body's elected president, and, second, the policy of disengagement from the civil rights and other social justice struggles during the revolutionary years following the 1954 Supreme Court decision concerning desegregation of public facilities.[68]

Lippy and Williams are a bit more accurate in their assessment of the role of civil rights noting that the schism was "...in part ...the desire of some church leaders for a more outspoken and progressive black denominational social stance."[69] In another survey, *Baptists Around the World*, Albert W. Wardin, using the *Directory of African-American Religious Bodies* as his main source, contends that the split was precipitated in part by the unwillingness of the NBC's leadership "to give Martin Luther King, Jr. and his defenders full support for their program and tactics in the civil rights struggle."[70] Wallace C. Smith, referred to earlier, is to be included in this number. He argued that the severance from the NBC was triggered by the desire of "Taylor supporters" to form a "new group devoted to a progressive Civil Rights agenda...."[71] While Smith mentions tenure for the presidency and the establishment of the position of General Secretary, he apparently ranks them as being less important than the civil rights agenda since the latter is placed first.

While the PNBC became the household of the civil rights movement among Black Baptists and provided a needed voice on the issue of injustice, this was not the originating impetus for the formation of the PNBC. This assertion is validated by the primary documents of the PNBC's formative meetings and other astute observers. In order to identify the driving motivation for the formation of any organization, an attempt must be made to get into the minds of those who were at ground zero when it was launched. Fortunately, there is no need to resort to any historical hocus-pocus. The availability of the primary documents for scrutiny and review can amply assist the student of history in probing the mind of the founder, L. V. Booth, who still lives and is able to speak in clarion tones about PNBC's genesis, and the thinking of others who pioneered with him. The former and the latter capture and convey with sufficient accuracy the living spirit that set the PNBC sailing on the uncharted sea of denominational existence.

J. Carl Mitchell, the PNBC's first secretary-historian and an attendee of the Call Meeting in Cincinnati in 1961, penned a piece entitled, *The Origin of the Progressive National Baptist Convention.* The salient thoughts from this brief sketch which are pertinent — (1) Mitchell traces the events that created the climate for the PNBC and (2) Mitchell endeavors to describe the founder's impetus for taking such a bold step.

> The Progressive National Baptist Convention is largely an outgrowth over "TENURE" and the office of Executive Secretary in the National Baptist Convention, Inc. The meeting, which culminated in a new organization, was called at Cincinnati, after several meetings had been held by outstanding ministers in the National Baptist Convention, Inc. over a period of years.
>
> The following meetings of the National Baptist Convention, Inc. were destined to widen the breach. In Denver, Colorado, we spent a whole session seeking to prevent the election of officers by vote of state delegations. The following year in 1957, when we convened at Louisville, Ky., a chair throwing session brought great disgrace to our Baptist Family. The two succeeding sessions marked a repeat in Baptist confusion in both Philadelphia, Pa. and Kansas City.
>
> The Reverend L. V. Booth of Zion Baptist Church, Cincinnati, Ohio left the convention at Kansas City, determined to call a meeting and allow the opposition to make a clear choice between tyranny and freedom and confusion and peace. Before many of the messengers had

reached their homes, a letter went out calling for all interested in Peace, Fellowship and Progress to attend a meeting in November.[72]

L. Venchael Booth, the "Architect [who] developed the plans, laid-out the foundation and structured the walls upon which [the PNBC is] building today,"[73] to quote former PNBC President Dr. Ralph Canty made an impassioned plea to the small assembly in Zion's Chapel. Mark the words of a servant of God possessed by a purpose:

Baptists are Confused into a State of Spiritual Paralysis

There are not many Baptist leaders left who are capable of a forthright decision. Defeat, doubt and bewilderment have so beset us that we have lost faith in ourselves. Some of us doubt now our ability to do anything. There are thousands afraid to assemble anywhere if they are called upon to make a clear-cut decision or take a decisive stand. We have become so victimized by our fears until we have surrendered almost completely to dictatorship, mob rule and high-powered politics. If this group here assembled cannot form an organization, elect a set of officers, it is just possible that we are unfit to serve our generation. Some of us have already become worshippers of "bigness." We think that our movement just has to be big to succeed. We think that our movement must rival all other movements and one in particular the one we are all going to be expelled from. We have forgotten the lowly Christ who said: "My kingdom is not of this world," (John 18:36) which set His mission in direct opposition and contrast to the kingdoms of His day. Our Lord also said: "The kingdom is like unto leaven, which a woman took, and hid in three measures of meal, till the whole was leavened." (Mt. 13:33). This description of Christ's kingdom belied bigness, pompousness and dazzling splendor, but it did not deny spiritual power. No one wants to be small anymore and by the same token, no one wants to be real anymore...for Christ's sake. In Christ's day, the

Romans were very big and the Christians were very small, but they changed the course of history.

We Must Not Procrastinate—
We Must Not Delay
Our Lord's Business.

My final word to you is—the call was honest—the call was sincere—the call was humble. We called you here to organize a new Convention. Our purpose has not changed. If you do not organize a new convention, it shall certainly not be the volunteer chairman's fault.

Please Don't Feel the Temptation to Save Me!

If I'm wrong let me perish. If I'm right sustain me! For God's sake do not do anything foolish just to save me. It is my prayerful hope that no one has made the sacrifice to come here just to save me. I'm not worthy of it. If you have come to save a cause, then your trip was worthy. Men must stop hazarding their precious lives on worthless missions. If you came with no greater passion than to save me—then you have come to our city in vain. There is either a cause to be saved or there is nothing to be saved. We either have a valid claim in assembling ourselves together, or we assemble ourselves as just another group of false prophets. We need men today who are certain about something. We need men today who are full of faith and charged with the Holy Spirit. We need men today who are not afraid to act and also who are not afraid of the consequences.

In this meeting your freedom to act as redeemed Baptists will not be denied you. When I'm through speaking, the meeting is yours. You may act by the program outlined, or you may act according to your choice. You are free to feel that I am no more than a sympathetic host. I seek no office. I covet no power. I simply seek to serve my precious Lord with earnestness, humility and faithfulness. I simply seek to serve diligently my age and generation. You are

> my Friends, you are my fellow-sufferers—I wish to bid
> you welcome to do your and my glorious King's business
> in the way that His Holy Spirit orders us to do it.[74]

Later the Convention itself would speak with one voice about its motivations for the schism. Its *Manifesto,* whose preparation was ably guided by Dr. W. H. R. Powell and was adopted by the PNBC in its Philadelphia session in 1962 as a "tangible expression of all persons present," [75] attempted to set the record straight about the PNBC's separation from the NBC. This document echoes in many respects the founder's thought except for the extensive detail to which it goes. It was divided into five sections—initiation, motivation, inspiration, dedication and commendation. In the section entitled "motivation," the Convention indicated that "they owe it to themselves, to their brethren, to the world, to their Savior, to set forth motivations for their action in such a way, that sane men and women can understand their compulsion and history their valor."[76]

Moreover, it was the intent of the *Manifesto* "to set forth humbly and prayerfully for the considerate judgment of mankind in some detail and with all the clarity to them possible, the reasons that have constrained them to form themselves into a new compact."[77] Any would-be-historians failing to give a proper weight to the *Manifesto* as they attempt to sort out what ushered the PNBC into existence would be like historians ignoring the Declaration of Independence in writing about the birth of our nation.

In the ten specific motivational bases for withdrawing from the NBC given in the *Manifesto,*[78] no reference was made to civil rights. This is not to say that civil rights matters were not dear to their hearts, but what it does say is that civil rights was not the heart of the matter.[79] Murphy, Melton, and Ward in commenting on the *Manifesto* also did not uncover any indication of a civil-rights agenda being the spark for igniting the Progressive flame. "The document," the authors contended, "cited the internal disharmony within the National Baptist Convention, U.S.A., Inc. as one rationale for the new convention's existence. It also affirmed that the election of officers of the new convention should be limited by tenure and the true spirit of democracy should prevail throughout the entire denomination."[80]

Other perceptive observers have identified the generative factor in the convention's coming to life as tenure not civil rights. Edward A. Freeman, a contributor on the subject of "Negro Conventions (U.S.A.)" in *Baptist Relations with Other Christians* wrote, "The court then ruled that the matter of tenure was invalid according to the Convention's own constitution. This led to the second split in Kansas City, Missouri, in 1961. Resulting from this separation was the Progressive National Baptist Convention, Inc."[81] Another Baptist resource, authored by H. Leon McBeth, echoed Freeman's assessment. In it, McBeth pointed out that the "question of tenure for officers, especially the President [which had continued] 'popping up',"[82] precipitated the change. Jini Kilgore Ross, authoring a paper as a graduate student on the history of the convention, came away with a similar finding that "The chief issues instigating the split were tenure and democratic governance...."[83]

A belated announcement about the convention's formation appeared in *The Twentieth Century Baptist*, a chronicle of the Baptist World Alliance. In the September 1965, newsletter, Carl W. Tiller reported, "The dispute centered around the issue of tenure in office...." In addition, noted theologian, Dr. J. Deotis Roberts, corroborated the above findings in this terse conclusion: "The Progressive Baptist Convention emerged from the 'Inc. Convention' more recently as a result of a dispute over the tenure of the office of president. (This was the chief area of conflict, but the designation 'progressive' indicates the initial program of the latter group.)"[84] Tenure was the bedrock issue spawning the new convention and that is an unimpeachable verdict of history.

Though the PNBC was not founded because of the Civil Rights Movement it definitely became a friend of the Civil Rights Movement. Dr. Booth was counted among the friends of Dr. Martin Luther King, Jr. and the movement. On his way to Oslo, Norway, to receive the Nobel Peace Prize, Dr. King made a stop in Cincinnati, Ohio, at the Zion Baptist Church, to preach the 122nd Anniversary message. In his introductory remarks, he had this to say about L. Venchael Booth:

> I certainly want to express my deep personal appreciation to your distinguished minister for his support. He has been one of those real consistent friends to me personally and to the cause for which I represent. And I can never think of a time when I have called on Venchael Booth to do anything for the struggle that he hasn't done it. So I want to thank him publicly and personally for this kind of moral and financial support as we struggle in this struggle to make America a better land and to make the brotherhood of man a reality.[85]

More recently, Mrs. Coretta Scott King, writing on the occasion of Dr. Booth's installation at the Church on the Rock in Anderson, Indiana, chose to this opportunity to make some choice comments about his relationship with her husband and the movement that clearly established Booth as friend of Dr. King.

> As you begin this new chapter of your distinguished career as one of America's preeminent clergymen, I want to thank you for your loyal support of my husband, Martin Luther King, Jr. and the Civil Rights Movement. You have also been a great friend to me personally, and I deeply appreciate your steadfast support of The King Center, as a loyal, creative and dedicated member of our Board of Directors. You have given so generously of your time and talents as a Christian minister who lives, as well as preaches, the social gospel.[86]

Formidable odds faced L. Venchael Booth in daring to launch the Progressive ship of state. Those who opposed, discouraged, and frustrated the formation of the PNBC, though good men, represented a veritable Who's Who among Black Baptists. Heading the list were Dr. Martin Luther King, Jr., Dr. Martin Luther, King, Sr.,[87] and Dr. Gardner C. Taylor, who, as noted earlier, did not condone the split. Dr. E. L. Harrison of the Shiloh Baptist Church of Washington, D.C., who would later become

President, cautioned Booth that the call should not come under the "signature of one man."[88] Prophesying that Booth's actions would "be most destructive to the cause of freedom and religion among the majority of Negro people of our Land,"[89] Dr. Herbert H. Eaton of the Dexter Avenue Baptist Church in Montgomery, Alabama, urged him not to proceed. Another of the top leaders, Dr. D. E. King, of the Monumental Baptist Church of Chicago, wrote, "...I do not feel that this is the time nor do we have the spiritual climate for beginning such a movement."[90] Dr. Thomas Kilgore, destined to become one of the president's of the PNBC, put a damper on things when he declared, "I feel along with many others that there is much to be done among our Baptist forces, but as much as I feel this way I am not yet committed to a new Baptist organization."[91] Then there was the Rev. Marvin T. Robinson, the spokesperson opposing the organization of the Convention at the Call Meeting in Cincinnati, who, shortly there-after, wrote a scathing article in *The Cleveland Call And Post* giving not only his reason for non-support of the fledgling body but that of others as well. In his rather personal attack on Rev. Booth, he noted: "Many Pastors ignored the Booth meeting because they felt it was ill-timed and a one-man call and the one issuing the call held no leadership position in the convention."[92]

The resident prophet among NBC pastors, Dr. L. K. Jackson, the self-anointed "Servant of the Lord's Servants" questioned Booth's sincerity:

> I think I have demonstrated as much altruistic interest in and philanthropic concern about the welfare and betterment of the National Baptist Convention as anyone in America. If you are calling a meeting to consider the betterment of the National Baptist Convention, how could you be sincere in your endeavour [endeavor] and ignore or disregard a person who has demonstrated the kind of interest I have over a period of twenty or more years?"[93]

Writing from Chester, Pennsylvania, Dr. J. Pius Barbour, mentor to many a Crozer Theological Seminary student including Dr. Martin Luther King, Jr., as well as the former editor of the *National Baptist Voice* (though at the time directing his attention to the American Baptist Convention), cautioned Booth "not [to] set up a lot of splitter [splinter] groups"[94] out of concern for the support of mission work in Africa. In closing his letter, Barbour offered his terse personal analysis:

> My experiences have taught me that it takes a lot of preparing to set up an organization locally and it takes much more to set up a national organization. I am not interested in joining a movement that will end in a debacle, so please write me at once and fill the letter with information so that I can show it to key men in the east. I told you at your home in Cincinnati that the devil cares nothing about the cross.[95]

Dr. Benjamin Elijah Mays, President of Morehouse College, noted Baptist educator and friend, regularly corresponded with Booth. In a handwritten postscript he assured Booth that "You and I differ on procedure only."[96]

The aging and fragile Baptist warrior Dr. J. C. Austin had some procedural concerns. In a letter to Booth on September 26, 1961, he spelled them out:

> I am also of the opinion that we should invite into this meeting the deposed heads of all auxiliaries of the National Baptist Convention, such as Mrs. Ross of the Women's Convention; Dr. Maxwell head of the National S. S. & B. T. U. Congress; [and] Dr. C. C. Adams of the Foreign Mission Board. I will join you in the effort to have them on hand.[97]

Dr. C. C. Adams (mentioned by Dr. J. C. Austin in his correspondence), having been ousted from the Foreign Mission Board of the NBC after Kansas City,[98] was compelled to "start from scratch"[99] to establish a new foreign mission organization. Yet he took time to commend Booth's effort. His plans, however, for coming to the Call Meeting in Cincinnati were at first frustrated by a "narrowness of mind"[100] which prompted him to come cloaked in secrecy, i.e., without any publicity. C. C. Adams overcame whatever obstacles confronted him, attended and preached at the historic Cincinnati session, but did not register or affiliate. Yet, he turned out to be the beneficiary of a generous gesture from the group that gathered—the receipt of the entire offering after expenses to further missions. Dr. J. C. Austin, however, did not make the meeting.

One who did not hesitate to be more caustic in his criticism was Rev. W. J. David, pastor of Mt. Moriah Baptist Church of Birmingham, Alabama, who challenged Booth's Christian faith in a strident way.

> Why be unchristian? Asking a new convention you all said if you got a fair vote. Ok. May I say you all are unfair and none Christians [non-Christians]. You will never succeed in your efforts for Christ is not with you in your spite work. Your trouble is you don't respect the voice of the majority.
>
> You so call [so-called] Christians need to go and get some religion, which you preach, to your people.
>
> I shall pray god [God] to convert all of you so call [so-called] gospel preacher's [preachers].[101]

These critical pieces of correspondence, all sent to L. V. Booth, are key evidentiary materials that identify him as the prime mover behind the PNBC. To the others who would stake their claim as founder, the question must be asked, "What price did you pay?" Dr. C. V. Johnson, first president of the Mid-West Region of the PNBC, wrote witih Spirit-stirring passion about the price the founder and others had to face in his reflections in 1977. "The 'Call Letter' and subsequest 'News Releases' were questioned, opposed, resisted, and I venture to say, many letters ended up in wastebaskets. Dr. Booth was persecuted, as were the persons who responded to his call. None but those who possessed an iron constitution could have lived through the turbulent days that followed...."

In a number of the references cited earlier, the name of L. Venchael Booth is not even mentioned in the same sentence with the PNBC.[102] Saddest of all is the fact that the PNBC in its marketing piece commissioned by Dr. J. Alfred Smith, Sr., prepared by Dr. Charles G. Adams and later recommissioned by Dr. Fred C. Lofton, failed to mention the name of Dr. L. Venchael Booth.

In a section of the leaflet entitled "Creative Leadership and Innovation,"[103] significant contributions by Progressive Baptists are highlighted, but a glaring omission regarding Dr. L. Venchael Booth's ascendancy to the position of vice-president of the Baptist World Alliance[104] was all too obvious an oversight. That Dr. Booth served from 1970-1975 is not listed. Moreover, it is notable that he also served as a member of the historic Nominating Committee of the Baptist World Alliance in 1965, which was responsible for electing the first person of color, Dr. William R. Tolbert as the BWA President. The thoughtful observer cannot ignore omissions like these.

Fortunately, numerous writers have referenced Booth in their histories, including Leroy Fitts, Lewis V. Baldwin, Edward Wheeler, Thomas J. Kilgore, Jini Kilgore Ross, Wallace C. Smith, Larry G. Murphy, J. Gordon Melton, Gary L. Ward, C. Eric Lincoln, Lawrence H. Mamiya, and William H. Brackney. Also taking note of Booth's role, but not mentioned earlier, were Daniel G. Reid,[105] J. Gordon Melton,[106] Bill J. Leonard,[107] and Edward Gilbreath in a more recent article in *Christianity Today* entitled "Redeeming Fire."[108]

C. Eric Lincoln and Lawrence H. Mamiya made the strongest statement regarding Booth's role when they wrote: "Rev. L. Venchael Booth *assumed leadership of the opposition* and, as the *chairman* of the 'Volunteer Committee for the Formation of a New National Baptist Convention,' *called* for a meeting in November 1961 at *his* church, Zion Baptist Church in Cincinnati."[109] However, even their descriptive language and designations like "under his leadership" or "issuer of the call" or "the leading voice"[110] does not begin to assess adequately Booth's contributions.

Conclusion

In recording history, it is crucial to provide an accurate representation of the past for the benefit of present and future generations. On the other hand, a history that is riddled with errors is a disservice to the readers and to those whose story is being told. Dr. L. Venchael Booth's role as founder of the Progressive National Baptist Convention, cited in *The Afro-American*, March 2, 1963 and *The New York Courier*, March 16, 1963,[111] warrants an accurate rendering for posterity. At stake is not simply his dignity, but the integrity of the PNBC as well. Documentation has validated that he appointed himself as chair of the "Volunteer Committee for the Formation of a New National Baptist Convention," called the meeting, set the rules for coming, set the date, set the time, set the place, set the program, issued the releases, hosted the meeting, underwrote the expenses, and served as the principal advocate for the new convention in the originating meeting for the PNBC. The record will show that Dr. L. Venchael Booth authored the convention song, designed the initial seal, and identified the foundational scripture. Finally, in a spirit uncommon in the annals of Black Baptist life, Dr. L. Venchael Booth as founder, though urged to become president of the fledging organization, deferred to Dr. T. M. Chambers in Cincinnati in 1961. Then again, in 1963, though in line to be re-elected as first vice president-at-large, Dr. L. Venchael Booth deferred to Dr. Gardner C. Taylor,[112] opening the way for his return to convention leadership among Black Baptists in Detroit, Michigan. Instead, Booth accepted and assumed the post of the Convention's first Executive Secretary. Such sacrifices of personal gain flowed from the parental heart of a founder who loved the cause more than an office.

More recently, a fresh wind of the spirit of truth was felt among Progressive Baptists. In the August 2000 edition of *Baptist Progress*, the official newspaper of the PNBC, Inc., Dr. L. Venchael Booth was referred to as the founder, first executive secretary, and third president. This fact is a welcomed move in the right direction. The PNBC now needs to codify in the Convention's history Booth's place as its founder.

On the eve of the PNBC's fortieth year, neither the integrity nor the credibility of the Convention is well served by denying Dr. L. Venchael Booth his rightful place as founder. L. Venchael Booth, in his bold and daring call to Black Baptists to form a new convention, built an important platform for Dr. Gardner C. Taylor, Dr. Martin Luther King, Jr., and the Civil Rights Movement. His light is not brighter than theirs; he simply illumined theirs more.

NOTES

[1] Among the histories chronicling the PNBC's beginnings are: William D. Booth, *The Progressive Story* (St. Paul Minnesota: Baum Press, 1980); Lewis V. Baldwin, *There Is a Balm in Gilead* (Minneapolis: Fortress Press, 1991), pp. 218-221; Leroy Fitts, *A History of Black Baptists* (Nashville: Broadman Press, 1985), p. 104; Jessyca Russell Gaver, *"You Shall Know The Truth": The Baptist Story* (New York: Lancer Books, 1973), pp. 144-166 [Jessyca Gaver in the pages noted simply lifts verbatim, and she acknowledged it, the material from my original manuscript for *The Progressive Story*.]; and Edward Wheeler, "Beyond One Man: A General Survey of Black Baptist History," *Review and Expositor* vol. LXXX, no.3 (Summer, 1973) p. 317.

[2] William H. Brackney, *Historical Dictionary of the Baptists* (Lanham, Maryland: Scarecrow Press 1999), pp. 337-338. This recent work exemplifies the inaccuracies which historical writings continue to perpetuate regarding PNBC's origins and which this article seeks to address.

[3] The National Baptist Convention, U. S. A., Inc. with its World Center Headquarters located in Nashville, TN was founded September 1895 and has a membership of 30,000 churches with a membership in excess of 7,500,000 as of September 1988. Clarence G. Newsome, ed., *Directory of African American Religious Bodies: A Compendium by The Howard University School of Divinity*, 2nd ed. (Washington, DC: Howard University Press, 1995), pp. 68, 69; M. C. Bruce, "National Baptists," *Dictionary of Baptists in America*, (Illinois: IVP, 1994), pp. 198, 199, drawing it latest figures from 1984 credits the NBC, USA, Inc., with 30,000 congregations and 7 million members. In any case compared to the National Baptist Convention of American with 3.5 million members, 2,500 churches and 8,000 ordained clergy as of September, 1987 [AARB, p. 59] or the Progressive National Baptist Convention, Inc., with 1,800 churches and 1.8 million members [AARB, p. 87], the NBC, USA, Inc., is clearly the largest even when compared with the AME with 3.5 million members and 8,000 churches or the Church of God in Christ with 5.5 million members, 1,000 congregations, and 10,5000 ministers [AARB, pp.110, 163].

A more recent report for the PNBC appeared in the General Secretary's Annual Report. In that report Dr. Tyrone S. Pitts presented the following statistics: "We have come a long way since our inception 39 years ago. From 33 persons who met in a church basement and raised $210 dollars in 1961 ["Church basement" is an inaccurate description of the meeting place. The setting for this historic session— Zion Baptist Church in Cincinnati, Ohio—was a modern edifice, having recently been erected in 1960 under the leadership of the Convention's founder, Dr. L. Venchael Booth. Instead of "church basement," Dr. Pitts should have referenced "church chapel." It was nothing like a basement for it was part of the one-floor plan which included the sanctuary, fellowship hall/kitchen, classrooms, and the administrative office complex. Moreover, Dr. Pitts also misstated the amount raised at the inaugural meeting. The actual amount raised was reported in the *Minutes of the First Annual Session* (p. 20) which hopefully is available in the convention archives recorded that "Total receipts for the two-day meeting: $721.26." It is disappointing that the top continuing officer of the PNBC would be so unfamiliar with the record as to make such factual blunders. If such historical slip-ups weren't characteristic of PNBC's generally loose handling of yesterday's record, this might have been viewed as an anomaly.] to over 2.5 million persons with an annual budget of $3 million dollars with over 1200 member churches in the United States and with affiliate conventions throughout the world. These affiliate conventions include 900 affiliate churches in Ghana, 267 affiliate churches in Cuba, 11 affiliate churches in the United Kingdom, 20 affiliate churches in the Bahamas, 1 affiliate church in both Nigeria and Costa Rica, and 252 churches in South Africa." Dr. Tyrone S. Pitts, "Annual Report of General Secretary," *Progressive National Baptist Convention, Inc., Minutes of the 39th Annual Session* (Louisville, KY, August 7-11, 2000), p. 3.

Verification of the amount received at the organizing session is provided in the correspondence of the then secretary-historian, Dr. J. Carl Mitchell. In that letter Dr. Mitchell wrote: "Our first meeting in Cincinnati, at which time we raised from all sources $721.26. At the close of the meeting, after expenses were paid, we turned over $378.60 to the treasurer. Representation from churches is not available at this moment. This total included monies raised for the Foreign Mission Bureau. I think you have a similar record of this meeting." Letter from J. Carl Mitchell to L. V. Booth 4 July 1962. [See Appendix 62]

[4] National Baptist Convention, USA, Inc., *Minutes of the 75th Annual Session* (Memphis, TN., September 8, 1955), pp. 11 & 63. On Thursday, September 8, 1955, Dr. Jackson delivered his annual address. In that address he made the following recommendation to the convention concerning the constitutional issue: "That Article IV, and the last sentence in section 1, the whole of Section 2, Article IV, and the whole of Section 6 of Article V, be lifted and committed for careful study and analysis; and to revamp (sic), reshape, amend or to reaffirm (sic) as they now appear in the constitution; and that said committee shall be appointed in this Annual Session." Dr. Gardner C. Taylor, according to the minutes, "glowingly commended the President on his address and moved that the address along with every recommendation be adopted. The motion received an overwhelming number of seconds and was carried without a dissenting vote." One the other hand L. V. Booth would issue a circular arguing for tenure and against its being lifted entitled *"21 Reasons Why Every Freedom Loving Baptist Should Vote for Retention of Tenure in our Constitution."* There is no way of assessing the impact of that circular, but there is no doubt of where Booth stood in relationship to J. H. Jackson on this matter. It further revealed the consistency and passion of his belief in tenure. Another outspoken critic of this action was Dr. L. K. Jackson who had been invited by Dr. J. Pius Barbour then editor of the *National Baptist Voice* to write an article on the topic, *"Seven Reasons Why Young, Trained, Christian Ministers Should Resist the Efforts of the 'Lift-Tricksters' and Support the Constitution."* In a searing invective, L. K. Jackson set forth his argument. This essay offers some excellent insights into the history of the NBC and takes us the behind the scenes unveiling the sullied motivations and sordid actions of servants of God. This sentence provides a glimpse of the vehemence of his contention. "Young, trained, Christian ministers should resist the 'Lift-Tricksters' and support the constitution for the reason that, the contention of the 'Lift-Tricksters' is one of the most inconsistent, illogical and ungodly arguments I have ever heard by Christian ministers." William D. Booth, *The Progressive Story: New Baptist Roots* (St. Paul, Minnesota: Baum Press, 1981), pp. 96-106.

[5] Cornell E. Tally, Letter (Mimeographed) to Rev. L.V. Booth, October 23, 1959. [See Appendix 1]

[6] Interview with J. Pius Barbour, Pastor of the Calvary Baptist Church, Chester, Pa., 11 April 1969. Dr. Barbour's remembrance was confirmed by the Founder's reflections as well. In the lead article in the pamphlet *"Reflections and Projections: A History of the Mid-West Region Progressive National Baptist Convention, Inc.,"* Dr. L. Venchael Booth set forth his sense of call to be an instrument of God in the founding of the PNBC and pinpointed the moment when the idea emerged and was concretized into an unshakable conviction.

"The Progressive National Baptist Convention is not an accident of history. It is totally wrapped up in God's purpose. It was not born in me, nor with me. I was called out, chosen and commissioned to do what needed to be done at that particular time in history. It is for this reason I have nothing to boast about, or glory in, save in the grace of God who not only works wonders, but does the impossible. The Progressive Convention is not a one-man creation. There is no way one man so weak, so vulnerable, so full of inconsistencies, could do such a noble work as to build a Convention. So, whatever has happened in the Progressive National Baptist Convention was not of man's doing, but was man plus God with man as the instrument.

The Apostle Paul explains what I am trying to say:

> But God hath chosen the foolish things of the world to confound the wise; and God hath chosen the weak things of the world to confound the things, which are mighty. And the base things of the world and things which are despised hath God chosen, yea, and the things that are: That no flesh should glory in his presence.
> 1 Cor. 1:27-29 KJV

The Progressive Convention grew out of a desire for unity. The Power Struggle in the Incorporated Convention was not only great, but bitter. So after many years of attending Conventions which for me began in Dallas, Texas in 1944, and continued through to Kansas City in 1961, it became a clear conviction to me that God had something better for his people to do. So, in 1957, in Louisville, Kentucky, I believe, that a light broke from heaven in my heart. It was there I offered the suggestion that if we wanted a convention that honored 'tenure,' we would have to organize one. My voice was so small that it was not even heard, nor was it heard in meetings following. It was following Philadelphia and Kansas City that it dawned on me that God had called me to offer my life as a living sacrifice to lift the Baptist Cause. My conviction became so strong that it never wavered from then until now."

[7] *Ibid.*

[8] Letter from Cornell E. Talley (Mimeographed), to L. V. Booth, (October 23, 1959).

[9] Dr. L. Venchael Booth would not only serve as host for the initial meeting leading to the launching of the Taylor Team but would become a strong supporter. Letter from M. L. King, Sr., to L. V. Booth (August 9, 1960) [See Appendix 2]; Letter from Gardner C. Taylor to L. V. Booth (October 10, 1960) [See Appendix 3]; Letter from Gardner C. Taylor to L. V. Booth (December 12, 1960) [See Appendix 4]; and Letter from Gardner C. Taylor to L. V. Booth (August 9, 1961) [See Appendix 5].

[10] William D. Booth, *The Progressive Story: New Baptist Roots* (St. Paul, Minnesota: Baum Press, 1981), p. 21.

[11] *Ibid.*, p. 23.

[12] L. V. Booth, prophet without portfolio and discernible following, stepped forth again and registered a protest about the Philadelphia debacle in a release entitled *"Baptists and the Philadelphia Dilemma."* [See Appendix 58] In it he raised serious questions about both Jackson and Taylor. "Why is President Jackson unwilling to submit to a voters' test? Why was he afraid in Philadelphia and thus threw his own Convention into bedlam by denying the people the right to vote? The true Philadelphia Story has to be understood only at this point. When President Jackson refused to allow the people to express themselves (both his supporters and opponents) he lost control of the Convention. On the other hand, why is President Gardner Taylor willing to step aside and accept the people's verdict and relieve the harmful tensions, which weaken and divide?"

[13] William D. Booth, *op. cit.*, pp. 31-45.

[14] C. Eric Lincoln and Lawrence H. Mamiya, "The Black Baptists: The First Black Churches in America," *Baptists in the Balance: The Tension between Freedom and Responsibility*, ed. by Everette C. Goodwin (Valley Forge: Judson Press, 1997), p. 113.

The reason for ousting of Dr. Martin Luther King, Jr., has often been linked to the

Jackson's jealousy of King's possibility as a potential rival, a contemporary version of a Saul vs. David scenario. While this argument may have merit, Jackson offers a dissenting view in his work on the history of the NBC. More seasoned students of history than I will have to decide what credence to give this opposing position.

"There was a special meeting of the Board of Directors held on Saturday morning, September 9, 1961. Among the items he, discussed was the matter of the office of the first vice-presidency of the Sunday School and B.T.U. Congress. There had been a great deal of agitation among the delegates to replace the current vice-president, and the members of the Board had to respond to this rather widespread movement. I had known Dr. Martin Luther King, Jr. for a number of years and felt, after listening to the open debate and frank discussion, that we could tolerate his actions at least for another year. He had not succeeded in achieving the goals that had been undertaken by the "Taylor Team" in 1959, 1960, nor 1961. The Convention, therefore, would have little or nothing to fear from his continuation in the office of the vice-presidency of the Congress.

At that point, the discussion—seemingly having reached an impasse—Rev. Julian Taylor of Connecticut asked to be recognized by the chair. He stated that he wished to make a motion but requested that he be allowed to preface his motion with a statement relative to the matter under discussion. Permission was granted, and he made the following statement,

We have seen and observed the actions of Dr. Martin Luther King relative to our Convention. He has used his influence and his technique to disrupt, confuse and disorganize our Convention and has done little or nothing to strengthen the fellowship between the Congress and the Convention, or to aid the Congress in its educational objectives. The truth is, we have his name but have not had his constructive support. The National Baptist Convention does not need Dr. King's name without Dr. King's loyalty. Mr. President, I move that the Board of Directors will recommend that the name of Dr. King be deleted as vice president of the Sunday School and B. T. U. Congress.

The motion was seconded and passed unanimously. It was then moved and seconded that the Board of Directors would recommend to the National Baptist Convention in session, that Rev. E. C. Estell would replace Dr. Martin Luther King, Jr. as the Vice-President at large of the Sunday School & B. T. U. Congress of the National Baptist Convention, U.S.A., Inc. And the motion carried. Later that morning the Board of Directors took the two motions in the form of one recommendation to the Convention, which had been assembled to hear commission reports as well as the report from the Board of Directors.

In reporting to the parent body the Board presented the following: "That Dr. E. C. Estell would replace Dr. Martin Luther King, Jr. as the Vice-President-at-large of the Sunday School and B.T.U. Congress of the National Baptist Convention, U.S.A., Inc. The recommendation was adopted." While Julian Taylor's remarks were not read to the parent body, they seemed to represent the sentiments of so many delegates who had lived through the horrendous days when the techniques of direct action had been applied to the Convention, which they loved so much.

The National Baptist Convention—in its repudiation of some of the persons who were members of boards—rejected them because of what the National Baptist Convention knew they had done against the rules of fellowship in opposition to and contrary to the principles and ideals of the National Baptist Convention.

Dr. Martin Luther King was not removed from the office of vice-presidency of the Congress of Christian Education of the National Baptist Convention in September 1961 because anyone feared his power or was jealous of his influence or popularity as a Nobel Peace Prize winner, but because of the anti-National Baptist Convention campaign he participated in during the years 1960 and 1961. The National Baptist Convention removed him from the position to which he had been elected in Omaha,

Nebraska, because of the type of militant campaign carried on against his own denomination and his own race.

The same was done regarding Dr. D. E. King, who was an assistant secretary of the National Baptist Convention. He was moved in September along with Dr. M. L. King, Sr., and Dr. Marshall Shepard. The few people who were removed from office or from the Board of Directors by the National Baptist Convention were not able to have themselves reinstated by any form of protest. Some of the brethren who were in the 1960 "sit-in" in Philadelphia and the "March-in" in Kansas City in 1961 came back in the Christian way and were received in the same way; some are now members of the official board and of the official family." J. H. Jackson, *A Story of Christian Activism: The History of the National Baptist Convention, U. S. A., Inc.* (Nashville, Tennessee: Townsend Press, 1980), pp. 483-435, 486, 487.

[15] The National Baptist Convention USA, Inc., opened it session in Kansas City in 1961 in confusion. The first order of business was a resolution read by Rev. E. C. Estell of Dallas, Texas, commending Dr. Jackson and recommending that he be re-elected for 1961-1962. Dr. Charles Hampton of San Diego, California entertained the motion and declared Dr. Jackson reelected. At this point the supporters of Dr. Taylor attempted to gain access to the speaker's platform. Amidst the shoving and pushing Rev. Ben F. Paxton, later indicated when questioned by a homicide detective, that he backed into Rev. Wright who was sitting in a chair. At that point, Rev. Wright reached for what he thought was a wall at the back of the platform, but it was only a curtain. He lost his balance and shouted, "Hold me." Rev. Paxton reached for and grabbed Rev. Wright. However, both men fell off of the platform with Rev. Paxton landing on Rev. Wright. On Thursday morning Rev. S. Wright, 64, an undertaker, minister, and reportedly a wealthy man, who had helped to fund Dr. Jackson's campaign, died. This tragedy placed an ominous cloud over NBC and spurred L. V. Booth to take the bold step of founding the PNBC. William D. Booth, *The Progressive Story: New Baptist Roots* (St. Paul Minnesota, Baum Press, 1981), pp. 35-36.

In his mammoth treatise, *A Story of Christian Activism: The History of the National Baptist Convention, U. S. A., Inc.*, Dr. Joseph Harrison Jackson presents his view of what took place that fatefully dark day in Black Baptist history. While Jackson's perspective has rarely been given much space and thought in any of the chronicles of the period, fairness and objectivity demand his side be heard. It was J. H. Jackson who at the time while President of the NBC called to the attention of the founder of the PNBC, L. Venchael Booth, the importance of "writing [as] part of our total responsibility." Letter from J. H. Jackson to L. V. Booth, February 4, 1975. And write Jackson did. Later L. V. Booth would be compelled to do the same to get a hearing for his side of the Progressive story. [Appendix 66]

Here is Jackson's view: "In a military and organized fashion Rev. Gardner C. Taylor and his supporters forced themselves into the auditorium, proceeded down the center aisle to the rostrum in order to take the auditorium by force. This was the same group which had carried on the 'Baptist Sit-In' in Philadelphia and now they were trying a new technique: a 'March-In.' Interestingly enough, although they had claimed throughout the year that they were the Convention and had publicized that the majority of the people were with them, their previous meetings on Tuesday, September 5, 1961, at the Paseo Baptist Church revealed that they did not have the following of the Convention. They could not even fill the church. The plan by the emissaries who came to speak with us on Tuesday afternoon for a compromise, which would see us turning over what was rightfully ours to them without a murmur, also failed. And now they—on some bad advice resorted to direct action.

... Members and leaders of the "Taylor Team" ... left the Paseo Baptist Church, the place where they had been meeting for two days as an independent body. They arrived at the Municipal Auditorium, which they had not rented and for which they held no contract. They were conducting their "Baptist March-In"; and without warning or notice, they moved toward a platform that was already overcrowded.

As they lunged upon the steps that led from the first floor of the auditorium to the platform, the wooden steps gave away with a loud crackle. Several marchers fell to the floor, but some of them were on the platform moving toward the front of it where the Convention's officers were standing and toward the rear. The Rev. A. G. Wright, in an attempt to make more space for the marchers in the aisle which was between his row of seats and the row in front of him, apparently thinking he was sitting with his chair abutting a wall, made an attempt to push his chair back only to discover too late-much too late-that there was only a curtain which separated the platform from the first floor level, seven or eight feet below.

No one had planned this tragedy; no group had willed it. While the planners, leaders, and participants in the 'March-In' did not intend the death of Rev. Wright, the planning of that kind of protest occasioned a series of events that caused the death of a fine, upright, Christian gentleman, an excellent preacher, and an outstanding pastor. Undoubtedly it was the kindness of Providence, which prevented even more grim results. Programs and plans of this kind of protest are potentially violent, it matters not by what name they are called." J. H. Jackson, *A Story of Christian Activism: The History of the National Baptist Convention, U. S. A., Inc.* (Nashville, Tennessee: Townsend Press, 1980), pp. 457, 488 and 489.

Dr. Gordon B. Hancock writing in his column for the *Associated Negro Press*, Behind The Headlines, offered two critiques – one of the behavior of Negro Baptists in Philadelphia and Kansas City and the other of "sectors of our press" for making too much of the events. "What happened there," Dr. Hancock in an unvarnished, scathing, but terse polemic said "was lamentable, deplorable, and regrettable, and not a little shameful, but not so graceful.

Certain sectors of our press have seized upon the unhappy doings of the Negro Baptists within the last year to make them look terrible in the eyes of the world, and the unfortunate death of a fellow minister in an accident has drawn the attention it would have merited if he had been shot down in cold blood in some hidden feud." Gordon B. Hancock, "Baptists Produce First Rate College Presidents," *Journal and Guide,* 14 October 1961, p. 8.

[16] "King Asks Retraction," *The Afro-American,* 23 September 1961, p. 7.

[17] *Ibid.*

[18] "Convention Victory for Jackson and Call to Close Ranks," *The Kansas City Star,* 8 September 1961. "Minister Dies After Floor Row: Dr. Taylor Loses In Bid For Presidency Of National Body," *Journal and Guide,* 16 September 1961, pp.1, 2. The *Journal and Guide* article reported Taylor's concession on this wise: "After the election, Dr. Taylor conceded with a statement that he would not run for the presidency of the National Baptist Convention USA, Inc. Dr. Taylor urged his supporters 'to get behind Dr. Jackson' and pledged his cooperation in all activities of the denomination, one of the world's largest Negro organizations."

[19] "Chicagoan Elected At Baptist Parley," *New York Times,* 9 September 1961.

[20] Alfredo Graham, "Election Satisfies Taylor," *The Pittsburgh Courier,* 23 September 1961.

[21] *Ibid.*

[22] After J. H. Jackson was elected to his fifth term in Louisville, Kentucky in 1957, he lifted the tenure amendment from the Constitution claiming that it was legally introduced on the wrong day. L.V. Booth took a conciliatory approach. To men of stature, long-standing friendship and trust he made pleas for intervention in the Convention's dilemma. Letters were sent to *Dr. Theodore F. Adams,* President of the Baptist World Alliance (October 19, 1957) [See Appendix 6]; to *Dr. Benjamin E. Mays,* President of Morehouse College; to *Dr. W. H. Jernagin,* President of the National Baptist Sunday School and BTU Congress; and to *Dr. Mordecai Johnson,* President of Howard University. Mays (Letter to L. V. Booth - October 21, 1957) [See Appendix 7] on the other hand felt that Booth was being "mighty optimistic"

to expect Jackson to be responsive to a plea for reconciliation and especially would he resent "three white men [coming in] to mediate the matter. Dr. W. H. Jernagin (Letter to L. V. Booth - October 24, 1957) [See Appendix 8] was comfortable with the reconciliation team considering them all "very fine and Christian." Yet he was pessimistic about J. H. Jackson's response noting that he was "hard boiled...ambitious...to be president." Adams (Letter to L. V. Booth - October 30, 1957) [See Appendix 9] felt it would be "presumptuous of him to step in" unless the leadership of the NBC made the request. Dr. Mordecai W. Johnson (Letter to L. V. Booth - November 7, 1957) [See Appendix 10] was amenable to the Booth's proposal but felt he wasn't "fully acquainted with the issues" and would need direct contact from Dr. Jernagin and Dr. Jackson.

[23] Eugene Peterson, *The Old Testament Wisdom Book in Contemporary English* (Colorado Spring, Col: NavPress Publishing Group, 1996), p. 359 (Ecclesiastes 3:2b).

[24] William D. Booth, *op. cit.*, pp. 44-45. [See Appendix 11]

[25] Edward Gilbreath, "The Pulpit King: The Passion and Eloquence of Gardner Taylor, a Legend among Preacher," *Christianity Today* (December 11, 1995), p. 28.

A more recent example of misstating Gardner Taylor's role in the origin of the PNBC occurred on August 9, 2000, at a White House ceremony. It was then that President William Jefferson Clinton presented the Medal of Freedom, the Nation's highest civilian award, to Dr. Gardner C. Taylor. Commander Gilday read the citation which included this sentence, *"As founder of the Progressive National Baptist Convention, Reverend Taylor helped to galvanize black churches all across America in the struggle for human rights."* [Taken from Note: S. 190, approved August 8, was assigned Public Law No. 106-258] Unmistakably this assertion of the citation, unlike the otherwise well deserved kudos of the declaration, does not square with history.

[26] Taylor Branch, *Pillar and Fire: America in the King Years 1963-65* (New York: Simon and Schuster, 1998), p. 25.

[27] Lewis V. Baldwin, *There is a Balm in Gilead: The Cultural Roots of Martin Luther King, Jr.* (Minneapolis, MN: Fortress Press, 1991), p. 219.

[28] *Ibid.*, p. 220 [see footnote 172].

[29] "New Split Threatens Baptists; Jackson Denies Rapping Dr. King," *JET*, 28 September 1961, p. 18.

[30] Trezzvant W. Anderson, "King Won't Fight Firing by Jackson," *The Pittsburgh Courier*, 23 September 1961, 2, Sec. 2.

[31] Gardner C. Taylor, *The Words of Gardner Taylor*, compiled by Edward L. Taylor, Vol. 1 (Valley Forge: Judson Press, 1999), 2. In his introduction to the volume, Edward Taylor noted in his biographical sketch the following: "During his college years, Dr. Taylor [Gardner] looked to Leland College President Dr. James Alvin Bacoats, who succeeded Washington Taylor at Mt. Zion, as his primary mentor."

[32] J. A. Bacoats, "Plea To Avert Split In Nat'l Baptist Convention," *Journal and Guide*, 14 October 1961, p. 9.

[33] Edward Wheeler, "Beyond One Man: A General Survey of Black Baptist History," *Review and Expositor*, Vol. LXXX, No.3 (Summer 1972), p. 317.

[34] C. Eric Lincoln and Lawrence H. Mamiya, *The Black Church in the African American Experience* (Durham & London: Duke University Press, 1990), 37.

[35] Letter from L. V. Booth to Gardner C. Taylor, November 21, 1961. [See App. 12]

[36] Letter from Uvee Mdodana-Arbouin to L. V. Booth, November 21, 1961. [See Appendix 13]

[37] Letter from Marvin T. Robinson to L. V. Booth, October 11, 1961. [See App. 14]

[38] Letter from A. Ross Brent to L. V. Booth, November 3, 1961. [See Appendix 15]

[39] Progressive National Baptist Convention, Inc., *Minutes of the First Annual Session* (September 4-9, 1962), p. 39.

[40] Letter from Gardner C. Taylor to L. V. Booth, July 8, 1963. [See Appendix 16]

[41] Progressive National Baptist Convention, Inc., *Minutes of the Second Annual Session* (September 3-8, 1962), p. 61.

[42] In a handwritten note on the Sheraton Cadillac Hotel stationery, Detroit, Michigan (Sept. 6, 1963) [see Appendix 17], Dr. Gardner C. Taylor assessed his role and that of Dr. L. Venchael Booth's in PNBC history this way: "I envy you! Today I become Vice-President of the Progressive National Baptist Convention—but you become saint and seer of a people's movement in response to the pushings and promptings of God. When my name is ... you will live in the grateful memory of a bruised people who responded to your vision and who must now venerate your name and memory as long as this convention shall last. Count me forever debtor and suppliant and aspirant to what you are." Gardner (Taylor).

[43] Letter from Gardner C. Taylor to L. V. Booth, September 9, 1963. [See App. 18].

[44] Letter from Gardner C. Taylor to L. V. Booth, September 13, 1963 [See Appendix 19]. [The ellipses are occasioned by an inability to decipher the handwriting of Gardner Taylor in the case of the first word and the case of the other word there is an absence of a word in the original letter. It seems, however, that the intent is to reference the newspapers in the respective cities and compare the efficiency of Booth's efforts positively to work done in those professional circles.]

[45] Letter from Gardner C. Taylor to L. V. Booth (December 27, 1963). [See App.20]

[46] Letter from Gardner C. Taylor to L. V. Booth (January 6, 1964). [See App. 21]

[47] Letter from Gardner C. Taylor to L. V. Booth (April 8, 1964). [See Appendix 22]

[48] Gardner C. Taylor, "Acting President Taylor's First Annual Address," *Minutes of the Fifth Annual Session of the Progressive National Baptist Convention, Inc.* (September 6-11, 1966), p. 67.

[49] Gardner C. Taylor, "The President's Message," *Minutes of the Sixth Annual Session of the Progressive National Baptist Convention, Inc.* (September 5-10, 1967), p. 42.

[50] Letter from Earl L. Harrison to L. V. Booth, September 19, 1970 [see Appendix 23]. Dr. E. L. Harrison was destined not to serve out his tenure as president of the convention. In fact, he did not get the opportunity to deliver his first annual address. L. V. Booth had to deliver it in his absence in Houston, Texas. (Letter from Earl L. Harrison to L. V. Booth, August 12, 1972) [See Appendix 24] In this correspondence sent to L. V. Booth prior to the Houston session. Harrison's faith shone through just as brightly as any of the venerated saints of the past. "I am in a tight conflict with my body. It is too soon to predict the victor or the victim. It is possible that I cannot get to the Houston convention. Just in case be ready to take over and carry on. The Lord's work must not be wanting because one worker drops out.

I am ready to go to Houston, stay in Washington or to go to my Lord.

Do not put out any alarm. Wait until opening day. If I can come I will.

God bless you. This is your day."

Earl Harrison

After Dr. Harrison's death Dr. L. Venchael Booth finally became president of the organization he founded. A congratulatory word was received from Owen Cooper, President of the Baptist World Alliance. In that correspondence Cooper said this: "May I extend my sincere congratulations for your having been elected President of the Progressive National Baptist Convention. Your devotion to the Convention and the inspired part you played in organizing the group certainly deserves the recognition that has come your way." Letter from Owen Cooper to L. V. Booth 12 September 1972. [See Appendix 59]

[51] Leroy Fitts, "Progressive National Baptist Convention of America," *Encyclopedia of African American Religions,* ed. by Larry G. Murphy, J. Gordon Melton, and Gary L. Ward (New York: Garland Publishing, Inc., 1993), p. 621.

[52] David J. Garrow, *Bearing the Cross: Martin Luther King, Jr., and the Southern Christian Leadership Conference* (New York: William Morrow and Company, Inc., 1986), p. 166.

[53] Wallace C. Smith, "Progressive National Baptist Convention—The Roots of the Black Church, " *American Baptist Quarterly* (September 2000), No. 3, p. 252. It is almost unthinkable that any scholar in a search for truth would have neglected interviewing the founder, Dr. L. Venchael Booth, as a primary source of data on the PNBC in preparing a significant paper for such an event as the "Baptist Together: A Common Witness in the New Millennium" co-hosted by Eastern College and Eastern Baptist Theological Seminary on the college's campus in St. Davids, Pennsylvania.

[54] The 23 registered Baptists were: Rev. W. H. Binford, Mount Zion, Michigan City, IN; Dr. L. V. Booth, Zion, Cincinnati, OH; Rev. A. R. Brent, Shiloh, Plainfield, NJ; Dr. T. M. Chambers, Zion Hill, Los Angeles, CA; Rev. W. V. Glover, New Virginia, Montgomery, AL; Rev. J. F. Green, Second, Detroit, MI; Dr. J. R. Henderson, Second, Los Angeles, CA; Rev. Joseph Hill, Tabernacle, Cincinnati, OH; Dr. S. S. Hodges, Pilgrim, Hamilton, OH; Rev. I. B. Lavigne, First, Farrell, PA: Rev. A. L. Mason, Grace, Columbus, OH; Rev. H. D. McBride, New Temple, Cincinnati, OH; Dr. J. C. Mitchell, Sixteenth Street, Charleston, W. VA: Rev. W. W. Parker, Antioch, Waterloo, IA; Rev. H. W. Patterson, Mount Carmel, Columbus, OH; Dr. Louis Rawls, Tabernacle, Chicago, IL; Dr. B. W. Robertson, Cedar Street, Richmond, VA; Rev. L. S. Sorrell, White Stone, Clarksdale, MS; Rev. C. E. Wagner, Zion, Cincinnati, Oh; Mrs. Thelma Walton, Antioch, Cincinnati, OH; Rev. J. A. Williams, Baptist Temple, Pittsburgh, Pa; Rev. J. B. Williams, New Zion, Pittsburgh, PA; and Rev. J. F. Williams, Messiah Baptist, Newport News, VA.

Dr. Sloan S. Hodges the successor to the Founder, L. V. Booth, as Executive Secretary chronicled "The First Hundred and Seventy Seven Days of PNBC – November 14, 1961 to May 10, 1962." In his chronicle, Hodges chalks up the discrepancies in the statistics on the day of organization between a listing of 23 messengers registering with 33 messengers participating over against 39 votes cast (19 for the motion not to organize and 20 against the motion not to organize) as "the trials and errors of getting off the ground on that first day." Moreover, Dr. Hodges listed the other persons who were present, some of them participated, but their names were not listed as registrants. "I personally know that Rev. and Mrs. D. C. Cosby from Second Baptist in Detroit were present. Rev. L. J. Alford, West Palm Beach, Florida has stated positively that he was there and so has Dr. Bennett W. Smith, now of Buffalo, N. Y., but then a member of Zion Baptist Church in Cincinnati. Mrs. Beulah P. Brent, later to become President of the Women's Department was there accompanying her husband, Dr. A. Ross Brent. Miss Peggy A. Garnett, a member of Zion and who also became President of the Women's Department was there, serving on the kitchen committee."

[55] Adam Fairclough, *Martin Luther King, Jr.* (Athens, Georgia: The University of Georgia Press, 1995), p. 53. In Faircough's book he confirms Dr. Martin Luther King's involvement in pressing for Dr. Gardner C. Taylor's pursuit of the presidency of the National Baptist Convention, USA, Inc. "King hoped to win the Baptist convention's backing for SCLC by ousting Jackson and replacing him with Gardner C. Taylor, a friend and ally. At a decisive meeting in 1961, however, Jackson quashed the Taylor-King challenge. He [Jackson] became one of King's most vociferous black critics."

[56] C. Eric Lincoln and Lawrence H. Mamiya, "The Black Baptist: The First Black Churches in America," *Baptists In The Balance,* ed. Everette C. Goodwin (Valley Forge, PA: Judson Press, 1997). p.112.

[57] William D. Booth, *op. cit.*, p. 59.

[58] Leroy Fitts, *op. cit.*, pp. 621- 622.

[59] L. V. Booth, "A High Call to Greatness," typewritten manuscript.

[60] Letter from C. T. Murray to L. V. Booth, October 23, 1961. [See Appendix 25]

[61] Progressive National Baptist Convention, Inc., *Minutes of the Second Annual Session*, (Sept. 3-8, 1969), p. 62.

[62] William Robert Miller, *Martin Luther King, Jr.: His life, Martyrdom and Meaning for the World* (New York, NY: Weybright and Talley, 1968), p. 126.

[63] Anne Devereaux Jordan and J. M. Stifle, *The Baptists* (New York, NY: Hippocrene Books, 1990), p. 116.

[64] Baldwin, *op. cit.*, p. 221.

[65] Progressive National Baptist Convention, Inc., *Minutes of the Sixth Annual Session* (September 5-10, 1967), p. 31.

[66] Baldwin, *op. cit.*, p. 221.

[67] Gilbreath, *op. cit.*, p. 28.

[68] Frank S. Mead and Samuel S. Hill (Revised by), *Handbook of Denominations in the United States*, rev. (Nashville, TN: Abingdon Press, 1995), p. 73.

[69] Charles H. Lippy and Peter W. Williams, eds., *Encyclopedia of the American Religious Experience: Studies of Traditions and Movements*, Vol.1 (New York: Charles Scribner's Sons, 1988), p. 575.

[70] Albert W. Wardin, ed., *Baptists Around The World: A Comprehensive Handbook* (Nashville, TN: Broadman & Holman Publishers, 1995), p. 416.

[71] Wallace C. Smith, *op.cit.*, p. 234. In another portion of his article Dr. Wallace C. Smith asserted in a more tellingly fashion his belief that the Civil Rights Movement blew the breath of life into the PNBC. "The Convention was largely founded on the Civil Rights beliefs of Martin Luther King, Jr."

[72] J. Carl Mitchell, "The Origin of the Progressive National Baptist Convention," *Minutes of the First Annual Session of the Progressive National Baptist Convention, Inc.* (September 4-9, 1962), p. 5.

[73] Quoted from Dr. Ralph W. Canty's letter appearing on the back cover of *The Progressive Story: New Baptists Roots* by William D. Booth.

[74] William D. Booth, *op. cit.*, 88-90.

[75] Progressive National Baptist Convention, Inc., *Minutes of the First Annual Session*, p. 37.

[76] *Ibid.*, p. 29.

[77] *Ibid.*

[78] *Ibid.*, pp. 29-31.

[79] W. H. R. Powell, "Towards The Creation of a New Convention Being a Declaration of the Organization, Principles and Aims of the Progressive Convention of America, Incorporated," *Minutes of the First Annual Session of the PNBC, Inc.* (September 4-9, 1961), pp. 29-31. [See Appendix 26]

Dr. Erich H. Ohlmann, Vice President/Academic Dean and Professor of Christian Heritage at Eastern Baptist Theological Seminary, drew upon Dr. W. H. R. Powell's "Manifesto" in his article, "American Baptist Churches, USA," appearing in the American Baptist Quarterly. In the section of Ohlmann's article headed "ABC and PNBC," his finding agrees with the Author that the primary basis for PNBC was tenure. No mention is made of the "Civil Rights Movement" as the motivation for the founding of the PNBC—confirming Powell's *Manifesto*. "One of the major bones of contention prior to the split was the issue of tenure for convention officers and particularly for the president. Efforts were made to introduce tenure by passing an amendment to the constitution, but they were frustrated, causing great resentment on the part of those who were eager for change. An integral part of this grievance was further discontent with election procedures. If elections had been conducted in a more agreeable manner, the issue of tenure may not have assumed the importance it did." Eric H. Ohlmann, "American Baptist Churches, USA," *American Baptist Quarterly* (September 2000), pp. 202, 203.

[80] Leroy Fitts, *op. cit.*, p. 622.

[81] Edward A. Freeman, "Negro Conventions (U.S.A.)," *Baptist Relations with Other Christians*, ed. James Leo Garrett (Valley Forge, PA: Judson Press, 1974), pp. 89-90.

[82] H. Leon McBeth, *A Sourcebook for Baptist Heritage* (Nashville, TN: Broadman Press, 1990), p. 594.

[83] Thomas Kilgore, Jr. with Jini Kilgore Ross, *A Servant's Journey: The Life and Work of Thomas Kilgore* (Valley Forge, PA: Judson Press, 1998), p. 223.

[84] J. Deotis Roberts, "Ecumenical Concerns Among National Baptists," *Journal of Ecumenical Studies* (Spring 1980), p. 38.

[85] Taped message of Dr. Martin Luther King, Jr., November 29, 1964, Zion Baptist Church's 122nd Anniversary, Cincinnati, Ohio.

[86] Letter from Coretta Scott King to L. V. Booth, April 26, 2001. [See Appendix 27] The sentiments of this letter had been previously expressed in an earlier piece of correspondence. Coretta in that letter said of L. V. Booth, "...your ministry has long been far larger than any single church. As a friend and devoted supporter of Martin Luther King, Jr. and as an energetic civil rights and religious leader in your own right, you have been in the forefront of the struggle for interracial justice, progress and reconciliation in our nation.

We deeply appreciate your friendship and your unflagging loyalty to the King Center and the King family, which has been a source of comfort and inspiration to us throughout the years. You have given generously to our efforts to carry forward Dr. King's unfinished work as an active member of our Board, and as a friend, advisor and confidant.

We have been profoundly inspired by your abiding faith and commitment to nonviolence and the teachings of Jesus Christ." Letter from Coretta Scott King to L. V. Booth, March 19, 1997. [See Appendix 60]

In an even earlier piece of correspondence to L. V. Booth, Coretta commended L. V. Booth for opening the door for her to speak before the PNBC. "I must say," Coretta wrote, "that you are a master strategist as you masterminded my appearance before the Progressive National Baptist Convention in a marvelous way. If it had'nt [hadn't] been for your artistry, I would never have appeared before the Convention." Letter from Coretta Scott King to L. V. Booth, October 5, 1976.

[87] Letter from J. C. Austin to L. V. Booth October 10, 1961 [see Appendix 26]. "After talking with a number of leading men, including Dr. E. L. Harrison of Washington D. C. and King of Georgia, I am persuaded to believe that such a move right now is not the best thing for us."

[88] Letter to L. V. Booth from E. L. Harrison, September 19, 1961. [See App. 28]

[89] Letter to L. V. Booth from Rev. Herbert H. Eaton, September 18, 1961. [See Appendix 30]

[90] Letter to L. V. Booth from Dr. D. E. King, October 12, 1961. [See Appendix 31]

[91] Letter to L. V. Booth from Dr. Thomas Kilgore, October 30, 1961. [See App. 32]

[92] Rev. Marvin Robinson, "Explains Why Many Baptists Ignored Newly Formed Group," *Cleveland Call And Post* (November 25, 1961).

[93] Letter from L. K. Jackson to L. V. Booth, September 15, 1961. [See Appendix 33] Another self-appointed prophet within the ranks of the NBC, Dr. Thomas E. Huntley, Pastor of the Central Baptist Church of St. Louis, Missouri, who frequently issued "manifestos" on the state of the convention urged Booth in a letter dated November 11, 1961, to "...go slow at this time until you read my Epistle. In the meantime since the meeting is call [ed], just have a good 'old fashion prayer meeting' with the boys who may atend [attend] and give them some good wholesome advise as you can do for this time." William D. Booth, *The Progressive Story: New Baptist Roots, op. cit.*, p. 167. [See Appendix 61]

[94] Letter from J. Pius Barbour to L. V. Booth, September 15, 1961. [See App. 34]

[95] *Ibid.*

[96] Letter from Benjamin E. Mays to L. V. Booth, September 21, 1961. [See App. 35]

[97] Letter from J. C. Austin to L. V. Booth, September 26, 1961. [See Appendix 36]

[98] Letter from C. C. Adams to L. V. Booth, September 28, 1961. [See Appendix 37]

[99] Letter from C. C. Adams to L. V. Booth, October 11, 1961 [See Appendix 38]

[100] Telegram from C. C. Adams to L. V. Booth, October 20, 1961. [See App. 39]

[101] Letter from W. J. Davis to L. V. Booth, October 18, 1961. [See Appendix 40]

Dr. C. V. Johnson of Chicago, Illinois, first President of the Midwest Region of the PNBC reflecting on the price paid by the founder and others who followed him left this on record: "The 'Call Letter' and subsequent 'News Releases' were questioned, opposed, resisted and I venture to say, many letters ended up in wastebaskets. Dr. Booth was persecuted, as were the persons who responded to his call. None but those who possessed an iron constitution could have lived thorough days that followed – even that would not have been sufficient except for the promise and assurance found in the Scriptures and the marvelous Grace of God. 'And they shall fight against them; but they shall not prevail against thee; for I am with thee, saith the Lord.' Jeremiah 1:19." *Reflections and Projections: A History of the Mid-West Region Progressive National Baptist Convention, Inc.* Pilot Edition, 1977 (Pages not numbered).

[102] The list of those who failed to mention L. Venchael Booth's name are as follows: Anne Devereaux Jordan and J. M. Stiffle, *The Baptists*, (New York: Hippocrene Books, 1990), p. 116; Edward Gilbreath, "The Pulpit King," *Christianity Today* (December 11, 1995), p. 28; David J. Garrow, *Bearing the Cross* (New York: William Morrow and Company, Inc., 1986), p. 166; H. Leon McBeth, *A Sourcebook for Baptist Heritage* (Nashville: Broadman Press, 1990), p. 594; Edward A. Freeman, "Negro Conventions (U.S.A.)," *Baptist Relations with Other Christians*, ed. James Leo Garrett (Valley Forge: Judson Press, 1974), pp. 89-90; Frank Mead, Samuel S. Hill (rev.), *Handbook of Denominations in the United States* (Nashville: Abingdon Press, 1995), p. 73; Carl W. Tiller, *The Twentieth-Century Baptist* (Valley Forge, PA: Judson Press, 1980), p. 5; and Albert W. Wardin, ed., *Baptists Around the World* (Nashville: Broadman Press, 1995) p. 416.

[103] Charles G. Adams, "Progressive National Baptist Convention, Inc.: A People of Faith and Action," PNBC publication, updated 1997.

[104] Bill J. Leonard, ed., *Dictionary of Baptists in America* (Downers Grove, Illinois: InterVarsity Press, 1994), p. 53.

[105] Daniel G. Reid, ed., *Dictionary of Christianity in America* (Downers Grove, Illinois: InterVarsity Press, 1990), p. 795.

[106] J. Gordon Melton, *The Encyclopedia of American Religions*, 3rd ed. (Detroit, Michigan: Gale Research Inc., 1989), p. 473.

[107] M. C. Bruce, "National Baptist," *Dictionary of Baptists in America*, ed. by Bill J. Leonard (Downers Grove, Illinois: InterVarsity Press, 1994), p. 199.

[108] Edward Gilbreath, "Redeeming Fire," *Christianity Today* (December 6, 1999), p. 42.

[109] C. Eric Lincoln, *op. cit.*, p. 37 [Italics in the quotation are mine].

[110] William H. Brackney, *Historical Dictionary of the Baptists*, p. 337.

[111] "Another State Joins," *The Afro-American*, 2 March 1963, p. 19 [see Appendix 41]; "In Business," *The New York Courier*, 16 March, 1963, p. 2. [See Appendix 41]

[112] William D. Booth, "Dr. L. Venchael Booth and the Origin of the Progressive National Baptist Convention, Inc., *American Baptist Quarterly*, XX (March, 2001), p. 89.

Appendices

Appendix 1

"One cannot hold another down unless he himself remains in the ditch"

Central Baptist Church

WYLIE AVE. & KIRKPATRICK ST.
PITTSBURGH 19, PENNSYLVANIA

REV. J. A. BRADLEY
ASSISTANT TO MINISTER

CHARLES P. PERNELL
CHAIRMAN TRUSTEE BOARD

ROBERT G. BAILEY
SUPT. SUNDAY SCHOOL

A. D. TAYLOR
DIRECTOR OF B. T. U.

OFFICE OF
CORNELL E. TALLEY, MINISTER
3066 IOWA STREET
PHONES: RES., MU. 2-5287 — OFFICE: AT. 1-1340

ALVIS R. ROSS
CHAIRMAN DEACON BOARD

ROBERT G. BAILEY
ASSISTANT CHAIRMAN

G. M. O. SAUNDERS
CHURCH CLERK

TWENTY-THIRD
OCTOBER
1 9 5 9

My dear Brother:

A group of pastors, who are definitely concerned about good administration in our National Baptist Convention, have been conferring recently over long-distance telephone and have decided to attempt a union of forces in a concerted effort to save both convention and our cherished fellowship.

We have no organization at present, therefore it has been suggested that I write urging your presence to a meeting for the initiation of plans and to form the nucleus of a great organization whose purpose will be to reclaim the Convention.

Our plans must be sound, foolproof, and constructive. Only a few men are being invited because it is difficult to work effectively with a big gathering. After our initial meeting, the crowd, who are like-minded, will be asked to join our crusade.

The meeting place is Cincinnati. Chicago would be ideal; but for obvious reasons, we feel that meeting in Chicago now would be unwise. You understand that this first meeting must be a top-secret. It is a secret, not that we fear retaliation from the administration; but others will want to know why they were not invited. We cannot risk the loss of one brother.

We ask therefore, that our proposed meeting not be discussed.

I have been in touch with Dr. L. V. Booth of 3415 Dury Avenue, Cincinnati. He has agreed to receive us and arrange hotel and meeting accommodations. To felicitate time and to insure secrecy, our meeting will be held at the hotel. So that arrangements can be completed in the minimum time, I suggest that you wire or call Booth at Captiol 1-4920. He will secure your accommodations.

Appendix 1, cont'd

-2-

The meeting is being called for Wednesday and Thursday, November fourth and fifth. I hope you will do everything possible to be present. This fight means personal sacrifices for all of us and our churches as well. Rest assured we mean business.

Write me, air-mail special, wire or call so that we may know if you can come. Please try to arrange to arrive by noon of November fourth. I have every reason to believe we can conclude our work and check out by 3 p.m. November fifth.

I hope that the purpose and plans are clear. With every good wish to you and yours, believe me to be

Cordially yours,

Cornell E. Talley

CET:vrf

Appendix 2

MU. 8-726

𝔈𝔟𝔢𝔫𝔢𝔷𝔢𝔯 𝔅𝔞𝔭𝔱𝔦𝔰𝔱 ℭ𝔥𝔲𝔯𝔠𝔥

407 - 413 Auburn Ave., N. E.
ATLANTA 12, GA.

MINISTERS:
M. L. KING SR.
M. L. KING JR.

August 9, 1960

Rev. L. Venchael Booth
Zion Baptist Church
430-432 Ninth Street
Cincinnati 3, Ohio

My dear Rev. Booth:

We are in receipt of your letter of August 4, 1960.

Thanks for your prompt reply stating you and Zion Baptist Church being willing to be placed in the "Selected Sixty", also the check for one hundred dollars ($100.00). I am forwarding your check on to "The Taylor Team Headquarters."

Things are shaping up quite well down this side and in other states where I have been.

Keep praying and keep working. We are in a struggle that is destined to win.

I am sure you will receive an official receipt from the headquarters.

Very truly yours,

M. L. King, Sr.

MLK:sr

Appendix 3

The Taylor Team Defense Fund

In Defense of our Basic Baptist Liberties
and the Integrity
of the

National Baptist Convention, U. S. A., Inc.

GARDNER TAYLOR, President (By the Will of the People)
833 MARCY AVENUE, BROOKLYN 16, N. Y.
Phone MAin 2-1819

NATIONAL OFFICERS

The Reverend Sandy F. Ray, New York
Chairman

The Reverend C. V. Johnson, Illinois
Co-Chairman

The Reverend George Lawrence, New York
Director of Public Relations

The Reverend M. L. King, Sr., Georgia
Finance Chairman

The Reverend Thomas Kilgore, New York
Secretary

The Reverend H. B. Charles, California
Treasurer

October 10, 1960

The Reverend L. Venchael Booth
430-432 West Ninth Street
Cincinnati 3, Ohio

My dear Reverend Booth:

Thank you for your good gift of $50.00 toward defense of our basic Baptist liberties in the National Baptist Convention, U.S.A., Inc. The check has been forwarded.

We have the greatest confidence in the outcome of the litigation into which we have been carried by those who lost the election at Philadelphia. Contrary to distorted reports, circulated by bitter, untruthful men, no court decision has been rendered other than one Judge saying his court does not have jurisdiction. Our attorney is now asking the Pennsylvania Supreme Court to hear the evidence. We are very anxious to have the evidence heard, since we have irrefutable recorded proof of what actually transpired.

Look forward to a crucially important meeting in the forseeable future which I hope you will attend.

Let us go forward together in the name of our God and our Baptist heritage.

Your Brother

Gardner Taylor

GT:wns

Appendix 4

NATIONAL BAPTIST CONVENTION, U. S. A., INC.

VICE PRESIDENT-AT-LARGE
VACANT

VICE PRESIDENTS
C. V. JOHNSON
F. T. GUY

ASSISTANT SECRETARIES
M. K. CURRY, JR.
A. A. BANKS, JR.
S. H. JAMES
KELLY MILLER SMITH

TREASURER
U. J. ROBINSON

GARDNER TAYLOR, PRESIDENT
833 MARCY AVENUE, BROOKLYN 16, NEW YORK

D. E. KING, SECRETARY
2200 WEST WALNUT STREET, LOUISVILLE 12, KENTUCKY

To contend for our basic Baptist

liberties and integrity.

HISTORIOGRAPHER
M. C. WILLIAMS

STATISTICIAN
R. W. NORSWORTHY

ATTORNEY
B. L. HOOKS,
COUNSELOR-AT-LAW

EDITOR, NATIONAL BAPTIST
VOICE
H. C. NABRIT

CHAIRMAN, SOCIAL SERVICE
COMMISSION
RALPH D. ABERNATHY

CHAIRMAN PUBLICITY
GEORGE LAWRENCE

December 12, 1960

The Reverend L. Venchael Booth
430-432 West 9th Street
Cincinnati, Ohio

My dear Reverend Booth:

I could not refrain from writing to thank you for your incalculable contribution to our recent National Baptist Convention meeting in Louisville. The warm enthusiasm of so many men was due in no large part to the service which you rendered.

I believe that bright, bright prospects open before our denomination. Let us spread the word of Louisville's success and the portents so many of us sense of a glad, new day in our denomination.

I am enclosing a copy of our registration income and expenditures for your information.

All blessings on your work!

Sincerely, as ever,

Gardner Taylor

GT:wll
Encl. 1.

Appendix 5

NATIONAL BAPTIST CONVENTION, U. S. A., INC.

VICE PRESIDENT-AT-LARGE
VACANT

VICE PRESIDENTS
C. V. JOHNSON
F. T. GUY

ASSISTANT SECRETARIES
M. K. CURRY, JR.
A. A. BANKS, JR.
S. H. JAMES
KELLY MILLER SMITH

TREASURER
U. J. ROBINSON

GARDNER TAYLOR, PRESIDENT
833 MARCY AVENUE, BROOKLYN 16, NEW YORK

D. E. KING, SECRETARY
2200 WEST WALNUT STREET, LOUISVILLE 12, KENTUCKY

To contend for our basic Baptist liberties and integrity.

HISTORIOGRAPHER
M. C. WILLIAMS

STATISTICIAN
R. W. NORSWORTHY

ATTORNEY
B. L. HOOKS,
COUNSELOR-AT-LAW

EDITOR, NATIONAL BAPTIST
VOICE
H. C. NABRIT

CHAIRMAN, SOCIAL SERVICE
COMMISSION
RALPH D. ABERNATHY

CHAIRMAN PUBLICITY
GEORGE LAWRENCE

August 9, 1961

The Reverend L. Venchael Booth
430-432 W. Ninth Street
Cincinnati 3, Ohio

My dear Reverend Booth:

I have received your generous gift of $200.00 to our Defense Fund for which I am very grateful, and am forwarding it to Dr. U.J. Robinson today.

I am thrilled at your enthusiastic and favorable response to our request. As we move toward the home stretch, let us permeate the atmosphere with victory.

Please keep praying and working. Victory is waiting for us. I am looking forward to seeing you in Kansas City.

With all good wishes, I am

Sincerely,

Gardner Taylor

GT:wll

Appendix 6

October 19, 1957

Dr. Theodore F. Adams
The First Baptist Church
Richmond, Virginia

Dear Dr. Adams:

I wish to take this opportunity to call to your attention the plight of
5 million Baptist who comprise the National Baptist Convention, Inc., a
member convention of the Baptist World Alliance. This convention is now
divided into two sharply opposing camps over the validity of their constitution as it relates to the question of "Tenure" for the office of president.
If you are not too familiar with this controversy, I should like to have you
confer with President J. H. Jackson of Chicago, and Dr. W. H. Borders
of Atlanta, Georgia. Dr. W. H. Jernagin of Washington, D. C. can give
you an impartial thesis on this question also.

My purpose for writing you is to inquire if you would be willing to
talk with leaders representing the two sides and advise us in this crucial
hour of fateful decision. It is my belief that God can use you in this hour
to help restore unity in this body of Baptized Believers. It is to be remembered that our report for the Evangelistic Advance that you have called for
in 1960 will be poor indeed if we continue to wrangle among ourselves. I
am certain also that you would not appreciate having another National Baptist Convention to represent in the next session of the Alliance.

Let me suggest therefore, as an immediate step that you will request
Dr. W. H. Borders, or Dr. W. H. Jernagin to advise our Attorney to delay
action until a real try at conciliation is made----a Mediation Board of "Top
Level" leaders be formed to hear discussions on this issue and aid in working
out a Compromise that will eventually restore unity and forestall further legal actions.

Appendix 6, cont'd

At a time in history when our whole world trembles in fear and unrest over the development of strange and powerful nuclear weapons, (for the destruction of mankind) Christian leaders can ill afford to persist in dispnity and strife. Moreover, more fortunate leaders can ill afford "to pass by on the other side" as though it is no concern of theirs. Therefore, Dr. Adams, I appeal to you because your help is needed in this perilous hour. I sincerely believe that the influence of your great office and particularly the influence of your strong character as a Christian could not be used more advantageously than to calm the unrest that now beseiges us and as a consequence threatens to destroy the Unity of this particular group of Baptists.

I shall prayerfully await your decision and replyl

Sincerely yours,

L. Venchael Booth

Appendix 7

MOREHOUSE COLLEGE

ATLANTA, GEORGIA

OFFICE OF THE PRESIDENT

October 21, 1957

Rev. L. Venchael Booth
432 West 9th Street
Cincinnati 3, Ohio

Dear Rev. Booth:

I have your good letter of October 17.

I am glad to know that you appreciate my article in the recent issue of the COURIER on the National Baptist Convention, Incorporated. I tried to write with restraint and I hope I have written constructively.

I hardly know what to say about your suggestion. You are mighty optimistic if you expect Dr. Jackson to accept any compromise proposal. I feel convinced that he has ruled that there is no tenure in the Constitution and that he was legally elected president of the Convention. From that position, I do not believe Dr. Jackson will retreat. I think he would even resent anyone suggesting that three white men come in to mediate the situation. I think your effort would be futile. I may be entirely wrong and if so I will apologize.

With kindest regards and best wishes, I am

Yours truly,

Benjamin E. Mays
President

BEM:J

Appendix 8

MRS BESSIE ESTELL, SECRETARY
BIRMINGHAM, ALA.

J. C. OLIVER, TREASURER
CHICAGO, ILL.

National Sunday School and B. T. U. Congress
U. S. A

DR. W. H. JERNAGIN, PRESIDENT
1728 WEBSTER STREET, N. W.
WASHINGTON 11, D. C.

Oct. 24, 1957

Rev. L. Venchael Booth
430-432 W. Ninth Street
Cincinnati 3, Ohio

My dear Rev. Booth:

Your letter of Oct. 17 was received and prayerfully considered. I have just returned from Toronto, Canada, last night, hence the delay in answering you.

Now in regard to your suggestions, they are very fine and Christian, however, we are up against this kind of situation - first, the suit may be filed by now; secondly, as hard boiled as J. H. is and as ambitious as he is to be president, I do not think he would pay any attention to what these two presidents might say if they agree to do it, knowing he has had his lawyer to give a written opinion on the constitution and then third, of course, these men are all in separate distant states who are signing this petition. It is not like we were here in Washington and together like in Louisville where I could talk with them together. They have put up the money and have ordered their attorney to go ahead with it. I read the affidavit they propose to sue on. I doubt very much now that I could get the attorney to wait until I could try to get hold of them. These are the petitioners: W. H. Borders, Georgia; T. M. Chambers, California; J. F. Green, Michigan; E. E. Hollins, Louisiana; L. K. Jackson, Indiana; Carl Mitchell, West Virginia; S. A. Owen, Tennessee; M. L. Shephard, Pennsylvania; E. C. Smith, D. C. and Roland Smith, Arkansas.

It seems that is a matter that has gone too far at this particular time for me to be able to accomplish what you suggested. Of course, Dr. Harrison has left for Texas. He was gone on my return from Canada and I could not talk with him, however, I am glad to see that your interest in what is best to do is alive and in accordance with the Scripture, but I fear you have waited too long to propose such a proposition.

We had a fine Executive Meeting of the Youth Conference of the Baptist World Alliance in Toronto, Canada, in preparing a program for next June.

Well, I want to say that not only was I delighted, but all of my friends as to the way you pictured me as a Christian last Monday night.

Appendix 8, cont'd

-2-

I want to thank you again for the scrap book. That was very thoughtful of you.

Mrs. Jernagin joins me in love to you and family.

Sincerely yours,

WHJ:cmh   W. H. Jernagin

Appendix 9

First Baptist Church

Monument Avenue and The Boulevard

RICHMOND 20, VIRGINIA

THEODORE F. ADAMS
PASTOR
O. J. HODGES
ASSOCIATE PASTOR
WALLACE E. PARHAM
ASSOCIATE PASTOR
WINIFRED TUMBLIN
ASSISTANT TO PASTOR
MARY EVELYN HENSLEY
CHILDREN'S WORKER

CHURCH STAFF
ROSALIE B. DIXON
ALTON L. HOWELL
MABEL N. BRIGGS
ETHEL OWEN
ELSIE S. PALMORE
JANE ROARK

October 30, 1957

Dr. L. Venchael Booth
Zion Baptist Church
430-432 W. Ninth Street
Cincinnati 3, Ohio

Dear Friend:

I was glad to get your letter. I appreciate greatly your confidence
in me and your concern in the present situation in the National Baptist
Convention, Inc.

Believe me I share your concern about the future of the Convention and do
want to help if it is possible to do so. I do, however, have an honest
question as to whether I should initiate any such effort.

If the leaders of the Convention, or the leaders in the controversy should
ask for some outside effort toward conciliation; I should, of course, be
happy to do anything I could but it would be rather difficult and a little
presumptious for me to suggest such a step myself. I do hope and pray that
the leaders in your Convention can get together, for certainly we want to do
all we can to strengthen our work rather than to divide it in these days.

With appreciation for your thoughtfulness and a prayer for God's guidance
in this whole matter, I am

Sincerely yours,

Theodore F. Adams

Appendix 10

HOWARD UNIVERSITY
WASHINGTON 1, D. C.

OFFICE OF THE PRESIDENT

November   Seventh

1   9   5   7

Dear Mr. Booth:

Please allow me to acknowledge and to thank you for
your recent letter with its proposal   for a conciliatory settlement
of the difficulties prevailing among our brethren in the National
Baptist Convention.   I agree with your proposal most heartily,
and I share your conviction that we have leaders who are wise
enough, impartial enough and just enough to help us through any
struggle such as this

You have done well, I think, to address yourself directly
to Dr. Jernagin. He is fully in touch with all the issues in the matter and he is a pure-hearted, wise and devoted leader. Unfortunate-
ly, I was not able to be present at the convention in Louisville and
I am not fully acquainted with the issues, therefore, as would be needful for one who took the initiative in this matter. If, however, Dr.
Jernagin and Dr. Jackson should call upon me for conciliatory help,
I would be glad to be of service in any possible way.

Once again, let me thank you for your letter and for the
spirit of concern and good will which your letter bears.

Sincerely yours,

Mordecai W. Johnson

Mr. L. Venchael Booth
432 W. Ninth Street
Cincinnati, Ohio

Appendix 11

A High Call To Greatness
by Dr. L. Venchael Booth

Once more the power of political might as demonstrated by a great machine has triumphed. Once more men of great ideals have been humbled to the dust. Once more men of great intelligence have been made to crawl before the powerful might of the ignorant, insecure and unstable of our time. Hopes have perished, dreams have faded and visions have been snuffed out. They would be conqueror and deliverers have been shamed, defeated and silenced. The voices of the mighty protest have been stilled. The glory of Philadelphia has melted into the tragedy of Kansas City. Generation to come shall murmur— "remember Kansas City, Mo. in '61."

They shall remember that here heroism died, militantism was crushed, and idealism was buried. Where are the men who boldly championed "Freedom must be restored in the house of our Fathers?" Where are the men who abhorred a split in the ranks—but silently accepted the loss of an innocent man's life as one of the tragic incidents of life? Did these men go to battle or did they start a war with water guns, or did they call others to battle with plastic bugles? Did they issue a false alarm to the enslaved children of God?

Why do men begin crusades without any alternatives other than surrender? Are we so poverty stricken in wisdom that we are bound to the weak walls of tradition? Is our mental telescope so short that we cannot see beyond the bridge? Is it really true that we have only one leader today who is certain about something and really going somewhere? Are we over-run by philosophers who cannot bear a rugged cross?

Is it true that we comprise a group that issued a call when there was not battle? Challenged the innocent when there was no war? Championed freedom while committed to slavery? What is the great crime of coming apart from those who defile us? Or what is the crime of separating from those who deny us our

Appendix 11, cont'd

freedom? Or parting from those who would crush our initiative? What is the crime? Shall we have unity at any costs?

There are thousands who do not believe that we must have unity at any cost. There are many in this group who have only a few years to share their wisdom and love with the present and on-coming generation. They must be provided a climate in which they can feel a sense of security. There are many in this group who are young, they must be given something worthy of their aspirations. We cannot call men and lead them nowhere except in beaten paths well-worn. We cannot f re their imaginations while our own senses are dulled. We must not preach a Gospel of Freedom while our own hearts are enslaved. We must be forthright, daring and sincere with a willingness to suffer as men who are certain about something.

The record should be set straight about who is splitting the Convention. We who separate at this time are not. We are simply trying to make the most of a tragic condition. The leader who creates disunity, expels members, throws out officers and banishes opponents is the real Convention splitter. We who separate are simply trying to salvage the dignity of a life-time struggle, preserve the contributions of our Fathers and bequeath to our children the best of our heritage. Our separation is for the purpose of restoring men to a sense of responsibility, spirituality, and service. Ours is a high call to greatness.

Appendix 12

November 21, 1961

Dr. Gardner C. Taylor
833 Marcy Avenue
Brooklyn 16, New York

My dear Dr. Taylor:

Once again I am deeply indebted to you for the sacred privilege of standing in your stead to speak to the magnificient array of women gathered in Concord last Sunday morning, together with a manifestly responsive group of men. It was a Day of Days for me! The inspiration I received, the delicious dinner, the ride to the subway with your Mother, the liberal honorarium - yes everything was most gracious. Not forgetting the privilege to participate in the unique evening Program so ably directed by Mrs. Taylor, to highlight the sanctity of Marriage. Can there be a stronger word than "Thank You?"

I am happy I went to the newly formed Ministers Conference yesterday. I had invited Rev. and Mrs. Brent to New York as my dinner guests, and I was proud of his courage to give that glowing report on the Cincinnati meeting. And when you later told me that you are "coming to help us" in due course, my heart leaped for joy. We all appreciate your position. You expressed our position when you said, in presenting Dr. Stamps for his address: "It is not a personality but a principle" that leads us on. Without you, Dr. Taylor, we will definitely forge head, out with you, we will more easily and quickly achieve the purpose which we are convinced is right. I understand that Dr. Borders did not go to Cincinnati nor send any word. However, God still has many souls who are not in the category of the little boy in your fighting joke - A Gideon's final number.

God bless you and continue to make you a blessing.

Most gratefully yours,

Appendix 13

Corona Council of Church Women

Affiliate of United Church Women of the National Council of Churches of Christ

Mrs. Uvee Mdodana-Arbouin, President
27-43 GILMORE STREET
EAST ELMHURST 69, L. I., N. Y.
Hickory 6-1030

November 21, 1961

Vice Presidents
Mrs. Gertrude Floyd
Mrs. Helen Troupe

Recording Secretaries
Mrs. Almeta Trent
Mrs. Ruth McLaughlin

Corresponding Secretary
Mrs. May A . Andt
40-35 Warren Street
Elmhurst 73, N. Y.

Financial Secretary
Mrs. Susie Atkins

Treasurer
Mrs. Marie Anderson

Dear Dr. Booth:

The Brents and Miss Fishburn haven given me a
fine report of the response to your CALL. Please read carefully
the enclosed copy of my letter to Dr. Taylor. It will save my
writing more on the subject here, except to say that this Ministers
Conference which was organized a few months after our Philadelphia
Convention is composed entirely of men who were active in the
Taylor Team. Yesterday they had installation of new officers and
Dr. Stamps is the new President. Dr. Stamps is also an officer
in the new Mission Bureau, hence I feel sure he will come to
help us. When Dr. Brent asked for the floor (you see he is not
on program) and brought greetings from the United Baptist
Convention of America, Inc. there was thunderous applause. You will
recall my telling you that the sentiment here is excellent, but
there are not many souls who will greatly dare. Now there is
the feeling that I think the folk must have had about Little
David of the Bible.

You should have the Negro paper I sent you by
this time. Rev. Arbouin is improving slowly and is much
interested. Let us have "your side" of the report, won't you?
Many men told Dr. Brent and me that they will attend the Board
Meeting which he announced.

I am eager to know what happened to Dr. Borders?
Was he bought? Surely not! Did you hear from him?

Personally, I am very proud of you. Your refusal
to accept the Presidency might help our Cause - it will at least
prove that your motive was not one of personal gain. "Keep
on believing - God will answer prayer."

Your co-worker,

Uvee Mdodana-Arbouin

PURPOSE: *"To unite Church Women in their allegiance to their Lord and Savior Jesus Christ, through a program looking to their integration in the total life and work of the Church, and to the building of a world Christian Community."*

Appendix 14

Friendship Baptist Church
MARVIN T. ROBINSON, PASTOR
PHONE MU. 1-5434

"The Friendly Church in Beautiful Pasadena"

OFFICE
OF THE
PASTOR

80 WEST DAYTON STREET
PASADENA 2, CALIFORNIA

October 11, 1961

Rev. L. V. Booth
630 Glenwood Ave.
Cincinnate 29, Ohio

Dear Booth,

Thanks for your letter of September 26. It was kind of you to honor me with a prompt reply.

Booth, don't think for once that my open letter suggesting that a top strategy meeting should preceed a call to the organization of a new National Baptist Convention, is to rival your meeting. I think your expression along with that of others in Philadelphia, Dallas and elsewhere are timely. I know how vacillation and how pastors will leave you holding the bag until it looks like victory and they pop up from no where. I sent out 100 letters which is intended to feel pastors out on what next in our national fellowship, and to date only about eight pastors have done me the courtesy to reply. After thirty or forty days I shall send out a second letter expressing the feelings of those who saw fit to answer. (no names will be mentioned) Booth, I don't plan to get out on a limb, as I can do nothing.

I cannot attend your meeting but I am prepared to meet with top pastors to set the stage for our future course.

You have my prayers.

Sincerely,

Marvin T. Robinson

MTR:ec

Appendix 15

November 3, 1961

Rev. L. V. Booth
Zion Baptist Church
630 Glenwood Avenue
Cincinnati 29, Ohio

My dear Dr. Booth:

There will be four in my party. We will be arriving by
Jet at 11:15 on Tuesday Nov. 14. *Mon. 13th.* Please make hotel reservations.

I suppose we are the last of the Mohecians . I reminded
our men in Miami that we would be sorry if they elected J. H.
Jackson. I was a member of the Olivet Baptist Church before
Dr. Jackson was pastor. hence I know many of his tactics.

Many of the men here in the east who are in favor of the
New Convention do not quite understand your avowed detachment
from the (Taylor Team) Do we not need their strength? We
will talk it over upon my arrival. If you would like to call
me collect I would be glad to talk to you.

Yours for a greater Baptist Fellowship,

A. Ross Brent

ARB/sr

Appendix 16

The Concord Baptist Church of Christ

AND

THE CONCORD BAPTIST ELEMENTARY SCHOOL

MADISON STREET AND PUTNAM AVENUE AT MARCY AVENUE

MAILING ADDRESS

833 MARCY AVENUE, BROOKLYN 16, NEW YORK

MAIN 2-1818

THE REVEREND GARDNER TAYLOR, D.D.

PASTOR

July 8, 1963

Rev. L. Venchael Booth
630 Glenwood Avenue
Cincinnati 29, Ohio

Dear Reverend Booth:

Thank you for your kind invitation to me to appear on the program for the 2nd Annual Session of the Progressive National Baptist Convention from September 3 - 8, 1963. I regret, due to congregational responsibilities, I cannot remain in Detroit until the week-end. Were it not for this, I would be happy to appear.

With all good wishes, I am,

Sincerely,

Gardner Taylor

GT/p

Appendix 17

I envy you! Today I become Vice-President of the Progressive National Baptist Convention — but you become saint and seer of a people's movement in response to the pushings and promptings of God. When my name is will live in the grateful memory of a bruised people who responded to your vision and who must venerate your name now as long as this convention shall last. Count me forever debtor and suppliant and aspirant to what you are.

Appendix 18

The Concord Baptist Church of Christ

AND

THE CONCORD BAPTIST ELEMENTARY SCHOOL

MADISON STREET AND PUTNAM AVENUE AT MARCY AVENUE
MAILING ADDRESS
833 MARCY AVENUE, BROOKLYN 16, NEW YORK

MAIN 2-1818

THE REVEREND GARDNER TAYLOR, D.D.
PASTOR

September 9, 1963

The Reverend L. Venchael Booth
Zion Baptist Church
630 Glenwood A^Venue .
Cincinnati 29, Ohio

My dear ~~Reverend~~ *Venchael* Booth:

Would you be so kind as to send to me a mailing list of
our delegates in Detroit, Michigan? I am hopeful of circulating
through the country some excerpts from the classic, "Towards the
Creation of a New Convention Being A Declaration of the Organization,
Principles and Aims of The Progressive Baptist Convention of America,
Incorporated." I hope to do this as a gift from our church at about
Christmas. Also, would you please send to me 100 copies or as many
as you can spare of the Minutes of the First Annual Session of our
convention.

All blessings on you and your work.

Sincerely,

Gardner Taylor

GT:wll

*P.S. You were magnificent, and I think in
the long run you will find that you can
do a more lasting job in your new post.*

Appendix 19

The Concord Baptist Church of Christ

AND

THE CONCORD BAPTIST ELEMENTARY SCHOOL

MADISON STREET AND PUTNAM AVENUE AT MARCY AVENUE

MAILING ADDRESS

833 MARCY AVENUE, BROOKLYN 16, NEW YORK

MAIN 2-1818

THE REVEREND GARDNER TAYLOR, D.D.

PASTOR

September 13, 1963

The Reverend L. Venchael Booth
630 Glenwood Avenue
Cincinnati 29, Ohio

Dear Booth:

I have received the material which you sent to me and
for which I am very grateful. Please advise me if this is the
enrollment of the churches that met in Detroit.I am most
anxious to have that list. Thank you for helping me out in
this matter.

With all good wishes, I am

Sincerely,

Gardner Taylor

GT:wll

_I'm confused at the speed with which you
got this to me & which led me to
wonder if this is the Detroit list
or Philadelphia_

Appendix 20

The Progressive National Baptist Convention, U. S. A., Inc.

THE REVEREND T. M. CHAMBERS, President

THE REVEREND GARDNER TAYLOR
Vice-President-At-Large

THE REVEREND L. V. BOOTH
Executive Secretary

OFFICE OF THE VICE-PRESIDENT-AT-LARGE
833 MARCY AVENUE
BROOKLYN 16, N. Y.

December 27, 1963

Dr. L. V. Booth
630 Glenwood Avenue
Cincinnati, Ohio   45229

Dear Venchael:

Thank you for your good letter of December 17th. I think you and I must be communicating strength, one to the other, since I felt a surge of confidence after our meeting. We must continue to do this.

As to my schedule, I am surely planning to be in St. Louis on April 21. I suggest that you reach John Nance about a church, not necessarily too close in location to his, where we can meet all day April 21, and that evening. We will need, I am sure, a church in which 5 or 6 groups can meet simultaneously and where a restaurant is not too far. President Chambers, to whom I am sending a copy of our correspondence, will, I am sure, suggest some names to you. We must get some of our very best minds. They ought to be divided among study groups on (1) Education (2) Budget (3) Relations to other Bodies (4) Publications (5) Public Affairs or Social Concern (6) Missions. One(1) and six (6) are really committees on Objectives, but I believe at this stage we need too much study of each matter to have them combined. What do you think? There may be other committees of which you might think. Seven or ten men to a group will be ideal, I think. The big job is getting men who will truly delve and plan. Melvin Watson in Atlanta would be an excellent man on the committee on Education. Unless President Chambers has other suggestions, I think we ought to press forward on our plans. This is vital for our future, I know. I am sending out a letter to Baptist pastors all through the country to announce how well we are moving and opening the door for them to throw in with us.

All blessings on your family in the New Year.

Sincerely,

Gardner Taylor

GT:wll

Appendix 21

The Progressive National Baptist Convention, U. S. A., Inc.

THE REVEREND T. M. CHAMBERS, President

THE REVEREND GARDNER TAYLOR
Vice-President-At-Large

THE REVEREND L. V. BOOTH
Executive Secretary

OFFICE OF THE VICE-PRESIDENT-AT-LARGE
833 MARCY AVENUE
BROOKLYN 16, N. Y.

January 6, 1964

Dr. L. Venchael Booth
630 Glenwood Avenue
Cincinnati 29, Ohio

Dear Venchael:

I feel very good about the seal on your stationery. It is
particularly gratifying to read your newsletter and your account
of gifts. You have genius for organized, sustained promotion.
This will largely determine our effectiveness. Let us stay at
it day in and day out.

Every blessing on you in the New Year.

Sincerely,

Gardner Taylor

GT:wll

P.S. Please find enclosed our first montly gift.
Encl.1.

*P.S. Let me see the list of those invited
as soon as possible. Carry on!*

Appendix 22

The Progressive National Baptist Convention, U. S. A., Inc.

THE REVEREND T. M. CHAMBERS, President

HE REVEREND GARDNER TAYLOR
Vice-President-At-Large

THE REVEREND L. V. BOOTH
Executive Secretary

OFFICE OF THE VICE-PRESIDENT-AT-LARGE
833 MARCY AVENUE
BROOKLYN 16, N. Y.

April 8, 1964

Dr. L. Venchael Booth
630 Glenwood Avenue
Cincinnati, Ohio   45229

Dear Venchael:

Thank you for keeping me abreast of things. I am elated
at the vigorous and enlightened way you are pressing the cause of
Progressive Baptists at the World's Fair and generally among American
Baptists and the National Council. I was commenting to Earl Harrison
and others in Washington of what inspired service you are rendering
to all of us.

As to St. Louis, our program is to be W O R K. I have
sent to each Group Leader some questions that have occured to
me. I am sending copies to you. We shall have brief devotions,
divide into Study Groups, and then reassemble for a worship service, and, if there is time, hear summations of the work which
are to be presented at Atlanta. Let me know if you think of some
other procedure we ought to follow.

I was pleased to see young Booth in Washington.

With all good wishes, I am

Sincerely, as ever,

Gardner Taylor

GT:wll
Encls.

Appendix 23

Earl L. Harrison, D. D., Pastor
Shiloh Baptist Church
1500 - 1508 NINTH STREET, N.W.
WASHINGTON, D. C. 20001
Phones: Office AD 4-6667 or DU 7-2046   Res. RA 3-5163

Sept. 19-70

Dear L. V.:

I was overwhelmingly pleased at your complete and unquestionable victory in the race for Vice President in K.C. Mo. last week.

This private, personal note comes to request that if you are in the east on any other business before Dec. 9, please see if I am home, and stop by. If you cannot stay over, I will gladly meet you at air port and we can talk between plans. Something you should know.

I hope you and yours are well.

Sincerely   E. L. Harrison

Appendix 24

Progressive National Baptist Convention, Inc.

EARL L. HARRISON, D.D., *President*
1500 - 1508 NINTH STREET, N.W.
WASHINGTON, D.C. 20001

Phones: Office AD 4-6667 or DU 7-2046   Res.: RA 3-5163

Headquarters:
SUITE 204, ETON TOWERS
1239 VERMONT AVENUE, N.W.
WASHINGTON, D.C. 20005
DR. S. S. HODGES
Executive Secretary

DR. VENCHAEL BOOTH, Ohio
1st Vice President

REV. H. A. SMITH, Ala.
2nd Vice President

August 12-71

Dear L.V.:

I am in a tight conflict with my body. It is too soon to predict the victor or the victim. It is possible that I cannot get to the Houston Convention, just in case be ready to take over and carry on. The Lord's work must not be wanting because one worker drops out.

I am ready to go to Houston, stay in Washington or to go to my Lord. Do not put out any alarm, wait until opening day. If I can come I will.

God bless you. This is your day

Earl Harrison

Appendix 25

Vermont Avenue Baptist Church

1630 VERMONT AVENUE, N. W.
WASHINGTON, D. C.
NORTH 7-1078

REV. C. T. MURRAY, *Minister*
1001 - 3rd Street, S. W.
Apt. #315 North
Tel. 347-2169

Ministerial Staff

REV. C. E. FIELDS
4412 Illinois Ave., N. W.
TU. 2-5742
REV. JOHN WHEELER
RA. 3-8815
REV. ALBERT R. WARD, JR.
LU. 1-4910
REV. FREDERICK DOUGLAS O'NEAL
RA. 3-0325

Personnel

DEACON KLINTON C. MOSS,
 Chairman Board of Deacons
LI. 3-7785
TRUSTEE JAS. L. COLES,
 Chairman Board of Trustees
DU. 7-2465
MR. DONALD VOWELS,
 Church Clerk
LU. 3-0549
MRS WILLYE MAE FREEMAN,
 ch Secretary
LA. J-2986
MRS. SALLIE D. LIGHTFOOT,
 Office Secretary
RA. 3-1141

Oct. 23, 1961

Rev. L. Venchael Booth
3415 Dura Avenue
Cincinnati, Ohio

Dear Rev. Booth:

Regret very much that the issues of the National Baptist Convention have come down in the churches. Many of the churches are divided on the issues. When ministers are invited for special occasions, a question is asked in some of the churches, "Is he a Taylor team man or a Jack man?"

We will have none of this in our Anniversary Celebration. Dr. W. C. Somerville, Executive Secretary of the Lott Carey Foreign Mission Convention, will be the Anniversary Speaker.

Regret so very much.

Yours very truly,

C. T. Murray

Appendix 26

Towards The Creation of a New Convention

Being

A Declaration of the Organization, Principles and Aims of

THE PROGRESSIVE BAPTIST CONVENTION OF AMERICA, INCORPORATED

Resolved and Authorized at Richmond, Virginia, Thursday Morning, May 10, 1962

INITIATION • MOTIVATION • INSPIRATION • DEDICATION • COMMENDATION

—I—
INITIATION

Pursuant to an urgent and widely publicized invitation to a Convocation, for the express purpose of considering the deep and wide-spread unrest persisting within our ranks, and to determine what should, or could, be done about it, and in what direction action, if any, should be undertaken, disturbed Baptist delegates, messengers and friends from fourteen states met in the Church Home of the Zion Baptist Church, Cincinnati, Ohio, Dr. L. Venchael Booth, Pastor, Wednesday and Thursday, November 15 and 16, 1961; and, after earnest devotions and prayer for divine guidance, entered into a wide and prolonged analysis of the problem for which they had been summoned, and concluded their deliberations in the following resolutions unanimously adopted. To wit, RESOLVED:

1— That the deep seated, persistent and progressively worsening dissension long existing among us as Baptists has come to that state of condition which ought no longer to be tolerated by honest, self-respecting and God-fearing men, and should now receive immediate corrective and constructive remedy.

2— That, inasmuch as all the long forbearance and democratic effort seeking reformation within the framework of our Communion have brought no hope of redress, there is, therefore, now nothing left for the aggrieved to do, but to seek such relief, as their sense of obligation to Christ and dedicated manliness demand, within the framing of a new and different contextus.

3— That this new context ought to be, and is hereby, through the perpetually reserved freedom of independent action belonging to us as Baptists, brought into being, and shall be known, and hereafter referred to as, THE PROGRESSIVE BAPTIST CONVENTION OF AMERICA, INCORPORATED.

4— That all such machinery deemed essential to the Incorporation of this New Body: make provision for its constitution: selection of its objectives: determination of its policies: and give life and purpose to its activities be, and is, here and now created: and shall continue to function until such time and place when the whole matter now disturbing us shall be reviewed again, acted upon and finally disposed, either by conciliation or confirmation.

5— That such officers as President, Vice-President, Secretary, Treasurer, Director of Publicity and Attorney, be here and now elected: and that these shall consist of Doctors T. M. Chambers, California, President; L. V. Booth, Ohio, Vice-President; J. Carl Mitchell, West Virginia, Secretary; Louis Rawls, Illinois, Treasurer; Andrews J. Hargett, Director of Publicity; and Honorable William W. Parker, Attorney.

6— That an extended session of this present convocation be held with the Tabernacle Baptist Church, Dr. Louis Rawls, Pastor, Chicago, Illinois, January 30 through February 1, 1962 at which time, all such action as has been taken in this initial meeting shall be reviewed, approved or disapproved, and permanently concluded.

Thus, notwithstanding, the deepest possible grief over the circumstances existing among us which make this action necessary, out of these initial prayers, deliberations and conclusions arrived at in the Cincinnati Meeting, confirmed and augmented by representatives from eighteen states and the District of Columbia assembled in a three day session, January 30 - February 1, 1962 in the Church Home of the Tabernacle Baptist Church, Chicago, Illinois, Dr. Louis Rawls, Pastor, and subsequently approved and enlarged by messengers and delegates from eleven states and the District of Columbia convened in a Second Regional Meeting in the Cedar Street Memorial Baptist Church, Richmond, Virginia, Dr. Benjamín W. Robertson,

Pastor, May 9-10, 1962, a new Convention known as The Progressive Baptist Convention of America, Incorporated, has been created, chartered and set upon a course of sincere goodwill, service to Christ and helpfulness to His people.

—II—
MOTIVATION

In the act of withdrawing from any Christian fellowship of which they have been long time members, to which they have given their allegiance, prayers, goodwill and support; whose fellowship and brotherhood have been deeply meaningful to them over a long period, for the purpose of creating a new and independent body that, in the very nature of things, cannot help but be parallel in its aims and in many respects a duplication of much that already exists, men of honor and high Christian integrity realize, that they have embarked upon a course of serious and far-reaching consequences; that their persuasions and motives toward such an act should be impersonal, Christian and of such solid worth that men of good judgment can approve and the Holy Spirit endorse; and that, concommitantly they owe it to themselves, to their brethren, to the world, to their Saviour, to set forth the motivations for their action in such a way, that sane men and women can understand their compulsion and history their valor.

Therefore, mindful of all such considerations, the promoters of the Progressive Baptist Convention of America, Incorporated, are more than pleased to set forth humbly and prayerfully for the considerate judgment of mankind in some detail and with all the clarity to them possible, the reasons that have constrained them to form themselves into a new compact. They have acted in this premise, as they have, because they believe:

1— That the time is overdue when Baptists should live, conduct their work,

Appendix 26, cont'd

and deport themselves in all their respective Conventions and Meetings in the Spirit of Christ and Christian brotherhood, and thus redeem themselves and their churches from the stigma and blight of the age-old tensions from which they have suffered so long, which have climaxed so rudely in these recent years, and which have thereby reduced His good name to the shame of His friends, and the sneering contempt of the enemies of our Lord Jesus Christ.

2— That believing themselves to be men of Christian maturity, free from the spirit of fanaticism, above emotional extravagance, opponents of cism, and capable of forming an intelligent concept of Christian procedure, the promoters of the Progressive Baptist Convention of America, Incorporated, declare it to be their unvarnished conviction, that all such incidents as of occurrence at Denver 1956; Lousville 1957; Philadelphia 1960; and Kansas City 1961 are indefensible, an embarrassment to Baptist churches, an offense to sober intelligence, an enduring impediment to Christian witness, and constitute a situation which reasonable men should not be expected longer to tolerate, or violate their conscience in support; so that the organization now taking shape is not a division for division's sake, but is an honest protest of honest men and women directed against a situation they believe long grown intolerable, and for which there does not appear at present any other solution.

3— That, in their judgment, there was not one question sparking either of these incidents of which they complain, ugly though they be, that could not have been resolved quickly by arbitration and democratic procedure, did the Spirit of our Lord Jesus Christ have His rightful place: that it is a sad commentary indeed upon our spiritual state that, in spite of all the sane, conscientious and brotherly advice given, together with the prayerful and painstaking efforts forwarded by some of the most saintly, pious, and inoffensive of our brotherhood, nothing could prevail to avert them; and that such a situation is itself evident revelation of the pain and anguish, good and self-respecting Christians have been compelled to endure across the years.

4— That no organization can hope to function in anything like harmony, the Spirit of Christ, and according to Baptist principles, without a proper constitution and by-laws, justly drawn, duly honored, faithfully observed, and without subjection to change, except and only through the knowledge and consent of the majority governed.

5— That the long continued methods of election illustrated in many of our annual meetings are painfully deplorable; that these procedures are a definite and continuous contribution to the woes and unrest by which our organizations have been plagued; and that, it is hopeless to expect peace and goodwill until the election of presidents and other officials become conducted in the spirit and after the manner common to the history of Baptists from their very inception.

6— That the time is now, when it is required that the president and other officers of our Baptist's Bodies be limited in their tenure of office; that this has been and still is the expressed desire of many of them is shown by their constitutions; that this provision has been in some cases set aside by procedural technicality; that all efforts to correct this technical error have been frustrated: and that in the very nature of things, there can be no harmony so long as the will of such Bodies is thus nullified and substituted by dictatorial control, defiance, and a challenge to all those members not willing to subscribe to such control, to withdraw and provide another fellowship according to their ideas.

7— That there is a vast difference between a "LEADER" and an "EXECUTIVE"—between dictation and executive: (Fidel Castro is a "leader"; John F. Kennedy is an "executive"); that there is no place in Baptist principles for "leaders"; that those principles provide for "executives" only; that in the very nature of democracy, no man can presume to dictate the policy and program of a Baptist institution; that there can never be one legitimate ruling by any president or moderator, on any matter pertaining to a Baptist Body, except and only in the spirit and sympathy with that which has been arrived at, and concluded by a majority of that institution in free and open debate; that at any time the program of a mutual fellowship becomes the program of the president or moderator, then, at that moment, that fellowship ceases to be a Baptist organization; and that, while it is right and customary for a president to think and give a Baptist body the benefit of his best judgment on any and all matters of concern, yet, he is, nevertheless, out of character should he undertake to force that judgment upon the membership of that body without their proper participation, judgment and consent, either directly or else encompass the same by manipulation.

8— That whenever any Baptist Institution becomes a fellowship only, with all of the rights of its members, supervision of its properties and determination of its policies transferred and lodged within an executive board, subject to self-perpetuation or executive appointment, either in part or whole, it is high time indeed for genuine Baptists to raise their protest, even to the point of dissolution, in order that the cause of Christ and the rights of His people be acknowledged and safeguarded.

9— That, so long as the business of any body in its annual session is conducted amid such noise and confusion, and under such circumstances that only a few favored ones around the president upon the rostrum can hear, know what is transpiring, have the right to the floor, be recognized by the chair, have an opportunity to express their opinion, or participate in the voting; so long as the administration of an association can determine arbitrarily the registration of the delegation and what churches shall or shall not become members, by such tactics as frustration, frequent and unannounced closing of the Registrar's Office, alleged failure of machines, summary demand of receipts of former annual representation for admission; so long as any member of any Baptist communion in good and regular standing becomes automatically suspect, prescribed and marked for embarrassment should he possess education, aptitude and talent, or illustrates leadership ability and espouses a program which, in his judgment, is suitable and contemporary with the needs of the people and the times in which he lives; so long as any individual can rent and control the place of meeting; privately purchase the hotel space of the city of a gathering and thus control the housing available to delegates; and so long as any one can then employ the local police to debar any and all other Baptists long time members of an institution in good and regular standing, not thought favorable to the policies of the administration, from entering the place of assemblge, or from participation in the deliberations of the body, there can be no hope of peace, reform or Christian atmosphere; but without which peace, reform and atmosphere no fellowship is worthy the name Christian, nor can it contrive to furnish the spiritual leadership so urgently needed by Baptists in times like ours.

10— And that, in view of their long continued experience, promoters of the Progressive Baptist Convention of America, Incorporated, cannot help but submit that experience as one of the finest examples to all of our churches of the tragic danger inherent in any thought of ecumenical unionism, and a timely warning that the New Testament pattern of independent local churches should be maintained at all costs; for if the present situation of which they complain be illustrative and meaningful in any one thing, it is in the fact that the Church of God can never have any other

Appendix 26, cont'd

Head than our Lord Jesus Christ, without endangering her liberties and forfeiting her rights.

Now therefore, in the presence of such circumstances: the prevailing atmosphere; and the apparent determination to resist even the most elementary reforms so imperatively needed, the promoters of the Progressive Baptist Convention of America, Incorporated, claim it their right and a clear responsibility to accept the contemptuous challenge thrown down to them, by creating another avenue wherein they may be able to carry on their God-given obligation in a way they believe consistent with Christian dignity and the Spirit of evangelical brotherhood; that this new creation shall gladly concede the right of individual members, and provide the medium through which the ever increasing number of young, talented and progressively minded Christian men and women among them can exercise freely their God-given talents and find expression for their leadership skill.

—III—
INSPIRATION

In keeping with good and sound Baptist tradition and practice from time immemorial, the promoters of the Progressive Baptist Convention of America find the inspiration and authority for what they have undertaken to do in what they believe to be the clear implications and forthright directives of the Holy Scriptures, which plainly show:

1— That, whereas, there may be the closest possible unity of purpose and harmony of effort within a church, convention, or other religious movement, yet, if the spirit of that purpose and effort of that church, convention, or movement is outside of the will and Spirit of God, then there should be deliberate and immediate separation.

"And the whole earth was of one language, and one speech. And they said, Go to, let us build us a city and a tower, whose top may reach unto heaven: and let us make us a name, less we be scattered abroad upon the face of the whole earth. And the Lord came down to see the city and the tower, which the children of men builded: So the Lord scattered them abroad from thence upon all the face of the earth."

2— That, whereas, there may be organizational unity within a church, con-

vention, or religious movement, yet, if there be continual strife, and shameful discord over a long and sustained period, with obstinate rejection of a fair adjudication of the rights and principles involved, then there should be brought to pass a new organizational arrangement.

"So that when all Israel saw that the King harkened not unto them, the people answered the King, saying, What portion have we in David? Neither have we inheritance in Jesse: to your tents, O Israel: now see to thine own house David. So all Israel departed unto their tents."

"And when Rehoboam was come to Jerusalem, he assembled all the house of Judah, with the tribe of Benjamin, a hundred and fourscore thousand to fight against the house of Israel to bring the Kingdom again to Rehoboam the son of Solomon."

"But the word of God came unto Shemiah the man of God, saying— thus saith the Lord, Ye shall not go up, nor fight against your brethren, the children of Israel: return every man to his house. FOR THIS THING IS OF ME."

3— That wherever there are those who seek to establish themselves as dictators either within a church, convention, or other religious movement, they should be strenuously and steadfastly rejected.

"But you are not to be called rabbi, for you have one teacher, and you are all brethren. And call no man your father on earth, for you have one Father, who is in heaven. Neither be called masters, for you have one master, the Christ. He who is greatest among you shall be your servant; whoever exalts himself will be humbled, and whoever humbles himself will be exalted."

4— And that, Christians are expressly exhorted to separate themselves from any devisive and offensive leadership which seeks to set aside the doctrines which they have learned.

"I appeal to you, brethren, to take note of those who create dissensions and difficulties, in opposition to the doctrine which you have been taught; avoid them. For such persons do not serve our Lord Christ, but their own appetites, and by fair and flattering words they deceive the hearts of the simple-minded."

—IV—
DEDICATION

In thus committing themselves to the establishment of the Progressive Baptist Convention of America, Incorporated, the promoters thereof do ordain and hereby declare it to be their purpose to dedicate themselves to the proposition:

1— That it is their sincere aim to create and operate a convention whose sole purpose shall be the exaltation of Christ by acting in His will, walking in His Spirit, seeking His glory, and by the maintenance of a reverent respect for his people.

2— That there is not now, nor shall there ever be any intentional bitterness, hostility, or deliberate antagonism on their part, towards any other existing fellowship, its auxiliaries, agents, or its membership; that were it not mandatory that their actions and motives be clearly defined and recorded, there would not be even now one reference at all to the unfortunate incidents of record by which they have been moved to take this step; and that notice is hereby served that, guided by the Holy Spirit, henceforward their emphasis shall be upon their work as they seek with all their God-given grace and might to spread the Gospel of our Lord Jesus Christ.

3— That they intend to maintain reverence for law, order and decency; for Baptist principles and procedure; for honor and justice; for becoming Christian conduct and for a sense of enlightened responsibility.

4— That their Convention shall be built around a constitution and by-laws painstakingly drawn, broad in coverage, detailed in content, fair in provision, steadfast in application, progressive in spirit, relevant in principle, and consistent in operation with contemporary church programs, and present day needs.

5— That the officers of their Convention shall be elected by a majority vote; shall be subject to a term of office; shall be not eligible to succeed themselves; and shall serve their office in the sense and spirit of an "executive" and not a "leader".

6— That their Convention shall have a business administration of such character and thought, as will secure proper accounting and audit from all boards, auxiliaries, and committees receiving funds in the name and on behalf of the Convention; and that all monies received

Appendix 26, cont'd

—V—
COMMENDATION

by the Convention shall be applied, without deviation, to the particular cause for which it was received.

7— That their Convention shall create and maintain all such boards, departments and machinery as shall be necessary to a proper function of the Convention in its program of Foreign and Home Missions; Religious Education; Ministerial Education; Evangelism; Social Welfare; Publication; and the general weal of Baptist interests.

8— That all property purchased within the framework of their Convention shall be so deeded that the title shall be and remain forever within the jurisdiction of the Progressive Convention of America, Incorporated, to own, to enjoy, to order, and to dispose of at will.

9— And that no right, authority, or privilege belonging either to the Convention or its members shall ever be delegated to, or lodged within any committee or board with discretionary authority, or dictatorial oversight; and that the proceedings, labor, and decisions, of all committees and boards shall be subject to the review and final disposition of the Convention itself.

COMPILATION
BY
W. H. R. POWELL, *Minister*
Shiloh Baptist Church
Philadelphia, Pennsylvania

And now, therefore, with the foregoing reasons and purposes for their actions clearly set forth; with a free and satisfied conscience that their motives are legitimate and Christian; with a belief that every courtesy and opportunity has been given to the end that there might be a fair and impartial adjustment of their grievances; with malice toward none and goodwill toward all; with a becoming appreciation for the long and continuous struggle incident to the course they have chosen; with a conscious expectation that their modest and limited beginning will issue one day in magnificent achievement; and with every confidence that a kind Providence will over-rule all to His glory, the organizers and promoters of the Progressive Baptist Convention of America, Incorporated, hereby commend themselves and their cause to a just and merciful God and to an understanding public.

And with this commendation, the brotherhood of this new Convention assembled in its second Regional Session at Richmond, Virginia, hereby extend a hearty and glad invitation to every pastor, church, state, Sunday School, B. T. U. district convention, and association; minister's conference, missionary board and circle within the jurisdiction of our great nation who believe in righteousness, peace, Christian culture, and a fair opportunity for all and sundry Baptists, to meet them in Philadelphia at the Union and Shiloh Baptist Churches, September 4-9, 1962 in the First Annual Session of the Convention, to share in its proceedings, enlarge its program, elect its officers, shape its constitution, and formulate its future policies.

T. M. CHAMBERS, *President*

L. V. BOOTH, *Vice-President*

J. CARL MITCHELL, *Secretary*

Appendix 27

THE KING CENTER

CORETTA SCOTT KING
Founder

DEXTER SCOTT KING
Chairman, President and
Chief Executive Officer

CHRISTINE KING FARRIS
Vice Chair, Treasurer

BERNICE A. KING
Secretary

April 26, 2001

Reverend L.V. Booth
1303 Duane Road
Muncie, IN 47304

Fax: (765) 378-1143

Dear Reverend Booth,

On behalf of The King family, Dexter Scott King and the King Center family, I write to express my warmest and wholehearted congratulations to you on your installation as pastor of The Church Up On the Rock.

As you begin this new chapter of your distinguished career as one of America's preeminent clergymen, I want to thank you for your loyal support of my husband, Martin Luther King, Jr. and the Civil Rights Movement. You have also been a great friend to me personally, and I deeply appreciate your steadfast support of The King Center, as a loyal, creative and dedicated member of our Board of Directors. You have given so generously of your time and talents as a Christian minister who lives, as well as preaches, the social gospel. Your new congregation is indeed blessed to have the benefit of your extraordinary experience and leadership.

With respect and admiration, I wish you many more years of good health and an ever-deepening sense of personal fulfillment. May God watch over you and give you strength and inspiration in all your endeavors.

Sincerely,

Coretta Scott King

THE MARTIN LUTHER KING, JR. CENTER FOR NONVIOLENT SOCIAL CHANGE, INC.
449 AUBURN AVE., NE ATLANTA, GA 30312-1590   (404) 526-8900   FAX: (404) 526-8901
E-MAIL: mlkctr@aol.com   WEBSITE: http://www.thekingcenter.com

Appendix 28

Pilgrim Missionary  **Baptist Church**

DR. J. C. AUSTIN, Minister
  Executive Secretary of African
    Exports and Imports, N.B.C., U.S.A.
  President, Square Deal Civic League
  State Chairman, Foreign Mission

  Pesidence: 3932 South Parkway
  Phone: ATlantic 5-9277

DR. J. C. AUSTIN, JR., Co-Minister
R. M. TURNER, Gen'l Chrm. Boards
J. C. OLIVER, Treasurer
LENA L. COMPTON, Financial Sec'y
CHARLES DAVIS, Church Clerk
Public Phone: DAnube 6-9828

3301 Indiana Avenue
Office Phone: VIctory 2-5830
CHICAGO 16, ILLINOIS

Oct. 10, 1961

Rev. L. Venchael Booth,
630 Glenwood Avenue
Cincinnati 29, Ohio

Dear Rev. Booth:

I am in a quandry as to my presence in your city, at the time you are setting
up sa new Convention. The quandry is this: In your letter you said you
wanted no one there who was not in harmony with organizing a new National
Baptist Convention.

After talking with a number of leading men, including Dr. E. L. Harrison of
Washington, D. C. and King of Georgia, I am persuaded to believe that such a
move right now is not the best thing for us.

I am sure you have received a letter from Dr. Harrison unto this end.

I will come providing we are to confer one with the other and decide here on
a meeting for the representative men who are anti-Jackson. This meeting
should come, as I see it, after our State Conventions shall have met and
authorized actions on our part.To have a National Convention means the
federating of all states of the nation and this cannot be done without the
voted consent of the majority in Convention sessions in all states or in
Board meetings.

Now, bear in mind, I am willing to come and confer with you, but if no one is
to be on hand who is not in line with organizing a new Convention, then my
trip would be useless and unwanted.

Believe me to be

            Your for the solution of our National Baptist
            problem and our fight for freedom,

                        J. C. Austin.

Appendix 29

Shiloh Baptist Church

NINTH AND P STREETS, N. W.

Washington 1, D. C.

EARL L. HARRISON, B. TH., D. D., *Pastor*
Residence: 1743 Webster Street, N. W.
RESIDENCE PHONE: RA. 3-5163   CHURCH: ADams 4-6667
STUDY: DUpont 7-2046

19 September 1961

Reverend L. V. Booth
630 Glenwood Avenue
Cincinnati 29, Ohio

Dear Brother Booth:

I have your letter-call for November 14,15, 1961. While I am in accord with the objective, I doubt very much the wisdom of procedure as follows:

1. The timing is under the influence of heated temper from Kansas City, Missouri. We should take time to cool off, think sober without the pressure of the recent fiasco.

2. The keynote speaker should not have been publicized, especially one of the ten. Nothing personal, but too many implications may be read into it.

3. The call should be made only after consultation and agreement of many men around the country, and not under the signature of one man.

4. It should not be made until after the Hot Spring meeting,- calling it before opens our hand to the attack of the opposition and will benefit Jackson by giving him a theme and a rallying point.

Instead of a call now we should capitalize on Luther King's undemocratic dismissal by sending a thousand telegrams and letters of protest to Doctor Maxwell from all over the country. King should be given approval by thinking Baptists. He should be our rallying point. Make Jackson ridiculous before the world. Do not send protests to him. Maxwell cannot do anything but the newspapers should be told every time one is sent. Work the nation up, then after Hot Springs call a meeting.

Just one man's thinking, however. Good luck, God bless you. Think over what I have said.

Sincerely yours,

Earl L. Harrison

ELH:bjm

Appendix 30

Dexter Avenue Baptist Church

454 Dexter Avenue

Montgomery 4, Alabama

Phone AMherst 3-3970

THE REV. HERBERT H. EATON, *Pastor*
309 South Jackson Street   September 18, 1961

Rev. L. V. Booth, Pastor
Zion Baptist Church
430-432 West 9th Street
Cincinnati 3, Ohio

Dear Rev. Booth:

I have just received the memorandum from your office concerning the formation
of a new National Baptist Convention. I shall not hesitate to say how utterly
disappointed I am that such an attempt is being made. This means that the
Negro Baptists of America are attempting to form a third split within the fellowship. I cannot think of a more tragic movement than this. I will agree with
you that the present leadership of the National Baptist Convention appears to
be most undesirable, to say the least. It is out of this conviction that I
went to this convention and casted my vote in the interest of Dr. Gardner
Taylor. I am naturally disappointed that Dr. Taylor did not -in the election.
However, does this mean that the way to solve christian religious problems is
to resort to Machiavelian principles? Quite the contrary to be sure, if Mr.
Jackson's administration is felt to exemplify principles that are not christian,
then it seems to me that a christian approach is to say what is precisely
unchristian about his administration and to address ourselves to this problem
by informing others what is unethical and why, and permit them to draw their
own conclusions as to whom they will follow. All sincere persons can make
themselves a committee of one to see that other ministers can understand what
is unethical and why about the Jackson administration. This will have, by far, a
stronger effect at unifying the Convention than forming another organization.

How can we as a Negro Baptist Group ever hope to participate in the world
ecumenical movement if we cannot unite among ourselves? We certainly cannot
hope to effect the type of unity desired by splitting of and forming another
convention, but we must stay within the organization and effect the desired
changes from within instead of from without. We know that if a new convention
is formed; naturally, officers will be elected to that convention; and with
our seemingly natural love for power, another tragic situation will be created
when the time comes for officers to relinquish their powers for the purpose
of reunity.

Appendix 30, cont'd

Rev. L. V. Booth, Pastor
Page 2
September 18, 1961

I can see nothing but tragedy ahead by splitting off and forming a new convention. I, therefore, hastened to inform you that I shall not be a part of any new split; and, that I shall not be present at any meeting in which such a suggestion is introduced.

I believe that your motives are good, and I also believe that the consequences of such action can be most destructive to the cause of freedom and religion among the majority of the Negro people of our Land. I, therefore, urge you not to proceed with the effort to form a new convention.

With every good wish, I am

Sincerely yours,

Rev. Herbert H. Eaton

HHE:hedm

Appendix 31

Zion Baptist Church

Twenty-Second and Walnut
Church Phone   SPring 5-8512
Home Phone   SPring 6-7315

900 S. 47th
D. E. KING, Pastor, ~~ARAB NYMMEHHOLD~~ Street, Louisville, Kentucky

October 12, 1961

Reverend L. V. Booth
3415 Dury Street
Cincinnati, Ohio

Dear Reverend Booth:

I have your recent letter pertaining to my appointment to be with you in
Revival services, November 12-19, and to a proposed new convention which you
are to organize during that same week.

Now about the revival! I had already accepted your invitation to preach
in your revival services on the above dates and had sent a photograph and data
sheet of myself for publicity purposes. Therefore, I do not understand why you
should ask whether or not I would be with you. I have wondered, however, how
could you conveniently hold a meeting to organize a convention for two days in
that same week. As I told you in the beginning I could definitely begin your
meeting on the night of November 12 and end on Friday night of that week. This
I will still do unless it is going to cause you embarrassment or inconvenience
with regards to the organization of a convention.

A word about the organization of a new convention! I am of the same opinion
as when I last talked to you. That is, I do not feel that this is the time nor
do we have the spiritual climate for beginning such a movement. For this reason
I cannot participate. On the other hand, if the above were not the case I still
could not participate on the conditions which you proposed the organization of a
convention. In the first place, I feel that a group, representing a cross section
of our denominational brotherhood should have been called by you to discuss the
advisability of organizing a convention. In the second place, since this was not
done I feel that such an allowance should have been made in the meeting which you
have called. Because you stated in your initial letter for persons not to come to
your meeting unless they came to organize a new convention, you did not make it
possible for persons to come to even discuss the matter. Therefore, I feel that the
door was closed to many interested persons along with myself.

Now I have talked with you frankly because you and I have always been able to
discuss issues objectively. If my coming to preach in your revival will cause you
any embarrassment because I will not participate in your movement, then I leave
it to your discretion as to whether it will be to your best interest to cancel
the engagement. Please be assured that if the engagement is cancelled, I will
neither be inconvenienced nor will our friendship be affected.

Appendix 31, cont'd

Zion Baptist Church

Twenty-Second and Walnut
Church Phone   SPring 5-8512
Home Phone   SPring 6-7315

900 S. 47th

D. E. KING, Pastor,   ~~3516 West Chestnut~~ Street,   Louisville, Kentucky

I very much regret that I do not have a new mailing list to forward you. As you know, I started with no records of the convention. Therefore, my entire mailing list was taken from the 1959 session held in San Francisco.

With sincere best regards, and hoping for you God's choicest blessings in all your endeavors, I am

Sincerely as always,

D. E. King

Appendix 32

Friendship Baptist Church

144 WEST 131st STREET

New York 27, N. Y.

Phone: FOundation 8-6223 - 4

OFFICE OF

PASTOR

30 October 1961

Reverend L. Venchael Booth
Zion Baptist Church
630 Glenwood Avenue
Cincinnati 29, Ohio

Dear Brother Booth:

        Thank you for your communications with reference
to a new Baptist Movement. I feel honored and flattered by the
comments in your letter of October 9th. I feel along with many
others that there is much to be done among our Baptist forces,
but as much as I feel this way, I am not yet committed to a new
Baptist organization. It is my feeling that we need to think and
pray at this point and in this light I must respectfully decline
your invitation to attend the meeting, and humbly thank you and
the others for mentioning me as a possible Executive Secretary
of a new movement.

        With all good wishes, I am

                        Faithfully yours,

                        Thomas Kilgore, Jr.

TK/sld

Appendix 33

The St. Paul Baptist Church

"The Church with a Dynamic and Spiritualizing Program, where
a Cordial Welcome is Always Extended."

REV. L. K. JACKSON, B.D., D.D., MINISTER

1938 ADAMS STREET

GARY, INDIANA

Church Phone TUrner 6-9313 - Res. TUrner 2-8851
Residence: 2541 Madison Street

• • •

MRS. ESTELLE JACKSON
Church Clerk
1536 Van Buren St. - TUrner 3-3307

September 15, 1961

Rev. L.V. Booth, Pastor
Mt. Zion Baptist Church
3415 Dura Avenue
Cincinnati, Ohio

Dear Rev. Booth:

I read every word of your document "So Much For So Little" and take this method of both commending and congratulating you upon the achievements you have made in Cincinnati.

I am informed that you have one of the most beautifully and most modernly equipped churches in the state. If you had let me know that you were building or had completed your building, I would have been among the first to congratulate you.

Several people have called me from Chicago, and some of the pastors here have informed me that you are calling a special meeting to consider the advisability of organizing a new National Baptist Convention.

I think I have demonstrated as much altruistic interest in and philanthropic concern about the welfare and betterment of the National Baptist Convention as anyone in America. If you are calling a meeting to consider the betterment of the National Baptist Convention, how could you be sincere in your endeavor and ignore or disregard a person who has demonstrated the kind of interest I have over a period of twenty or more years?

Under seperate cover, I am sending you a complimentary copy of my 18th Anniversary as pastor of St. Paul Baptist Church; also a copy of a sermon I preached on Sunday morning, August 27. Please read them over carefully and give me your reaction to same.

I am

Yours very truly,

L.K. Jackson

"The Servant of the Lord's Servants"

LKJ:lnd

Appendix 34

1614 Second Street
Chester, Pa.
September 15, 1961

Rev. L.V. Booth
630 Glenwood Avenue
Cincinnati, Ohio

My dear friend:

The enclosed circulars will give you an idea whats
churning in the minds of some of the brethren. Now let's
be careful and not set up a lot of splitter groups under;
under all circumstances we must not let the monies given
for our brethren in Africa become involved in convention
politics. We will keep you informed as to how matters
are proceeding, but at the present time we are taking
steps to conserve our missionary set up.

Personally as you know, I have been out of the convention since Louisville and have directed my interest to
the American Baptist Convention and the Foreign Mission
Board. I would appreciate it if you would write me in detail so I will know what's what as the only communication
I have had from you are these two circulars.

My experiences have taught me that it takes a lot of
preparing to set up an organization locally and it takes
much more to set up a national organization. I am not
interested in joining a movement that will end in a debacle,
so please write me at once and fill the letter with information so that I can show it to key men in the east.
I told you at your home in Cincinnati that the devil cares
nothing about the cross.

Let me hear from you at once.

Your friend,

J. Pius Barbour

JPB/aw
Encl: 2

Appendix 35

MOREHOUSE COLLEGE
ATLANTA, GEORGIA

OF▭ ▭ OF THE PRESIDENT

September 21, 1961

Rev. L. Venchael Booth
Zion Baptist Church
430-432 W. Ninth Street
Cincinnati 3, Ohio

Dear Rev. Booth:

I thank you for your letter of
September 18.

I hope things will turn out well.
I still feel that it would have been
much better to have had a meeting of
12, 15, or 20 people before announcing
the separate convention. We will watch
developments with real interest. I cannot promise you now that I will be
available. On November 14 I am in New
York that weekend attending my fall
Board meeting.

Sincerely yours,

Benjamin E. Mays
President

BEM:mej

*N. B. you & I differ on procedure
only.
BEM*

Appendix 36

Pilgrim Missionary  **Baptist Church**

DR. J. C. AUSTIN, Minister
  Executive Secretary of African
    Exports and Imports, N.B.C., U.S.A.
  President, Square Deal Civic League
  State Chairman, Foreign Mission

  Residence: 3932 South Parkway
  Phone: ATlantic 5-9277

DR. J. C. AUSTIN, JR., Co-Minister
R. M. TURNER, Gen'l Chrm. Boards
J. C. OLIVER, Treasurer
LENA L. COMPTON, Financial Sec'y
CHARLES DAVIS, Church Clerk
Public Phone: DAnube 6-9828

3301 Indiana Avenue
Office Phone: VIctory 2-5830
CHICAGO 16, ILLINOIS

Sept. 26, 1961

Rev. L. Venchael Booth
Zion Baptist Church
630 Glenwood Avenue
Cincinnati, Ohio

Dear Rev. Booth:

I am in receipt of your letter and am planning to be in
your meeting.   Kindly secure for me hotel reservation
for two.   I regret to say, but I prefer a white hotel,
one of the best.

I am writing this letter with the feeling that you are a
man, not only bit a trained mind but an open mind.   You
are ready for suggestions, especially when they come out
of the years of rich and ripe experiences.   I regret that
you areputting in front of the movement old material, such
as my very personal friend Borders of Atlanta, Ga.   The
very fact that the hand of David is soiled with blood makes
it vitally necessary that a young Solomon would be our key
man.

If I have an acceptable suggestion, it would be that we go
all out to draft Martin Luther King for leadership.

Now, I don't mean to meddle with your affairs; from the
tone of your letter, this is an independent movement on
your part and you are asking very positively that nobody
comes who is not concerned in a new set up.   I can't
criticize your statment, for the reason no insurrectionist
should be on hand, and yet we must leave room for different
opinions.   We must concede to every man the right of an
opinion, the privilege to express the same, and at the same
time have the objectives so clear, so positive, so real,
so essential that no one can oppose.

Appendix 36, cont'd

Pilgrim Missionary | **Baptist Church**

DR. J. C. AUSTIN, Minister
Executive Secretary of African
Exports and Imports, N.B.C., U.S.A.
President, Square Deal Civic League
State Chairman, Foreign Mission

Residence: 3932 South Parkway
Phone: ATlantic 5-9277

DR. J. C. AUSTIN, JR., Co-Minister
R. M. TURNER, Gen'l Chrm. Boards
J. C. OLIVER, Treasurer
LENA L. COMPTON, Financial Sec'y
CHARLES DAVIS, Church Clerk
Public Phone: DAnube 6-9828

3301 Indiana Avenue
Office Phone: Victory 2-5830
CHICAGO 16, ILLINOIS

Page Two

Rev. L. Venchael Booth Cont.

I am also of the opinion that we should invite into this
meeting the deposed heads of all auxiliaries of the
National Baptist Convention, such as Mrs. Ross of the
Women's Convention; Dr. Maxwell head of the National S. S.
& B. T. U. Congress; Dr. C. C. Adams of the Foreign
Mission Board. I will join you in the effort to have
them on hand.

Please accept these suggestions out of the heart of one
who hopes for an honest-to-goodness National Baptist
Convention composed of Christian leaders and members.

Yours sincerely,

J. C. Austin

JCA:c

Appendix 37

𝔅aptist 𝔉oreign 𝔐ission 𝔅ureau, 𝔘. 𝔖. 𝔄.

1908 FITZWATER STREET

PHILADELPHIA 46, PENNSYLVANIA

September 28, 1961

Rev. L.V. Booth
432 W. 9th St.
Cincinnati, Ohio

Dear Rev. Booth:

Because of recent events in Kansas City and out of
our God-given autonomy as a Baptists, a group of ministers
and laymen assembled in the Union Baptist Church, Philadelphia, Pa., September 19, 1961 and pledged themselves to
restore our former dignity as Baptists by embarking on a
new and expanded Foreign Missions program. This was done
because we believe the purpose of the church and its
ministry is to evangelize the world. Due to our lack of
confidence in the present Foreign Mission Board, U.S.A.,
Inc., we could do no other. Our aim is not to destroy
but to save. We are in the process of obtaining a charter
under the laws of the State of Pennsylvania.

We are appealing to all men with like convictions to
join us in this positive movement. We have no convention
ties whatsoever; we have no candidates for office and
are seeking none. Our sole purpose is to keep the mission
fires burning with the assurance that what we give will be
used only for the purpose for which it is given.

We prayerfully solicit your support in this venture
that as of this early date appears destined for greatness.

Yours in Christ,

C.C. Adams, Cor. Sec'y.

CCA/aw
p.s.   Enclosed is a card inviting you to become a member
of our Board of Directors. Please sign and return
immediately.

ALLIES FOR AFRICA & THE WORLD

Appendix 38

REV. H. J. TRAPP, Chairman

REV. J. E. KIRKLAND, Honorary Chairman

REV. E. T. LEWIS, Treasurer

REV. J. A. YOUNGER, Recording Secretary

REV. C. C. ADAMS, Secretary

REV. R. A. CROMWELL, Asst. Secretary

REV. O. M. LOCUST, Special Asst. Sect.

Baptist Foreign Mission Bureau, U. S. A.

1908 FITZWATER STREET
PHILADELPHIA 46, PENNSYLVANIA

Oct. 11, 1961

Dr. L. V. Booth
432 W. 9th Street
Cincinnati, Ohio

Dear Dr. Booth:

I congratulate you on your initiative and effort to bring divided Baptists to some sense of meaning and order out of the confusion that plagues our national unity. I hope from the effort and those who think similarly with you that there may come a rebirth, dignity, democratic and christian procedure in an organization where brotherly fellowship may prevail and we can be forever done with high-handed dictatorship and undermining treachery.

I hope I may be able to be present at your meeting. I thank you for your letter and returned card accepting membership in our new missionary organization, Baptist Foreign Mission Bureau.

We had to start from scratch in opening up head-quarters, without one cent on hand and it has been a costly endeavor. If I or some representative comes to your meeting, I pray for time for a brief statement of purpose of this new organization and an opportunity to make an appeal to those who might desire to help us to meet the cost of setting up this new head-quarters.

Again with best wishes and success in your efforts, I am

Yours truly,

C. C. Adams, Cor. Sec'y

CCA/mb

ALLIES FOR AFRICA & THE WORLD

Appendix 39

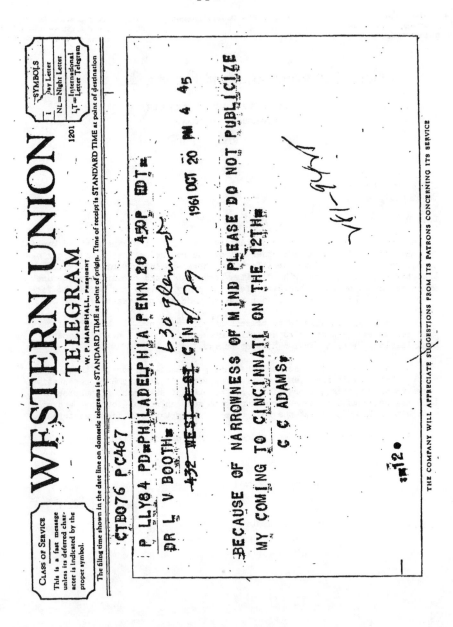

WESTERN UNION
TELEGRAM
W. P. MARSHALL, PRESIDENT

CLASS OF SERVICE

This is a fast message unless its deferred character is indicated by the proper symbol.

SYMBOLS
i — Day Letter
NL = Night Letter
LT = International Letter Telegram

1201

The filing time shown in the date line on domestic telegrams is STANDARD TIME at point of origin. Time of receipt is STANDARD TIME at point of destination

CTB076 PC467

P LLY84 PD=PHILADELPHIA PENN 20 450P EDT=

DR L V BOOTH=

432 WEST 8 ST CIN=   1961 OCT 20 PM 4 45

BECAUSE OF NARROWNESS OF MIND PLEASE DO NOT PUBLICIZE

MY COMING TO CINCINNATI ON THE 12TH=

G C ADAMS=

THE COMPANY WILL APPRECIATE SUGGESTIONS FROM ITS PATRONS CONCERNING ITS SERVICE

Appendix 40

SERVICE HOURS: 11:00 A.M. and 7:00 P.M.

𝔐t. 𝔐oriah 𝔅aptist ℭhurch

Mildred and Beall Street
BIRMINGHAM 8, ALABAMA

REV. W. J. DAVIS, A.B., D.D.
Minister
408 5th Way
Birmingham 8, Ala.
Res. Phone 56-8868

Church Office Phone _____

Notary Public
State-at-Large

Trustee Selma University

Noted Evangelist

Contributing Editor
Baptist Leader

Member Transportation Committee
Alabama State Convention

HENRY LATHAM
Chairman Deacons' Board
1315 Hattie Street
Phone 56-5593

JOHN HUNTER
Chairman Trustee Board
1132 LaFayette Street
Phone 56-9511

WILLIE J. REYNOLDS
Treasurer
1405 LaFayette Street
Phone 56-5016

ARCHIE MOORE
Church Clerk
1201 Hattie Street
Phone 56-4422

MRS. MILDRED WOODRICK
Finance Secretary
607 Carline Ave.
Phone 56-5341

10-18-61

My dear;
Dr. Booth:
This comes in reply to a request, and
invitation to all who are interested
in Organizing a new national Baptist
Convention. May I say to you and
all who asked for a fair vote.
you asked, & got it. Why be
un christians asking a new convention
you all said if you got a fair voi
OK. May I say you all are unfair
and none christians. you will never
over

Appendix 40, cont'd

succeed in your efforts for
Christ is not with you in your
spite work. Your trouble is,
you dont respect the voice of
the majority.

You So call christians
need to go & get some religion
which you preach to your people.

I shall pray God to convert
all of you, so call gospel
preacher's-

Respectively

W. H. Davis

Appendix 41

THE AFRO-AMERICAN,   MARCH 2, 1963   **19**

ANOTHER STATE JOINS — The Rev. L. V. Booth, Cincinnati, founder and vice president at large of the newly organized Progressive National Baptist Inc., congratulates Dr. C. S. Stamps, pastor of Metropolitan Baptist Church, New York, and president of the recently organized New York Progressive State Baptist Convention. Seen in center, from left are, the Rev. John Nichols, vice president and Raymond Dunn, secretary.

Appendix 42

2   THE NEW YORK COURIER   March 16, 1963

IN BUSINESS — Officers of the newly-organized Progressive New York State Baptist Convention are congratulated by the Rev. Dr. L. V. Booth of Cincinnati, founder and vice president-atlarge of the Progressive National Baptist Convention. Occasion was the first eastern regional meeting of the New York group, attended by more than 250 delegates from Washington, D. C., Boston, Los Angeles and New York. Left to right: Dr. Booth, Dr. J. H. Nichols, vice president; the Rev. J. Raymond Dunn, recording secretary; Dr. C. S. Stamps, president and host pastor of Metropolitan Baptist Church. — Gilbert photo.

Appendix 43

THE NATION'S PRAYER CALL

PRAYER—FELLOWSHIP—SERVICE

"If my people, which are called by my name, shall humble themselves and Pray . . ."
2 CHRON. 7:14

Vol. 2   Cincinnati, Ohio   July-August No. 4

Will Baptists Vote Against Integration?

As the Convention session approaches us it becomes more and more apparent that the fight to preserve Tenure in the constitution is not a mere clash involving personalities. No longer is it the opinion of "thinkers" that we shall meet in Louisville to accept or reject a certain personality. But, the real issue is, are we going to join the evil forces, we so greatly o p p o s e in their fight against Integration? In the face of all the charges and counter-charges there arises one question — Can Negro Baptists afford "to bow at a time like this?"

It has become crystal clear that our fight is a moral fight rather than a political one. The cry for "the old way," is reaching loud proportions and nothing is being left undone to make it heard. We hear arguments of the negative effects of Tenure and its possible harm to the convention down to the local Church. These are but the dying groans of an old order about to be buried. The outstanding brilliancy of its leadership cannot save it. Indefinite Tenure of office has outlived its day even among Baptists who are thought to be unwieldy, unmanageable and unprogressive. There are those who think that Baptists are so unthoughtful and gullible that "change" is impossible. These opinions do not even have to be argued, or debated because Baptists generally are for Tenure.

Since much has been written and talks have been carried on for months, it will not be necessary to preach a sermon on this issue now. Let me offer three simple reasons why Tenure will prevail in the National Baptist Convention, Incorporated, despite arguments to the contrary. They are as follows:

1. We cannot admit **now** that we are different.

2. We cannot admit **now** that we are limited in leadership.

3. We cannot admit **now** that we are not ready for integration.

There are many other reasons, but these three are the most basic ones. Too many Baptists have

Appendix 43, cont'd

fought for a "new day" to be defeated now that it is in sight. To do so would betray all that Dr. Martin Luther King, Jr., and all of the other militant Baptist leaders have fought for and accomplished. There is no turning back of the hands of the clock now! The pendulum has swung forward and it is taking us all along with it. We are marching in a new day and we simply meet in Louisville to affirm it. Therefore, it will be better not to fight, maim and kill, but rather to give thanks and offer praise to Almighty God who has led us into the Sunlight of this hour.

Let us go to Louisville determined that we shall be "brothers in Christ." There is no earthly reason why we cannot conduct our business with charity, dignity and order. Let us close ranks and end the disunity, enmity and disharmony that have characterized our convention too long. If the forces for the Constitution win, then all of us will win. And, what is more important the cause of Christ will win. Baptists will not vote against Integration because our basic belief is Unity!

Appendix 43, cont'd

The Nation's Prayer Call

L. V. Booth

IS IT WORTH IT?

Scripture: Lk. 9: 23-27

Thought for Today:

"But seek ye first the kingdom of God, and his righteousness; and all these things shall be added unto you." (Matt. 6:33) "Then he answered and spake unto me, saying This is the word of the Lord unto Zerubbabel, saying, Not by might, nor by power, but by my spirit, saith the Lord of hosts."
(Zech. 4:6)

Many of us who are members of one of the great Conventions among Christians are witnessing one of the greatest power battles of the century. It promises to loom much larger and possibly erupt into legal conflict and division. All who are engaged in it are committeed to the Prince of Peace and His rule in the world. Any casual visitor however to one of our meetings would never guess this fact just by observation.

The central figure in this struggle is one of the most able and gifted men of our time. It could very well be imagined that Angels cease their harp-playing when he preaches the gospel. Friend and foe alike agree that he is a speaker of unusual brilliance and power.

What a paradox! One so gifted and so able has been compelled by friends to become a target for Political battle! Surely all will agree that such talent could be used far more advantageously in soul winning than in Political warfare.

The day must soon come when leaders will deny themselves of all Political Power for the sake of the kingdom. In the next generation or so, we must make meaningful our call and commitment to the Gospel. Baptist must de-emphasize offices and get on with objectives. Let's pray that we shall not awake to this imperative too late.

Prayer: O God, our Father, we have become confused about values. Save us lest we miss thy Kingdom's goal. Amen.

Meditations from the National Prayer League, 432 W. 9th Street, Cincinnati, Ohio.

Appendix 44

PROGRAM

OF

THE UNITED BAPTIST CONVENTION

OF AMERICA, INC.

CONVENING

NOVEMBER 14,.15, 1961

AT

ZION BAPTIST CHURCH

630 GLENWOOD AVENUE

CINCINNATI 29, OHIO

L. VENCHAEL BOOTH, PASTOR

Appendix 44, cont'd

Attention Delegates

Note: All Devotional Leaders listed for
each service are requested to start
hymn-singing and prayer (10) minutes
before the scheduled program to insure a creative worship experience.

THANKS to Attorney Norris Muldrow for
preparing the proposed outline of The
Constitution and to all the officers and
members of Zion for their splendid cooperation in every day.

A Word On The Name

The United Baptist Convention of
American, Inc. is a good name for our
Convention because:

1. It is clear and distinct from any
   other Baptist body in America.

2. It is an inclusive name which in-
   vites the merger of existing
   conventions.

3. It describes the loftiest aspirations
   of all Baptists to enjoy unity.

4. It is a testimonial against any
   effort of division.

Appendix 44, cont'd

TUESDAY NOVEMBER 14, 1961

10:00 A. M.

Devotional Service Led By: Dr. John F. Williams, Va;
Dr. A. W. Moore, Miss.; and Dr. Joseph McRae, Г'a.

Opening Hymn------------------"What a Fellowship"

Scripture Lesson----------Rev. Andrew J. Hargrett
                              Chicago, Ill.

Prayer Period------------------Led By Committee

Hymn #204------"Must Jesus Bear The Cross Alone"

Welcome and Statement of Purpose-Rev. L. V. Booth
(Agreement to Follow Robert's Rules of Order)

Nomination and Election of Temporary Chairman-Body

Nomination and Election of Temporary Secretary-Body

The Call for the Meeting by the Secretary----------

Resolution for the Formation of a National Organization

Appointment of Committees:

    A. Credentials Committee
    B. Nominating Committee
       (After By-Laws are adopted)
    C. Constitution Committee
    D. Program Committee

Hymn #213------------"Am I A Soldier of The Cross"

- 1 -

Appendix 44, cont'd

TUESDAY NOVEMBER 14, 1961

10:00 A. M.

Introduction of Speaker------Dr. T. M. Chambers
                         Los Angeles, Calif.

Hymn #181----------------------"Amazing Grace"

Sermon-----------------------Dr. W. H. Borders
                         Atlanta, Ga.

Offering------------------------------Congregation

Benediction-----------Rev. J. Van Alfred Winsett
                      Owensboro, Kentucky

AFTERNOON SESSION 3:00 P. M.

Devotional Service Led By: Dr. A. Haney, Miss.,
Dr. P. A. Cantrell, Ill., Dr. A. H. Hogan, Ala.

Opening Hymn----------------"What A Fellowship"

Scripture Lesson-------------Dr. A. Ross Brent
                         Plainfield, N. J.

Prayer------------------Dr. Marvin T. Robinson
                       Pasadena, California

Hymn #154------------------"There Is A Fountain"

Information Regarding Our General Discussion.

   1. To allow wide participation we are suggest-
      ing a time limit of 2 minutes for each speaker
      on a series of topics listed below related to

- 2 -

Appendix 44, cont'd

AFTERNOON SESSION 3:00 P. M.

the general theme. Will 2 hours be sufficient?.

2. We should like to accomplish the following
    mile-stones at the close of this discussion:

    (a) Agree on organizing a new Convention.
    (b) The Name of the New Convention.
    (c) The Next Meeting Place and the Dates
         of the Meeting.

Discussion on the Theme will be led and conducted
by------------------- Dr. J. Raymond Henderson
                           Los Angeles, Calif.

THEME: "How to Build A Democratic Convention
          Dedicated to Christian Objectives"

1.	Action	9.	Love
2.	Brotherliness	10.	Missions
3.	Education	11.	Patience
4.	Endurance	12.	Prayer
5.	Evangelism	13.	Stewardship
6.	Faith	14.	Tenure
7.	Fellowship	15.	Understanding
8.	Good Conduct	16.	Unity

Summation Address------Rev. Andrew J. Hargrett
                              Chicago, Ill

Intermission Music----Mrs. L. C. Manggrum-Bush

The Call for a Vote on a New Convention------Body

The Call for a Vote on the Name------------Body

A Welcome to the Baptist Foreign Mission Bureau
into the Membership.

- 3 -

Appendix 44, cont'd

TUESDAY EVENING - 8:00 P. M.

Devotional Service Led By: Rev. A. E. Banks, Ala;
Rev. C. J. Brown, Ill; Rev. W. Leo Hamilton, N. Y.

Opening Hymn----------------"What A Fellowship!"

Scripture Lesson------------------Rev. L. J. Burt
                                    Detroit, Mich.

Prayer-----------------------Rev. D. R. Royal
                                Greenville, Miss.

Hymn #350---------"Jesus Keep Me Near The Cross"

Introduction of Speaker-----Dr. W. Owen DeVaughn
                            Los Angeles, Calif.

Hymn #223------------------------"Come Thou Fount"

Speaker-------------------------Dr. T. M. Chambers

Benediction-------------------Dr. H. J. Trapp
                                Philadelphia, Pa.

Note: All Evening Sessions will have Music
furnished by Zion Baptist Church Combined
Choirs under the direction of Mr. James V.
Roach, Minister of Music.

Music during Day Sessions will be provided
by Mrs. L. C. Manggrum-Bush and
Mr. Emmet Anderson.

- 4 -

Appendix 44, cont'd

WEDNESDAY NOVEMBER 15, 1961

10:00 A. M.

Devotional Service Led By: Rev. M. H. Wheeler,
Mich; Rev. W. D. Burton, N. Y.; Rev. W. L. Baxter
Conn.

Opening Hymn #359------------"Blessed Assurance"

Scripture Lesson-------------Dr. W. H. R. Powell
                              Philadelphia, Pa.

Prayer------------------------- Rev. L. A. Burrus
                              Jamaica, N. Y.

Hymn #384-----------------"Have Thine Own Way"

Report of Nomination Committee--------------------

Report of Committee On Time and Place-----------

Intermission Music---Mrs. L. C. Manggrum-Bush

Brief Talks---------Visitors and Special Messengers

Feature Address--------Mrs. Vivian Carter Mason
                              Peace Corps
                              Washington, D. C.

Hymn #274-----"O Master Let Me Walk With Thee"

Offering--------------------------- Congregation

Benediction----------- Dr. J. Raymond Henderson

- 5 -

Appendix 44, cont'd

WEDNESDAY AFTERNOON - 3:00 P. M.

<u>Devotional Service Led By:</u> Rev. W. D. Mosley,
Ohio; Rev. S. L. Taylor, Ohio; Rev. Ctis Moss,
Ohio.

Opening Hymn #244-"The Church's One Foundation"

Scripture Lesson------------Rev. W. P. Halbert
                                    Cincinnati, Ohio

Prayer------------------- Dr. J. Pius Barbour
                                    Chester, Pa.

Hymn-----------------"Wonderful Words of Life"

Introduction of Speaker------- Rev. W. D. Mosley

The Living Word----------Dr. J. W. Montgomery

Hymn #203----------- -"A Charge To Keep I Have"

Offering---------------------------Congregation

Election of Officers------------------Delegates

Hymn #43------"Guide Me O Thou Great Jehovah"

Benediction-------------------President Elect

- 6 -

Appendix 44, cont'd

WEDNESDAY EVENING - 8:00 P. M.

Devotional Service Led By: Dr. John F. Williams,
Va; Dr. R. A. Cromwell, Pa; Dr. L. S. Sorrell, Miss.

Opening Hymn #133---------"All Hail The Power"

Scripture Lesson------------Rev. W. A. Anderson
                                        Philadelphia, Pa.

Prayer------------------------Dr. C. C. Stamps
                                        New York, N. Y.

Hymn #264--"O Zion Haste Thy Mission High Fulfilling

Presentation of Speaker--Dr. J. Raymond Henderson
                                        Los Angeles, Calif.

Speaker-----------------------Dr. C. C. Adams
                                        BAPTIST FOREIGN
                                        MISSION BUREAU
                                        Philadelphia, Pa.

Invitation and Challenge-----------------Speaker

Offering------------------------------Congregation

Benediction-------------------Dr. C. C. Adams

- 7 -

Appendix 44, cont'd

SOME A, B, C'S OF CHRISTIAN CONDUCT

Baptists are faced with the challenge of creating a new and better image of their Christian integrity and intelligence. Each must feel his great responsibility if progress is to be made. These A, B, C's are presented for your thinking.

A. As ye would that men should do to you, do ye also to them likewise. Lk. 6:31

B. Bless them which persecute you: bless, and curse not. Ro. 12:14

C. Come now, and let us reason together, saith the Lord: Is. 1:16

D. Depart from evil, and do good; seek peace, and pursue it. Pr. 34:14

E. Enter into his gates with thanksgiving, and into his courts with praise. Ps. 100:4

F. Fret not thyself because of evil doers, neither be thou envious against the workers of iniquity. Ps. 37:1

G. Give unto the Lord the glory due unto his name; bring an offering, and come before him: worship the Lord in the beauty of his holiness. I Chron. 16:29

H. Hatred stirreth up strifes: but love covereth all sins. Pr. 10:12

- 8 -

Appendix 44, cont'd

I. I have set the Lord always before me: because
he is at my right hand, I shall not be moved.
Pr. 16:8

J. ...Jesus of Nazareth ...went about doing good.
Acts 10:38

K. Keep thy tongue from evil, and thy lips from
speaking guile. Ps. 34:13

L. Let nothing be done through strife or vainglory;
but in lowliness of mind let each esteem other
better than themselves. Phil. 2:3

M. Mercy and truth are met together; righteousness
and peace have kissed each other. Ps. 85:10

Appendix 44, cont'd

LEANING ON THE EVERLASTING ARMS

What a fellowship, what a joy divine,
    Leaning on the everlasting arms;
What a blessedness, what a peace is mine,
    Leaning on the everlasting arms.

Chorus

    Leaning, leaning,
    Safe and secure from all alarms;
    Leaning, leaning,
    Leaning on the everlasting arms

Oh, how sweet to walk in this pilgrim way,
    Leaning on the everlasting arms;
Oh, how bright the path grows from day to day,
    Leaning on the everlasting arms.

What have I to dread, what have I to fear
    Leaning on the everlasting arms;
I have blessed peace with my Lord so near,
    Leaning on the everlasting arms.

A WORD OF THANKS

THANKS to all of you who have
come from far and near. Zion is grateful along with her pastor that you have
responded so nicely to the call for this
meeting.

We wish for you a pleasant and
happy stay in our city.

Appendix 45

A VOLUNTEER COMMITTEE

FOR THE FORMATION OF A

NEW NATIONAL BAPTIST CONVENTION

CONDUCTS A WORKSHOP

AT

ZION BAPTIST CHURCH

630 GLENWOOD AVENUE

CINCINNATI 29, OHIO

NOVEMBER 14, 15, 1961

- THEME -

"HOW TO BUILD A DEMOCRATIC CON-
VENTION DEDICATED TO CHRISTIAN
OBJECTIVES"

L. VENCHAEL BOOTH, PASTOR

Appendix 45, cont'd

I. THE CONFESSION

1. A split of our present National Baptist
   Convention, is certainly not desirable in
   this age of mergers and unity, but the
   Baptists of our age deserve a choice between Tyranny and Freedom. We seek to
   offer them freedom. We believe that Baptist blood still runs red with a desire for
   freedom.

2. We owe the nation something better than
   law-suits, stage-fights and mob violence.
   Some of us cannot bow to what we believe
   to be brazenly and grossly wrong. We are
   fighting much too hard to gain freedom on
   other fronts to forfeit our rights for freedom in our National Convention.

3. We think it is far more righteous to
   separate in the interest of peace than to go
   to a convention in the fear of returning in
   a shroud.

II. THE CALL

A Cordial Welcome Is Extended

To the valiant elder statesmen of our Baptist
Family whose contributions will always bless
our denomination.

To the youthful and promising who must meet
the challenge of today and tomorrow.

- 1 -

Appendix 45, cont'd

To all who need encouragement, uplift and the
pure breath of Freedom.

To all who believe that they are the chosen and
called out sufferers of Christ.

To all who are willing to start small with
righteous principles and trust God to grow
large by His grace.

To all who are faith-filled and unafraid to
stretch out on the promises of God.

To all who believe that God is still a Friend
and will not withhold anything good from all
who walk uprightly.

To all who cherish peace, brotherhood and
dignity above wealth, property and power-
politics.

To all who love Christ and His Church our
welcome is extended in humility and love.

III. THE COMMITMENT

We suggest that our new organization be named
The National Baptist Association, Inc.

We suggest that our CONSTITUTION provide
for the following:

1. A voluntary association of regular Baptist
   Churches, Pastor's Conferences, District
   Associations and State Conventions and
   Regional Conventions.

Appendix 45, cont'd

2. An association that practices Tenure for all of its elected officers.

3. An association that elects its officers by secret ballot.

4. An association that fosters as its primary objectives:

   (a) Evangelism
   (b) Missions
   (c) Education
   (d) Stewardship

5. An association whose conduct is guided by the New Testament with particular emphasis upon Mt. 18:15f; Ph. 2:3; Eph. 4:32; I Cor. 6:1-7 and all other injunctions to peace among Christians.

6. An association that engages in fellowship with other Baptist bodies and all other New Testament Christians whenever possible to do so without any breach of Baptist Doctrine.

7. An association that encourages the Fellowship of Prayer among its member churches.

8. An association that encourages lay activites for youth and age with special emphasis on help for the needy and handicapped.

9. As association that employs an Executive Secretary as a continuing officer between changes of administrations.

- 3 -

Appendix 45, cont'd

10. An association that has a unified Budget to
    which its members might make monthly and
    quarterly contributions.

11. An association that conducts a Placement
    Bureau for bona fide ministers and Christian
    Workers.

12. An association that supports Freedom Fighters
    and the cause of freedom for all mankind.

13. An association that provides a climate for both
    security and fellowship for its officers and
    constituents.

14. An association that protects the rights of
    every member and holds that every man's
    right to vote is sacred.

15. An association that helps its needy member
    churches both spiritually and financially.

16. An association that practices Christianity in its
    politics and programs.

17. An association that practices sound financing
    of its objectives.

18. An association that publishes an Cfficial
    Organ for the purpose of publishing articles
    of Baptist interests including important sermons,
    addresses and resolutions.

Appendix 45, cont'd

19. An association that recognizes the office of parliamentarian as a necessary assistant to the presiding officer that it will never be necessary for him to bear the burden of a parliamentary ruling.

20. An association that provides for the Christian discipline of its members who will not abide by its rules and regulations.

21. An association that provides for representation for its member churches in the following amounts:

   (a) Smaller Churches $25.00 - $100.00, annually - payable monthly.

   (b) Larger Churches $100.00 - $1,000.00, annually - payable monthly.

   (c) Pastor's Conferences, District Associations and State Conventions $100.00 - $1,000.00 annually - payable monthly.

22. All members 70 years of age and above should be awarded an honorary life membership.

Appendix 45, cont'd

ZION BAPTIST CHURCH
690 Glenwood Avenue   Cincinnati 29, Ohio
I. VENCHAEL BOOTH, Minister

Appendix 46

Statement of Welcome and Purpose

For a great door and effectual is opened unto me,
and there are many adversaries. 1 Cor. 16:9.

For a great opportunity has opened for effective work,
and there is much opposition. (NEB)

Fellow Baptists, Sisters and Brothers in Christ, Greetings and welcome to Cincinnati and to Zion:

The most difficult thing for mortal man in our age of drift and decline is to make a choice or come to a decision. This is especially true if that choice is related to his religious beliefs — if it cuts across his traditional mores, feelings and emotions. Unhappily for man though, even in this age, his world gives him no choice, but to make a choice and suffer the consequences if he is to be true to his inner-self. Ever so often man is called upon to choose between good evil; freedom and tyranny; truth and falsehood—even life and death.

We are convinced that the problem of choice confronted Israel in her early history and was highlighted by Elijah on Mt. Carmel when he met in a contest with the prophets of Baal: His words are lucid and challenging: "How long halt ye between two opinions? if the Lord be God, follow him: but if Baal, then follow him." (1 Kgs. 18:21) This same idea was expressed another way by Joshua who declared:

> And if it seem evil unto you to serve the Lord, choose
> ye this day whom ye will serve: whether the gods
> which your fathers served that were on the other
> side of the flood or the gods of the Amorites in whose
> land ye dwell; but as for me and my house, we will
> serve the Lord. (Josh. 24:15)

It is not easy for men of weak convictions to take a stand, or embrace a choice that is not popular and assured of success. Weak men do not wish to be on the losing side, though that side is eventually destined to win. We cling to expediency, the

Appendix 46, cont'd

comfortable ringside, the well-filled arena where popularity is prized above security—and empty shouts above inner satisfaction. There is a moment in history when a decision can be crucial. At such a time as this—weak men choose to talk endlessly on important items so as to avoid decision. We have witnessed endless debates going on in State Halls, Congress Halls and even at the United Nations. This same malady has infected men of religion who would rather talk than think; argue than meditate; fight than pray.

Before we can do business in this meeting, we must puncture the theory that a "convention split" is a tragedy. If so we are either now are, or once were former members of a tragic convention. In truth and in fact, the National Baptist Convention, Inc. has been split for sometime. The split simply has not been given for mal recognition. It began to split in 1952 when the Convention adopted "tenure" in its constitution. It split a little more in 1957 when tenure was ruled unconstitutional. It split just a little bit more when an outstanding pastor was drafted to run for the office of president against an incumbent who refused to recognize any opposition, or the right of another to aspire for this office. Our Convention is now hopelessly split and cannot be united without a complete overhaul job in this generation.

There are sentimentalists among us who feel that in some way and somehow, we can go on together at any cost. We can go on despite taxation without representation. We can go on despite mediocrity replacing ability. We can go on despite the failure to recognize the rights of any man. We can go on despite reprisals without redress. No amount of instability, insecurity and inefficiency in operation convinces them that there is a time of separation and there is a time when only separation can be honorable. These sentimentalists who reject these facts are simply desirous of being part of the crowd whether with honor or without it.

As much as we hate disunity, we cannot avoid some degree of frustration and skepticism. We are very skeptical about the possibility of progress toward peace and freedom in an organization

Appendix 46, cont'd

now governed by a charter conceived many years ago. It is my understanding that the charter of the National Baptist Convention, Inc. which is now being invoked for apparent political reasons and spiritual insecurity; was born long before the fire Or freedom burst into flames and the whole world became ablaze with a desire for equality and liberty. It cannot possibly serve a generation geared to the Space Age and infused with a spirit of freedom which cannot die.

The need for a new convention existed long before our last meeting in Kansas City, Mo. We all agree that there should not have been this need. This need arose because of stubborn refusal of men to keep pace with the times. The reluctance to change even when light appeared. The ungodly deceit which has been meted out to one generation after another has made a new convention necessary. We have not built anything that supports our youth nor anything that our youth can respect. Clearly speaking, we have failed miserably as good stewards of the manifold of grace of God. There are many in our nation who seriously indict us: Here is the commentary of one person who might be representative of many:

> We have glorified ignorance; sanctified evil and crucified righteousness. We have used our power to divide the strong; strangle the aggressive and crush the weak. Our convention has been one big parasite. Our financial contributions have gone on a one way journey to satisfy the greedy and corrupt the weak. There has been little or no help forthcoming to raise the level of falling humanity.

> Our convention builds no churches—educates no illiterates and strengthens no visible cause of righteousness.

> It has become a place for weak men to get drunk; for fast women to play prostitutes and a happy hunting ground for the sordid and spiritually sick.

Appendix 46, cont'd

Baptists are Confused into a state of Spiritual Paralysis.

There are not many Baptist leaders left who are capable of a forthright decision. Defeat, doubt and bewilderment have so beset us that we have lost faith in ourselves. Some Or us doubt now our ability to do anything. There are thousands afraid to assemble any where if they are called upon to make a clear-cut decision or take a decisive stand. We have become so victimized by our fears until we have surrendered almost completely to dictatorship, mob rule and high powered politics. If this group here asser1bled cannot do business under one of the most clear-cut calls for business ever issued, there is little possibility left of our ever doing business somewhere else with a larger crowd. If this small group cannot form an organization, elect a set of officers, it is just possible that we are unfit to serve our generation. Some of us have already become worshippers of "bigness." We think that our movement just has to be big to succeed. We think that our movement must rival all other movements and one in particula— the one we are all going to be expelled from. We have forgotten the lowly Christ who said: "My kingdom is not of this world," (Jno. 18:36) which set His mission in direct opposition and contrast to the kingdoms of His day. Our Lord also said: "The kingdom is like unto leaven, which a woman took, and hid in three measures of meal, till the whole was leavened." (Mt. 13:33). This description of Christ's kingdom belied bigness, pompousness and dazzling splendor, but it did not deny spiritual power. No one wants to be small anymore and by the same token, no one wants to be real anymore...for Christ's sake. In Christ's day, the Romans were very big and the Christians were very small, but they changed the course of history.

We must not Procrastinate—
We must Not Delay our Lord's Business.

My final word to you is—the call was honest—the call was sincere—the call was humble. We called you here to organize a new Convention. Our purpose has not changed. If you do not organize a new convention, it shall certainly not be the volunteer chairman's fault.

Please don't feel the temptation to Save Me!

If I'm wrong, let me perish. If I'm right sustain me! For God's sake do not do anything foolish just to save me. It is my prayerful hope that no one has made the sacrifice to come here just to save me. I'm not worthy of it. If you have come to save a cause, then your trip was worthy. Men must stop hazarding their precious lives on worthless missions. If you came with no greater passion than to save me— then you have come to our city in vain. There is either a cause to be saved or there is nothing to be saved. We either have a valid claim in assembling ourselves together, or we assemble ourselves as just another group of false prophets. We need men today who are certain about something. We need men today who are full of faith and charged with the Holy Spirit. We need men today who are not afraid to act and also who are not afraid to take the consequences.

In this meeting your freedom to act as redeemed Baptists will not be denied you. When I'm through speaking, the meeting is yours. You may act by the program outlined, or you may act according to your choice. You are free to feel that I am no more then a sympathetic host. I seek no office. I covet no power. I simply seek to serve my precious Lord with earnestness, humility and faithfulness. I simply seek to serve diligently my age and generation. You are my Friends, you are my fellow-sufferers—I wish to bid you welcome to do your and my glorious King's business in the way that His Holy Spirit orders us to do it.

Appendix 47

INTRODUCTION

Executive Secretary's First Annual Report

"Give thanks unto the Lord, call upon His name, make
known His deeds among the people."   I Chron. 16:8

President Chambers, Officers and Messengers of the Progressive National
Baptist Convention, Inc., assembled here in the Wheat Street Baptist Church
of Atlanta, Georgia. This great church, pastored by the world renowned Dr.
William H. Borders, is in truth my church home. It was here that I received
my inspiration to strive for greatness, and it was here that I was ordained to
the Christian Ministry. With this personal testimony, let me end all personal
remarks and turn to the business at hand.

It is a great privilege to stand before you and present an account of our
stewardship as Executive Secretary of this great Convention. As far as possible,
we shall resist the temptation to magnify our labors, trials and difficulties since
accepting this honored post and major on the joys, triumphs and successes of
this great venture. The hand of the Almighty has led us in all our efforts to
advance the work of our Convention. In our human weakness, we have sometimes been too blunt, and sometimes too sharp, both in written communications
and from the public platform. In whatever we have done, a sincere effort has
been made to advance the cause of Christ and this great Convention. We have
always tried to avoid promoting our own small selfish cause.

Our work with all the officers, beginning with our beloved President and
extending to officers of auxiliaries, has been pleasant and inspiring. Your
acceptance of this office has been nothing short of remarkable. You have
shown by your cooperation that one day our Convention shall be listed along
with other great bodies that have a Christ-centered plan and purpose. Our
Convention has shown great maturity despite its youthfulness. This is not
surprising, however, when we consider that we have gathered here some of
the best minds and hearts in this nation, represented in our senior pastors, as
well as in our young pastors of pronounced quality.

Our faith is beginning to grow, our confidence is beginning to solidify as
we work with each other. We are losing our fear, timidity and doubt. The
righteous arm of the Lord is being revealed and man is recognizing that he is
a mere instrument in the orderly plan of God. We know by experience the
tragedy of human exaltation and the dethronement of Divinity. God must be
exalted high and reign supreme in all our actions, or we are doomed before
we start.

As your Executive Secretary, we have been at the call of the President,
Members and his Cabinet and Committee Chairmen to render whatever service
was possible to be rendered. We have not counted the cost in sending out
communications, making phone calls, or taking unscheduled trips. The salary
allowed our office has been largely spent in promoting the work of the Convention. Our church personnel and facilities have been used more greatly at
times for Convention work than for our Church work. We have served you
while being fed and supported by others. This cannot continue for any long
period.

There must be serious consideration given to establishing a Headquarters
and the employment of a full-time Executive Secretary to carry on this important work.

We must accept help. We cannot allow ourselves to ignore the generous
spirit of the American and Southern Baptist Conventions, nor can we turn
aside from the generous offer made by the David C. Cook Publishing Company.
We can cooperate with all of these friends without becoming subservient to
any one of them. They seek not domination but cooperation. It will be wisdom
on our part to meet them half-way.

Our report is fairly extensive and informative. It contains a body of facts
and figures which time will not allow us to give in this session. You will need
to buy it and let it serve as a Study Guide for the next year. We have within
these pages an outline of the duties of the Executive Secretary, important reports from experts, statistics on our Convention from its origin, which no one
else can give. You will see for the first time a real accurate account of the
membership of this Convention. Our report on financial contributions by regular and generous supporters is revealing. No one can read this report and

Appendix 47, cont'd

content himself with giving once a year a measly representation fee. The Comments made by some of our leaders are inspiring. The entire gamut of our work is covered including the expenses of the office and the travels engaged in. You will read notes of our contributions to the creation, development and growth of the Convention. And above all else, you will see yourself and the great contribution you have made to the most challenging movement among Baptists today in America. We are indebted to many, but most of all to you who have honored us by making us your servant.

A VOLUNTARY MONTHLY SUPPORT PLAN FOR THE PROGRESSIVE NATIONAL BAPTIST CONVENTION

The Progressive National Baptist Convention faces the righteous imperative to bring to the nation a Stewardship Program that will lift it from a mere "protest" group to an "action" group as soon as possible. The nation has little patience with people who are merely "against" something. It is ready to applaud those who are "for" something. Historically Negro Baptists have not distinguished themselves as being "cause-centered." Too often we have been looked upon as an "untrained mass of Christians" with an "hit-and-miss" program for the advancement of Christ's Kingdom. Our numbers have been our shame rather than our glory. We have won souls to Christ, but we have neither harnessed them or kept them. Our tendency to ignore Stewardship Principles has resulted in many local congregations resorting to Fund Raising practices that are detrimental to Christian dignity and culture. Many of them can no longer be identified as the Missionary Baptist Churches.

Our record collectively is much less impressive than our record individually. We have not developed career evangelists, missionaries, and Christian Education Specialists and almost no Christian Writers because we have had no program of support that would offer them any security. We have neglected to produce institutional and military chaplains and have shown only a spasmodic interest in our education institutions. Our Conventions have largely served our political interests. They have often been reduced to political arenas where ambitious office seekers fought for offices.

The young minister with holy ideals and lofty dreams is often robbed of these virtues and made over after our image and likeness. Only God knows how much we have robbed His kingdom of workers largely because of our un-Christian attitude toward money.

If the Progressive National Baptist Convention proves to be no different from what we have already had — then the nation will have to wait for another half-century or more for a new movement to arise. Our generation will not suffer repeated "calls" that are false and deceitful. In fact, some of us sincerely believe that we have only ONE DECADE to prove our claim to be "progressive" before we shall be banished from the minds of dedicated men. Nothing could be more serious than to declare righteousness and be found practicing evil.

The Progressive National Baptist Convention must practice Christian Stewardship or close shop. There are great doors of opportunity open to us because of our claim to serve a righteous cause. These doors shall not remain open if we falter — if we procrastinate — if we prove untrue.

The Voluntary Monthly Support Plan is presented in the hope that it might serve until faith grows strong and God reveals another Plan. It is not the last word, but it is a hopeful word. Moreover, it has been adopted by us in Executive Session and every member is under obligation to follow it, or present a better plan. Let us heed the timely admonition: "Let nothing be done through strife or vainglory; but in lowliness of mind let each esteem other better than themselves." (Ph. 2:3)

THE PROGRAM IN A NUT SHELL
SETTING FORTH
AN EASY PROGRAM OF FINANCING OUR CONVENTION

I. The Argument

One of the outstanding needs of the Progressive National Baptist Convention is a Unified Financial Program to support its growing objectives. The outstanding weakness of our Baptist Family has been for many decades now, our failure to do anything in concert, or unison. We must conclude even at this point in our development that there is absolutely no significant reason for a new Convention among Baptist unless it is going to offer a better program of

Appendix 47, cont'd

securing the unity that we seek. There must not be a duplication of the same disorganized effort that has characterized our work in the past.

Our inconsistency has plagued all our efforts and rendered invalid much of what we have tried to do. Consistent with all the effort we have made to guarantee Tenure for all elected officers is the need for (1) Unified Action, (2) Unified Support, and (3) A Unified Budget. This unity cannot afford to be postponed until every District can have a Missionary, every State Convention a Headquarters and our Progressive National Baptist Convention a highly paid Executive Secretary. Unless our efforts are unified soon and independent collection agencies are removed from the field — the public will have to assume that there is nothing really "progressive" about us and that we are the same "disunified army" appearing in new uniforms.

The Voluntary Offering each month from the member churches of the Progressive National Baptist Convention will enable us to support all of our objectives with a greater degree of regularity and consistency. Our monthly contributions can be allocated before it is received by agreement of The Executive Board. All that is needed is to divide the dollar percentage-wise and multiply it by the amount we receive. Every College and Seminary represented in our Membership can receive some support and every Board and Auxiliary can be assured of greater strength. The Convention will profit greatly by the dignity and orderliness of the operation of its Boards and Auxiliaries. All that is needed is a group of dedicated leaders with intelligence enough to divide a dollar into significant parts.

Highly emotional, competitive efforts by ambitious leaders can no longer be truly representative of the Christian Challenge. We need more than ever to visualize needs, estimate potentials and reach for significant goals. Our Auxiliaries must not become competitive armies . . . even dividing us in our loyalties, sympathies and support. Unless our present methods are checked, studied and revised, we shall find ourselves facing a greater evil than we have witnessed. Even our Annual Appeals must be organized, coordinated and unified. Some of the methods now being used are confusing, degrading and defeating to our high Christian Objectives.

If each Pastor of a Member Church of the Convention will ask for a Voluntary Offering based upon a Unified Budget and supported by Unified Action on the same Sunday in the month and report the same by Money Order or Certified Check to the Office of the President or Executive Secretary each month — The Progressive National Baptist Convention will be able to justify its existence among other Baptist Conventions within one decade.

We must strive to grow according to Stewardship Principles and to be content with moderate and orderly growth. The proclamation of a new look will not suffice unless we rid ourselves of old practices. From the local churches up to the Progressive National Baptist Convention, there must be an absolute conversion to a New Way of life.

Every Progressive National Baptist Church must embrace Stewardship Methods that will be sane, solid, and spiritual. Every member church must distribute Christian Tracts, equip pews with Bibles, Hymnals, and all the other necessary Christian tools for the enlightenment and spiritual growth of its members. Sporadic drives, secular schemes, and unscriptural Financial Programs must be eliminated as swiftly as possible. Foreign Missions must be balanced with Home Missions. Evangelism must parallel with Christian Education and every Auxiliary and Board must be freed of every evidence of personal greed and graft. Churches who entertain the Convention in any of its activities must not do so to make a profit.

A Unified Budget is a must. A Unified Approach is a must. A Stewardship Emphasis is a must.

II. The Proposal

1. A Unified Budget for all our Objectives. This would require all Boards and Auxiliaries to report their receipts to One Common Treasurer — the Treasurer of Parent Body. Legitimate expenses can be estimated and provided for between sessions. The Treasurer must be well approved and beyond reproach.

2. An invitation should be extended to all our Baptist College Presidents, of colleges represented in our Convention, to form a Committee to work out a plan for "United Baptist College Fund." A brochure must be developed setting forth the offerings of the several colleges.

Appendix 47, cont'd

3. The United Budget will be raised by Progressive National Baptist Churches by adopting the "Voluntary Monthly Plan" of supporting the Convention. Each church will report monthly by certified check or money order to the office of the President or the Executive Secretary.

4. The Convention might designate one night of its Annual Session as "William Henry Jernagin Night," and invite a noted speaker. This night should be dedicated to aid our youth in getting an education. A number of scholarships should be given from the proceeds to young people who are going into full time Christian Service. This effort can be further supplemented by Christian College Sunday in May and Christian Education Week in September.

III.   The Implementation

1. If there is believed to be any conflict in this program with our constitution, let us revise it to make possible a "Voluntary Monthly Plan of Support."

2. Let each Auxiliary help to plan a Unified Budget and have representation on the "Committee for Unified Action." This Committee should be empowered to plan a Unified Budget and develop a strategy for a Unified Financial Goal.

3. Let us select an Executive Secretary who will serve in every way possible to carry out the objectives of the Convention. This officer should be a person who has succeeded in the pastorate or some comparable field. In the absence of such a person there should be no discrimination against one who is presently serving in a substantial pastorate.

4. Let us adopt the Voluntary Support Plan and set aside each First Lord's Day in the month as the day every member church will take an offering and send it in on the Monday following.

5. Let the Executive Board be authorized along with such members who might be added by the President to allocate such funds received quarterly and send a Quarterly Report to each member church participating, accounting for both Receipts and Disbursements.

6. Let us engage in a Unified Prayer Period each Saturday night before the First Lord's Day when the offering is to be taken.

7. Let each Pastor take out a Life Membership in the Convention by giving $100.00 above his regular Church representation in any Regional or Regular Session.

Appendix 47, cont'd

A COOPERATIVE PROGRAM OF SHARING FOR PROGRESSIVE AND AMERICAN BAPTISTS

At the invitation of Dr. Paul Madsen, Associate Executive Secretary, Division of Church Missions, a visit was made to Detroit, Michigan, in early November, 1963, and followed up in March, 1964, by a visit to Valley Forge, Penna. Our conferences were conducted on a very high spiritual plane and we arrived at the following areas of concern of mutual interest.

1. Building counsel. A full-time staff is available to give guidance in modification of existing buildings or assisting with counsel about new buildings.
2. Participation in "The Secret Place." Here we have the opportunity to contribute meditations and perhaps sponsor and distribute this world-wide periodical.
3. General Commission on Chaplains and Armed Forces Personnel. Two American Baptists are on the Executive Committee. They visit Chaplains throughout the world on a two-year cycle. They offer to work cooperatively to represent PNBC.
4. Development of Stewardship Materials.
5. Training of local church leaders in Every Member Canvass and development of rounded budgets in local churches.
6. In-service training for ministers. They conduct a number of schools each year designed for ministers in particular kinds of fields, i.e., inner city, Town and Country, depressed communities. Schools can be developed for a particular need. This is an intensive sixteen day experience in an academic atmosphere, away from all pastoral responsibilities.
7. Christian Education
    a. Writers for curriculum materials
    b. Use of special materials
    c. Participation in development of materials over long range planning periods.
    d. PNBC Director attend Bi-ennial Director's Conference.
8. Radio and TV training and participation in Laymen's Hour broadcasts on national basis.
9. Development of special Evangelism programs. Training in existing programs on regional or area basis.
10. Preaching missions on an exchange basis.
11. Regional Workshops
    a. Administration
    b. Missionary education
    c. Church extension
12. Joint Mission enterprise
    a. ABHMS now works cooperatively with various Negro State Conventions. This could be extended or re-designed for special needs, not now being met.
    b. Possible overseas project to be developed in the same manner with Foreign Mission Societies.
13. ABC works on the campuses of many colleges and universities. Officially, they might be able to represent PNBC also. Some Chaplains are Negro.
14. Cooperative Women's Work in many areas.
15. Participation in Minister's Council of ABC with PNBC in over-all concern for personal growth of minister.

The proposals made to us by our friends in the ABC should be seriously considered by us in our Convention. Such proposals are in keeping with Christian Fellowship and should be pursued genuinely and enthusiastically. As we grow, we shall be needing friends in many places. We are more than fortunate to have the great ABC to make such generous proposals to us at this time.

PROPOSAL OF THE
DAVID C. COOK PUBLISHING COMPANY TO THE
PROGRESSIVE NATIONAL BAPTIST CONVENTION

The basic Sunday School literature proposal is this — the David C. Cook Publishing Company to provide all of its literature and services, indicated in

Appendix 47, cont'd

the original proposal; i. e., imprinting, especial Negro art, order processing, shipping, billing, bookkeeping — and to do this for 80% of the established retail selling price. Therefore, 20% of the retail selling price would be turned over to the Progressive National Baptist Convention.

Look at what this financial provision would mean. Let's use the Sunday School figures provided the Yearbook of American Churches by your Department of Christian Education.

548,898   Sunday School pupils, Progressive National Baptist Convention (your figure).

Multiply this Sunday School enrollment by an average annual expenditure per pupil of $2.00 (a low estimate)

$1,097,796.00   Estimated annual expenditure for Sunday School literature, if all churches subscribe and spend an average of $2.00 annually per pupil.

$ 219,559.20   Annual amount to the Progressive National Baptist Convention, under terms of the 80/20% imprinting-sales proposal.

Admittedly, the above figure is based on two assumptions — (1) the $2.00 average per pupil per year — although this is a low figure, and (2) that all Convention churches will fully participate in your literature program — although so many Convention churches are now using David C. Cook literature that its acceptability within your church is already clearly established.

Appendix 48

Executive Secretary's Report

INTRODUCTION

Dr. L. V. Booth, Executive Secretary

"For a great door and effectual is opened unto me, and
there are many adversaries."   I Corinthians 16:9

President Chambers, Officers and Messengers of the Progressive National
Baptist Convention, Inc., assembled in the "Exciting World" of Los Angeles,
California, at the Zion Hill Baptist Church pastored by our beloved and
esteemed President. It is with deep gratitude for God's grace and mercy that
I bring to you my Second Annual Report as your Executive Secretary.

It is a great honor and privilege to serve a growing convention like ours.
The trials are many and the untraveled way is often hard. There is the great
consolation, however, that our Lord has seen fit to call us to this task in this
particular hour. From one session to the other real effort is made to be faithful
and true.

As we look back over the past year we can truly say that great strides
have been made and many doors have been opened which can lead to greater
fellowship, progress, and peace. Our great need is to keep in mind the purpose
for which we were born and the task to which we are called.

In the time allotted to me, I should like to call our convention to consider
three basic ideas for the advancement of the work we now seek to foster.
The text which we have chosen serves as a basis for our thinking.

I. POSSIBILITIES AND POTENTIALITIES

There is a great door open to us in these crucial times. They are readily
discernible in the areas of (a) Christian Education, (b) Christian Stewardship
and (c) Christian Evangelism. In the area of Christian Education our possibilities are unparalleled. There are many Baptist students needing a helping
hand in the many colleges across the country. We could start meeting their
need by deputizing ministers of character and training in close proximity to
colleges and universities to lend a helping hand. This could take the form of
making transportation and facilities available to these young people. This concern might be followed up by implementing the program offered by Dr. Gardner C. Taylor, Vice President-at-Large, to give scholarships to young ministers
of our Baptist family without regard to convention affiliation.

As we consider the area of Christian Stewardship, we have particular
reference to proportionate giving and tithing. Every Progressive Church should
begin a strong emphasis on tithing. The weakest spot in our Baptist religion
is seen in the area of Giving. Pastors must lead the way by tithing themselves.
This should be followed by monthly support to the Convention. We have seen
less than 100 pastors keep the Convention going between sessions this year.
Your monthly giving has added a new dimension of character and sacredness
to the work of our Convention. We need to conduct Stewardship Workshops
in every region of our Convention and teach both pastors and laymen God's
Plan for financing the Church.

The rallying force of the Church is Evangelism. This is that part of the
Great Commission to tell the world about Christ wherever possible. Progressive Churches should conduct united evangelistic efforts at an appropriate
season of the year.

If these three basic concerns are activated in Progressive Churches across
this nation, a great revival will break out thus energizing and strengthening
our effort. The individual local church will be revived and pastors will face
fewer problems; even those of equipment and personnel will be solved.

II. PROBLEMS AND PROPENSITIES

The local church is weak and ineffective far too often because of problems
and propensities. These are the simple day-to-day troubles which vex our
spirits and try our souls. They manifest themselves in (a) insecurity and
doubt, (b) divisiveness and jealousy and (c) lethargy and ignorance. There are
far too many laymen who feel that all the work of the Church is done from
the pulpit or by the man in the pulpit. Aside from "sitting" complacently on
boards and annoying the pastor many otherwise mature people are mature
everywhere but in the Church. For some reason we have reserved this area

Appendix 48, cont'd

for acting immature. Through our Christian Education Department, we must conduct workshops and training sessions that will relieve the Church of its deadwood by transforming it into live coals of fire. The Church must STOP DIAGNOSING and START TREATING.

III. PROGRESS AND PEACE

On the national front there must be an increasing awareness of our possibilities. We can relieve ourselves of much embarrassment by learning to pull together on causes that concern us all. The real mistake of Baptists across the years has been the localizing of Kingdom interests. Our colleges have been state colleges. Our important boards have been restricted to state organizations and leadership largely of the same state.

Today we need to launch out and build an enduring structure to undergird our efforts in the field of education. The time is ripe for a United Baptist College Fund that will include several Baptist colleges in allocation. We cannot achieve harmony through unequal distribution of the funds which are gathered from all over the nation. We must stop being siphoned off by one section to the detriment of all other sections.

Our Convention must keep striving toward a Unified Program and a Unified Budget. Every unit, auxiliary, and department of our Convention must feel related to the whole. We must cease separate treasuries held by individual units. Beginning with our registration to the closing hymn of the Convention, we must have a sense of ONE-NESS. Our Regional Conventions must be brought into harmony with the Parent Body and cease their independent existence. Their records must be understood to be the property of the Convention and their money as well. We must cease to pay each other generous honorariums and invite expensive guests to regional meetings without the consent of the Parent Body. Our Regional Conventions must become larger feeding tributaries of the mainstream. Likewise the Women's Convention, Moderator's Council and all other units must be brought into a harmonious whole.

We must stop holding annual meetings with different themes. We now have two buttons symbolizing different ideas. We cannot be a Progressive National Baptist Convention with a lot of independent units going in different directions. There needs to be a Budget Committee to ascertain the financial needs. There needs to be a Program Committee to ascertain our spiritual needs. We should try to develop one program printed between the same covers that can be understood by the same people. Now that we are nearly five years old, we need to examine ourselves and see if we can walk — uprightly without stumbling and falling,

In the interest of Progress and Peace, we must always be willing to take time and negotiate matters of vital interest to our great Convention and try to reach a consensus of agreement.

Not a single department submitted a report for financial consideration. In this connection we do not need the usual bombardment that follows each Annual Session. If you cannot express your needs in figures and facts, then we should spare our words and thus spare unnecessary debate.

The time is out for responsible Negro church bodies to forget causes and objectives while disbursing sacred money. We have a "charge" to keep and it extends from our prayer-life to our financial-life. Far too often leaders cheapen the image of church organizations by cheap unworthy actions. Every officer of the Convention should feel a real obligation to see that his affairs are conducted with dignity and integrity. We must stop spending thousands of dollars and hazarding our lives to conduct side-shows and circus-like performances.

Our Convention has achieved distinction and recognition. We are now recognized by the following organizations:

1. The Yearbook of American Churches
2. The National Council of Churches
3. The American Bible Society
4. The Baptist World Alliance
5. The National Commission on Chaplains

and others of long standing. We must respond through substantial support and payment of membership fees. We must not falter in these matters. As God

Appendix 48, cont'd

gives us strength and power, we must honor Him with worthy deeds and actions.

There must arise a growing number of pastors who are not ashamed to tell their churches that there is a Progressive National Baptist Convention, Inc., and also add that they belong to it. Most pastors who do not support do not tell the story of a Movement designed to set men free. WE MUST TELL IT! WE MUST SELL IT! WE MUST SUPPORT IT! Our possibilities are unlimited; our potentialities are great. Our problems are normal ones; our propensities are as natural as the noonday sun. Our progress is up to us; our peace is God's Gift and God's Trust.

Progressive National Baptists, let's face forward — until the light of God reflects its rays in our hearts and in our lives.

SOME REASONS WHY YOUR CONVENTION NEEDS STATISTICAL INFORMATION
by the Executive Secretary

Many Pastors refuse to worry about progress reports in our member churches because they place more emphasis on the things of the spirit than they do on material progress. A close examination will show that they are related and one is dependent upon the other.

Every good pastor should know how many members he is serving and how much property his church controls. To be derelict in these matters could result in the loss of his trusteeship. God wants somebody He can trust over the welfare of His people. It is almost impossible to make progress when one operates blindfolded or in the dark. It will pay each pastor to become more diligent and accurate in the keeping of Church Records.

A casual study of the "Parable of the Pounds" will suggest to us all that God expects us to handle with care the gifts He entrusts to us. (Read: Luke 19:13-27.)

Please consider why your Convention needs your response to questions on your Registration Blank:

1. It helps us as a National Body to check our progress from year to year.
2. It lifts us out of the category of being uninformed.
3. It tells other religious bodies that we are enlightened and concerned about advancing Christ's Kingdom.
4. It keeps us from being "just another backward group."
5. It enables us to give accurate figures to the National Council of Churches, and other religious bodies which require statistical information.
6. It will help the Baptist World Alliance to know whether our Convention is an addition or subtraction to its membership roster.

Appendix 48, cont'd

HERE IS WHAT KEEPING ACCURATE RECORDS WILL DO FOR YOUR CHURCH

1. It will strengthen your stewardship efforts. Members will serve better when they are cultivated.
2. It will convince your flock that you are sincere about serving them.
3. It will make your membership more stewardship-conscious; more faithful in attendance and more faithful in giving.
4. It will make your place as pastor more significant and influential.
5. It will give you a real "push forward" when you seek a loan or attempt to make some worthy expansion.
6. It will put you in the rank of forward and enlightened leadership.
7. It will save you from careless, slipshod management of our Lord's business.
8. It will save you from coming to the Convention to fill out your Registration Blank when you can do it much better at home.

Your careful and prayerful attention to all that we have stated can transform your ministry. It will not only help us serve you better, it will make you more able to serve. Whenever you do good to someone else, you are the real beneficiary.

Please send in your Registration Blank at once — with or without money. Please Send in Your Blank.

PROGRESSIVE NATIONAL BAPTIST CONVENTION CHURCH CONVENTION GROWTH

State	1961 Cinti.	1962 Phila.	1963 Detroit	1964 Atlanta
Alabama	1	7	16	25
Arkansas	0	1	0	1
British West Indies	0	1	0	0
California	2	14	15	10
Colorado	0	0	0	1
Connecticut	0	2	1	1
District of Columbia	0	18	23	26
Florida	0	3	6	10
Georgia	0	7	9	32
Illinois	2	23	47	43
Indiana	1	1	4	5
Iowa	1	0	0	0
Kentucky	0	12	21	17
Louisiana	0	1	1	3
Maryland	0	3	5	4
Massachusetts	0	0	1	1
Michigan	1	6	21	17

Appendix 48, cont'd

Mississippi	1	3	4	12
Missouri	0	8	8	14
Nevada	0	1	2	1
New Jersey	1	12	15	12
New York	0	41	52	48 .
North Carolina	0	10	7	11
Ohio	5	6	9	9
Oklahoma	0	0	1	2
Pennsylvania	2	46	32	27
South Carolina	0	14	20	28
Tennessee	0	6	8	9
Texas	0	3	1	2
Virginia	2	22	15	15
West Virginia	1	6	7	3
Wisconsin	0	0	1	1

SUMMARY STATEMENTS:

	Number of States Represented	Number of Churches Enrolled
1961	12	20
1962	25 (District of Columbia and British West Indies)	277
1963	28 (District of Columbia)	352
1964	29 (District of Columbia)	390*

The aggregate figure of churches enrolling in Detroit and Atlanta is **428**.
*This figure also includes those new churches which have come in since the annual session in Atlanta.

SUGGESTIONS FOR PROGRESSIVE BAPTIST GROWTH

1. IT WILL PROMOTE THE CONVENTION'S GROWTH if we would support the Headquarter's Drive beginning January 1966 and ending January 1971 with Dr. E. L. Harrison, leader extraordinary, serving as chairman.
2. IT WILL PROMOTE THE CONVENTION'S GROWTH if the small auxiliary treasuries are eliminated.
3. IT WILL PROMOTE THE CONVENTION'S GROWTH if the Executive Secretary is given authorization to supervise or organize a Committee to publish a "Progressive Baptist Hymnal," "Baptist Church Guide," and Doctrinal and Devotional Literature.
4. IT WILL PROMOTE THE CONVENTION'S GROWTH if the Minutes of Regional Meetings are turned over within ten days to the Recording Secretary or the Executive Secretary with a request for a return receipt.
5. IT WILL PROMOTE THE CONVENTION'S GROWTH if we would exchange pulpits with Southern pastors in troubled areas and thus extend the Civil Rights Drive so nobly executed under the matchless leadership of Dr. Martin Luther King, Jr.
6. IT WILL PROMOTE THE CONVENTION'S GROWTH if Area Meetings are held with Progressive Baptist churches where no District Association or Convention is organized.
7. IT WILL PROMOTE THE CONVENTION'S GROWTH if the planning for all meetings, Regional and National, is done as far in advance as possible, for short planning often makes for poor performances.
8. IT WILL PROMOTE THE CONVENTION'S GROWTH if Christian Education Sunday in September is observed, if the Scholarship Program to aid worthy Baptist Students is supported, and if our National Sunday School Congress and other Educational Endeavors are backed by our enthusiastic efforts.
9. IT WILL PROMOTE THE CONVENTION'S GROWTH if Progressive Convention Sunday in November is observed and its purpose and program emphasized.
10. IT WILL PROMOTE THE CONVENTION'S GROWTH if "Relief Sunday" for fire or flood victims is held on an appropriate Sunday.
11. IT WILL PROMOTE THE CONVENTION'S GROWTH if we would support the move to develop a nation-wide Stewardship Commission and

Appendix 48, cont'd

follow through by including stewardship texts in the Congress curriculum and all other Workshops and Institutes.

12. IT WILL PROMOTE THE CONVENTION'S GROWTH if we would support the Foreign Mission Bureau Monthly.
13. IT WILL PROMOTE THE CONVENTION'S GROWTH if we would join the March of Progress by enrolling in the Voluntary Monthly Support Plan and reach our goal of "Every Church supporting the Convention Monthly."
14. IT WILL PROMOTE THE CONVENTION'S GROWTH if we encourage a compilation and organization of photographs of leaders to comprise a group picture of "Leaders in the Formation Period of the Progressive National Baptist Convention."
15. IT WILL PROMOTE THE CONVENTION'S GROWTH if we would accept the invitation of Dr. S. A. Owens and the Pastors of Memphis, Tenn., to host our Convention in 1966.
16. IT WILL PROMOTE THE CONVENTION'S GROWTH if we would organize Bus Tours, Train Specials, and Air Groups to the Annual Sessions and wherever possible to the Congress and to future Regional Meetings.
17. IT WILL PROMOTE THE CONVENTION'S GROWTH if officers and leaders of the Convention would send in articles of interest and promotion to the Executive Secretary's Office anytime during the year.
18. IT WILL PROMOTE THE CONVENTION'S GROWTH if all Moderators reported the vacant Baptist Churches in each District and if the Regional Presidents would request such a report in the regional session after which said report would be sent to the Office of the Executive Secretary.
19. IT WILL PROMOTE THE CONVENTION'S GROWTH if all of us would seek to cultivate and convey a SPIRIT OF BROTHERHOOD to one another.

A significant paragraph from the text of Dr. Gardner C. Taylor's address on

"FREEDOM AND RESPONSIBILITY"

delivered at the Baptist World Congress of 1965 held in Miami, Florida

"Freedom is responsibility and without freedom responsibility is a mockery of mind and a blasphemy against God. Can any nation hope to build an enduring and worthy society while rejecting the great foundation stones of a religious faith? Can a negative assumption about the sacredness of life establish a society of Justice? Is there any greater assault on justice than to hold a human soul responsible while withholding the exercise of that freedom in which men alone can act with responsibility? Is there any greater affront to the God of justice than to hold men responsible for civilized conduct while denying to them those communal institutions by which men come to understand how one acts civilized? Is there a larger sin against God than to hold men responsible for drudgery involved in building a community while denying to them the freedom for participation in that community into whose building their blood and toil have been poured? To refuse a human the liberating experience of schooling and then to hold him responsible as intellectually unfit, to sentence any soul to the bondage of living in a filthy ghetto and then to brand him as irresponsible because he is dirty, to deny a person the freedom of employment and then to hold him responsible for not being ambitious, to degrade any human soul by epithet and systematic scorn and then to demand of him dignity and to hold him responsible for breaches of personhood is a brutal violation of one's own moral apparatus and an insult to God whose dignifying stamp is in every human soul."

Appendix 49

EXECUTIVE SECRETARY'S
THIRD ANNUAL REPORT

THE SHIPS ON OUR VOYAGE

"They that go down to the sea in ships, that do business in great
waters, these see the works of the Lord, and His wonders in
the deep."—Ps. 107:23-24.
"And when they had sent away the multitude, they took Him
even as He was in the ship. And there were with Him other
little ships."—Mk. 4:36.

Mr. President, Officers and Messengers, Visitors and Friends: It is with
great humility and gratitude that this attempt is made today to give an account
of my stewardship as your Executive Secretary for the past Convention-year.
It is a great privilege to serve in this capacity and be of service to the very
fine constituency of our Progressive National Baptist Convention, Inc. This has
been another great year in the service of the Lord. Let me admit before beginning that this is not intended to be a detailed account of the past year, nor
is it a chronological account. For the most part it will simply be a few impres-
sions of what we have experienced over the months. This report will not carry
many of the congratulatory letters I have received from all sections of the
country, nor will there be an accounting of every trip taken in the interest of
the Convention. As your Executive Secretary, I have played whatever role that
has been necessary to keep the Convention a living force in this nation. This
is not going to be a sermon, nor will the texts selected be developed. It
is a brief resume of many important events and a lot of dedicated living of
many fine people who comprise this great Convention.

We reflect with pride upon the wonderful session we had in Los Angeles,
California in the former Church of our beloved President Chambers. Despite
his illness and the devastation of the Watts Riot we were royally treated by the
members of this Church, who were destined later to become the pillars of
True Love which is now a blessing and a reality.

In the session at Los Angeles we were highly hopeful that the long step
could have been made which would have set us on the course toward acquiring
a Headquarters Building. It was mine to discover at the end of the session that
I had picked the wrong time and location to begin this effort. The building
selected by your Executive Secretary was in Cincinnati, very close to the highway and not too far from our Church. The Convention passed a Constitutional
provision locating the Headquarters in Washington, D. C., and our Acting President made the suggestion that his matter be deferred until he could give it
much more planning and thought. It was a real pleasure to follow the advice
of our great leader because in him we have a man who not only has followed
faithfully our great chieftain, but is a real leader in his own right.

Our Report for the past two succeeding Conventions was published by
the David C. Cook Publishing Company as a compliment of Mr. James W.
English. We shall always be grateful for this very helpful service. It was dis-
continued at the suggestion of your Executive Secretary and not at the suggestion of the donor. It was the Secertary's view that our Convention must never
involve material consideration in matters of principle. Likewise, it was deemed
wise that this fine Company discontinue its quarterly contributions to our Headquarters Fund. In the case of the American Baptist Convention, there was no
thought of publishing our literature when she began supporting our office. They
were allowed to continue because of this reason. Where there is a Family relationship such as we have with the American Baptist Convention, no one
could accuse the Secretary of compromising the Convention by accepting support.

At this time the Executive Secretary's Office only receives help from the
American Baptist Convention for travel and there are no strings attached because this money comes from another Department unrelated to the Publication
Division. This great Convention has contributed money faithfully across the
months without any suggestion of future consideration. This Convention will
continue to help us regardless of the outcome of our decision on Literature.
Their record of helping dates back across more than 100 years.

Appendix 49, cont'd

It is apropos at this point to express my delight in working with the fine group of Officers who will retire under Tenure Law this year. This Convention was blessed to be launched by some of the finest men and most capable ones in our land today. They have set high standards which will challenge those who follow in their footsteps. There has been cooperation and contest. There have been no "rubber stamps" in this wonderful group. They will continue to be faithful as supporters and advisors when they are no longer in office.

With the foregoing introduction, let me turn now to a general discussion of the texts that have been presented. Life is a voyage and all who embrace life are akin to those who journey in ships. There is no possibility of discovery on the shore. Those who would reach far away places must launch out into the deep and go journeying in ships. Ours is a glorious voyage, but a dangerous one. We shall need someone to accompany us who knows all about the troubled sea. The wise traveler does not embark without seeking His companionship for the journey. We begin this journey because of Him. It is a call which impels us to leave the familiar shores about us and launch out into the deep. We journey because we seek to behold the works of the Lord and the wonders of the deep. Few realize it, but there is the world of the sea even as there is a world of the land. Both worlds are wonderful because both were created by the same source. Our God is the Commander of the sea as well as Master of the land. There is no escape from Him whether on land, sea, or in the air. There is something however about the sea which bids man to make greater preparation than for his usual habitat. Progressives in my humble opinion are destined to go down to the sea and do business in deep waters. Many will confront us with "get-rich-quick" offers and will make them sound so real that we are likely to succumb to them. There is a need however to realize that there is no easy path to victory. There is an easy road to slavery and we must seek God's guidance that we do not travel this road. We must stand strong and tall for the grace that set us free. As Baptists our heritage is a strong heritage. We follow those who placed the cause of Christ above their lives. They sought freedom above advantage; independence above slavery; and suffering above servitude. As we move forward we must avoid with all our might and power any proposition that will make for compromise of the highest principles we hold.

As we take this voyage we are not alone. Accompanying the Master Ship are also "other little ships." We believe that our Progressive Convention has an awareness of these ships. If we had the time and opportunity to discuss them — they would reveal themselves to us as: 1. Discipleship, 2. Fellowship, 3. Leadership, and 4. Stewardship. In the coming year let us build on these as we carry forward the great work entrusted to us. These other little ships have room enough for every Progressive to lose himself in complete devotion to the Master's cause. As we face the future, let us not seek subsidy from any source, but rather let us tap more deeply our own resources given by God to those who faithfully serve and trust in Him.

We claim no infallibility regarding the accounting of funds. Your corrections are always welcomed and our acknowledgment will be always forthcoming. Please feel free to help us help you.

The Executive Secretary and Staff.

Appendix 50

FOURTH ANNUAL REPORT
of
THE EXECUTIVE SECRETARY
of
The Progressive National Baptist Convention, Inc.
SEPTEMBER 1966 — JULY 1967

Sixth Annual Session
September 5-10, 1967

ZION BAPTIST CHURCH, 630 GLENWOOD AVE., CINCINNATI, OHIO

President Taylor, Officers, Messengers and Friends here assembled for the Sixth Annual Session of the Progressive National Baptist Convention, Inc., Greetings and Welcome to the Birthplace of the Convention. The way over which we have come to this Session has not been an easy one. In addition to the usual trying circumstances under which we labor, some of us have lived in cities which have experienced riots, unrest and tension. These experiences have made their demands, taken their toll, and exacted their sacrifices. Because of the great challenges we have faced here both as a leader and your host, this Report will not be as inclusive as in previous years. Some items will not be accounted for until in our Extra Session in January. Our usual message will not be printed here in the interest of both brevity and economy. We beg you to accept and consider the following Recommendations:

1. Increase the Office Secretary's salary $5.00 per week bringing it up to a "take-home pay" of $54.98 instead of $49.98.

2. Consider the purchase of the property located at 3756 Reading Road for an Information Center and to house the expanding records of the Convention. The Executive Secretary's work would also be carried on from this location.

3. Set meeting sites from 3-5 years in advance for effective planning and Convention arrangements.

4. Appoint Program Committee for the Annual Session in September. Invite major speakers in January. Complete the Program in June.

5. Adopt the Voluntary Monthly Support Plan as a constitutional provision. It need not carry a penalty, but could be a requisite for office holding.

6. Encourage the use of new Seminary graduates as Assistant pastors, ministers of Christian Education, chaplains in Institutions and military service.

7. Increase the productivity of unemployed ministers who are not theologically trained by helping to start missions and churches wherever possible.

8. Support the Crusade of the Americas and encourage union evangelistic services in every community where we have churches.

9. Encourage the observance of Baptist World Alliance Sunday and urge each church to take an offering for the Convention's Annual Membership Pledge and its Relief contribution to the BWA.

10. Under the leadership of our President, let us designate "One Great Sunday of Sharing" on the Sunday preceding Thanksgiving for the purpose of Schools and Colleges, New Churches, heavily mortgaged churches and churches burned, or damaged by some act of God.

11. Encourage recruits to the ministry by providing small quarterly scholarships to students in Bible Schools and Seminaries.

12. Encourage the use of Hol Reba Bible School as a Summer Retreat for members of both the Convention and the Congress.

Appendix 50, cont'd

Our Convention is now a reality and a living entity of the Baptist Family. We must strive with all diligence to be a worthy member of this Family.

The question raised by the Psalmist challenges us. "If the foundations be destroyed, what can the righteous do?" (Ps. 11:3.) In times like these, there are certain foundation stones on which we must build. To take any other course will be an excursion into folly. Among the foundation stones for Progressives must be (1) Fidelity, (2) Humility, (3) Integrity. With these we can build a future that will lift man and honor God.

Your Humble Servant,
L. VENCHAEL BOOTH, Executive Secretary

Appendix 51

FIFTH ANNUAL REPORT

OF

THE EXECUTIVE SECRETARY

OF

THE PROGRESSIVE NATIONAL BAPTIST CONVENTION
Incorporated

July 1967 / June 1968

SEVENTH ANNUAL SESSION

September 3-8, 1968

SHOREHAM HOTEL
CONNECTICUT AVENUE AT CALVERT STREET
WASHINGTON, D. C. 20008

EXECUTIVE SECRETARY'S ANNUAL REPORT

1968

President Taylor, Officers, Messengers and Friends here assembled for the Seventh Annual Session of the Progressive National Baptist Convention, Inc., Greetings and Best Wishes for a fruitful Session while here in the Nation's Capital. We are truly thankful that we are privileged to come together again in another historic session.

Our meeting in Cincinnati last September at our Birthplace established a new norm for our Convention. The drastic step made by meeting at the Netherland Hilton Hotel gave us a new outlook for future Conventions. Now we know that there are definite advantages in holding our meetings under one roof. We also know that proper living conditions also serve to make our work more effective. We must learn to use all these comforts to the glory and honor of God. Just as we have learned to accept the best in physical accommodations, we must also move forward and learn to accept no less in our spiritual aspirations. Our Convention must set a new high in program maturity and motivation. We must avoid stormy debates over minor matters. We must do more "home-work" and less "floor-work." It is painful but true that great emphasis on matters of little significance make them no greater because of it. We must learn to accept "self-appointed interpreters" of the Convention's objectives in the light of their deeds and not their words.

We must develop a generation of leaders who will concentrate on IMAGE and ACHIEVEMENT. No leader should allow any Convention matter to upset him to the extent that he loses his spiritual balance and posture. Far too many

Appendix 51, cont'd

of us who are sincere have been found to be sincerely wrong. Our burned and scarred cities would suggest that we "cool it" in terms of unbridled emotions in our Church affairs, or lose our influence in community affairs. The Apostle Paul's admonition is most timely for our Convention: "Let nothing be done through strife or vainglory; but in lowliness of mind let each esteem other better than themselves." (Phil. 2:3.)

Our real need is Christian Militancy. Our clergy wants so much to be militant. Our congregations want us to be militant. They want us to be militant in Prayer, Preaching and Peace-making. How wonderful such militancy could be in an age like this! So many have lost their way and there are so few (MMC's) militant messengers of Christ to lead the way home. Our burning cities tell of cool preaching and half-hearted praying. Our divided communities tell of feeble faith and lukewarm spirits. Our worship of power tells of our lack of love for God and our fellowman. Our indifferent attitude toward our own country tells of our loss of vision and our sense of destiny.

When God goes — all else goes. We need not doubt the relevancy of Christ. We can doubt the relevancy of our Christian witness. It is not difficult for any trusting soul to believe and witness to the great truth: "Jesus Christ the same yesterday, and today, and forever." (Heb. 13:8.)

The recommendations which were presented last year are presented again for adoption this year. The first is a must if we are to continue operation. The whole set is vital:

1. Increase the Office Secretary's salary $5.00 per week bringing it up to a "take-home pay" of $54.98 instead of $49.98.

2. Consider the purchase of the property located at 3756 Reading Rd. for an Information Center and to house the expanding records of the Convention. The Executive Secretary's work would also be carried on from this location.

3. Set meeting sites from 3-5 years in advance for effective planning and Convention arrangements.

4. Appoint Program Committee for the Annual Session in September. Invite major speakers in January. Complete the Program in June.

5. Adopt the Voluntary Monthly Support Plan as a constitutional provision. It need not carry a penalty, but could be a requisite for office holding.

6. Encourage the use of new Seminary graduates as Assistant pastors, ministers of Christian Education, chaplains in Institutions and military service.

7. Increase the productivity of unemployed ministers who are not theologically trained by helping to start missions and churches wherever possible.

8. Support the Crusade of the Americas and encourage union evangelistic services in every community where we have churches.

9. Encourage the observance of Baptist World Alliance Sunday and urge each church to take an offering for the Convention's Annual Membership Pledge and its Relief contribution to the BWA.

10. Under the leadership of our President, let us designate "One Great Sunday of Sharing" on the Sunday preceding Thanksgiving for the purpose of Schools and Colleges, New Churches, heavily mortgaged churches and churches burned, or damaged by some act of God.

11. Encourage recruits to the ministry by providing small quarterly scholarships to students in Bible Schools and Seminaries.

12. Encourage the use of Hol Reba Bible School as a Summer Retreat for members of both the Convention and the Congress.

We meet this year with a sense of great loss. Among our several fallen leaders of the past Conventional year is Dr. Martin Luther King, Jr., who fell victim to an assassin's bullet. He left us a great legacy. Our Convention is richer because of his fellowship with us. Our Convention was founded to provide a platform from which great men could express great thoughts. The late Dr. King visited us and did just that in Memphis, 1966, and in Cincinnati in 1967. In the midst of our sorrow we are filled with great pride. Providence has bequeathed us a great legacy; it becomes our duty to make it a legacy of greatness. The Progressive National Baptist Convention, Inc., offers its prayer and support to Dr. King's family, the organization he founded and to Morehouse College's memorial projects.

Appendix 52

VIII — PRESIDENT L. VENCHAEL BOOTH'S — ANNUAL ADDRESS
THE CALL OF GOD

Mr. Vice President, our distinguished former Presidents, Officers of all Departments of our Progressive Family, Messengers and Friends here assembled at our 11th Annual Session, greetings in the name of our Lord and Saviour Jesus Christ. Let me assure you that this message will be directed at the heart of matters which affect our Convention and will not be an effort at literary excellence, nor an excursion into statesmanship.

CHICAGO: A CITY OF MEMORIES

Our meeting in Chicago at this 11th Annual Session strikes me as being an act of Providence. Our second meeting following our organization was held in this Great City. We were welcomed by the Tabernacle Baptist Church and her great pastor, Dr. Louis Rawls.

As for me, to some degree, it is a return to a place that was once home to me. During the early forties, I attended the University of Chicago. I lived on the South Side before moving on campus. It was my great privilege to become the first black elevator operator to serve Harpers Memorial Library. My family and I became the first black family to integrate a small apartment building on campus. Before that, I served as an Inter-University Scholarship Student with an office in Rockfeller Chapel. As significant as these experiences were, my most significant experiences came through working with our black leaders in our black Baptist churches. My small world included such great personalities as Dr. J. L. Horace, Dr. J. C. Austin and Dr. J. H. Jackson. There were a host of others, but these stood out most prominently in my experiences. I became a member of the great Olivet Baptist Church and when I received a call to pastor the First Baptist Church in Gary, Indiana, I was installed by my pastor, Dr. Joseph Harrison Jackson.

Chicago, then, is one of my favorite cities because I became a man here at the tender age of 26. I became acquainted with the struggles and vicissitudes of church politics. Once I tried to get a church here and was successfully beaten back by the religious hierarchy. In those days, I became acquainted with Dr. C. V. Johnson, Dr. W. L. Lambert and a host of other prominent pastors here. While in Gary, Indiana, I felt the fierce winds of national Baptist politics and was made aware of the consequences of choosing the wrong side. All of this was to prepare me for a latter day when I would issue the call for the organization of a new Convention.

Chicago is not only a so-called "Windy City," it is also a "Wonder City." Legend has it that when Chicago was being planned as a metropolis, one of her founders rose and spoke: "Make no little plans, they have no magic which stir men's souls . . . make big plans." Even the great Chicago Fire in 1871 could not daunt the spirit of this great city. Someone wrote during this period, perhaps one year following the Great Fire:

> The first frost appeared before the ashes had cooled, and the ground remained frozen until Spring was far advanced. At first, it was supposed that no permanent building could be commenced until the return of warmer days; but massive structures began at once to rise, and the work steadily progressed throughout the entire winter.

I heartily concur with the civic leader who said:

> There's a vitality, a strength about the city . . . something left from those days following the Chicago Fire.

He said further, "The spirit has continued right on down for a hundred years now."

I personally would not take anything for having passed this way as a student, a newly wed and as a pastor next door for eight beautiful years. As a Radio Pastor in Gary, Indiana, I was heard in this area for three years. Tonight I feel like a wandering boy come home. Like all of you who have passed the half-century mark — I have passed through many troubled waters. Sometimes, the giant streams have swollen before me; the sound of Pharoah's chariots have frightened me and quickened my footsteps, but there has always been a Guiding Hand that has led me onward.

And so, I come tonight to report to you of my stewardship since the home-going of our Chieftain and the celebrated pastor of the Shiloh Baptist Church in Washington, D. C.

Appendix 52, cont'd

In my statement to this Convention, after confirmation by the Executive Board, I expressed my inability to follow such an extraordinary leader. Nevertheless, because time, duty and opportunity brought me to this office, I yielded myself to God and your call.

Since his departure, word has reached my office that several others have followed in his train. The names which I shall call may not be all of our Progressive Pastors, but these are the ones which have been brought to my attention.

Beginning with our President I ask that we pause and remember our Sainted Dead:

1. Dr. Earl L. Harrison — Washington, D. C.
2. Dr. D. D. Clay — Illinois
3. Dr. W. H. Gray — Pennsylvania
4. Dr. E. D. McCreary — Virginia
5. Dr. R. L. Rollins — Washington, D. C.
6. Dr. R. A. Lowe — New Jersey
7. Dr. S. A. Grayson — New York
8. Dr. L. H. Mills — Virginia
9. Dr. C. A. Cherry — South Carolina

I have called the names which are known to me and sincerely apologize for those which are not known.

At this time, I would like to present to the Cenvention a list of recommendations which I feel should be placed under careful consideration by each member.

RECOMMENDATIONS

1. Let the Regional Conventions consider prayerfully the possibility of meeting in cities over a weekend to involve the laity. Preachers attending the Regional Convention will preach in city pulpits on Sunday morning and a Mass Rally will be held in the afternoon, highlighting Foreign Missions and Home Missions.

2. Let churches supporting Regional Conventions plan to register with $25 - $100, realizing that living costs and operational costs are higher.

3. I recommend that we combine the two Southern Regions for meeting purposes through a visitation plan. One will meet with the other on an alternating basis until plans for reunification can be worked out. This might become a practice for other Regional Conventions where geographical boundaries will allow.

4. The compilation of a list of our Sainted Dead. The formation of a Committee on Necrology is recommended. Its purpose would be to create and study the feasibility of a special memory roll at the Headquarters.

5. The consideration of a retirement plan for Ministers and Christian workers.

6. A committee to research both Eastern and Mid-Western proposals and draw up an insurance package for our Progressive Family; and prepare an in-depth study for consideration.

7. A national chairman with a complete national committee to coordinate the observance of Martin Luther King, Jr. Sunday, our Martyr's birthday.

8. A professional audit of our books each year.

9. The selection of 50 State and Major City Captains to lead our "Progressive Dollar" Drive and gain support for it.

10. The adoption of Morehouse College School of Religion is recommended.

11. A regional program of reporting Progressive News and a committee comprised of Regional Reporters to broaden our news base for news in "Baptist Progress." Work cooperatively with the women's department in the selection of Regional Reporters to feed news to "Baptist Progress" editors. Feature items on "The Strength of Small Churches" and the Executive Secretary's report on churches contributing monthly to causes.

12. I recommend that our Convention consider a Field Secretary who will work out of the Executive Secretary's office, who might be paid out of the Publishing House receipts. His duties may include:
    (a) Putting Progressive preachers in contact with vacant churches.
    (b) Seeking unaffiliated churches, District Associations and State Conventions who might join the PNBC.
    (c) Gathering news for "Baptist Progress" and enlisting new Sunday Schools to purchase Progressive Literature.
    (d) Collecting delinquent literature accounts.

Appendix 52, cont'd

(e) Helping to promote Mission Drives.
(f) Helping to organize Union-Revivals.

13. Hold mid-winter meeting, alternating, in Atlanta, Georgia and Washington, D. C. for larger understanding of our objectives:
    (a) Morehouse College School of Religion
    (b) Headquarters
    (c) Nannie Helen Burroughs School
    Let each meeting constitute and include an effort to support these institutions.

14. A committee on honorariums: to study the feasibility of giving honorariums, or to honor leaders through the support of causes.

15. Recommendations to consider concerning future Conventions:
    (a) Capacities of meeting rooms.
    (b) Local committees' contributions to Convention.
    (c) Our commitment to other religious bodies.

Next. I would like to place before you some goals toward which all Progressives should be striving mightily.

SOME GOALS FOR "PROGRESSIVES"

1. A Bible Readers Fellowship — looking toward developing a devotional publication.
2. Strive for "togetherness" with purpose: Progress, Fellowship and Peace. Read our Progressive Scripture: Romans 12:9-21.
3. Pray earnestly for a Spiritual Revival in Progressive Churches; souls must be won to Christ.
4. Youth Cultivation: Keep in touch with young people and love them whether they are "turned off," or "turned on."
5. Senior Citizen Preservation: Visitation — Housing — Fellowship — "Tender Loving Care."
6. Pulpit Pentecost: A renewed emphasis on preaching and the power of the Spoken Word. Seek a return to Apostolic zeal and power.
7. Pew Exaltation: Increased participation of the pews in decision making. Greater use and cultivation of the laity.
8. Greater support of Home and Foreign Missions. Monthly support of the Executive Secretary's Office.
9. Freedom for all mankind — support for the continuing Civil Rights Struggle for the equality and dignity of all peoples.
10. Enroll 2,000 churches by 1974.
11. Enlist smaller churches in small towns and rural communities.
12. Work for the underprivileged. Champion the cause of the oppressed — working through organizations such as NAACP, SCLC, OIC, UNCF, PUSH, URBAN LEAGUE.
    And now, I would like to bring to your awareness some important matters.

MATTERS WHICH SHOULD HAVE THE SUPPORT OF ALL PROGRESSIVE BAPTISTS

1. **The Voluntary Monthly Support Plan** — One of the creative plans set forth in the early days of the Convention was the Voluntary Monthly Support Plan. This plan still holds the greatest possible promise for our Convention's success. Somehow we need to find a way to think of our Convention and its causes more. than three times a year. If we truly believe in the Progressive Concept of Fellowship, Progress and Peace, we must support it. Any church among us with 1,000 members should not give less than $300.00 per year. This should not include gifts to Foreign Missions and Home Missions. We need to lift our sights to see the needs about us at home and abroad.

2. **Foreign Missions** — Progressives need to be aware of the fact that the property of the Baptist Foreign Mission Bureau has been transferred to the PNBC. It needs our support to make possible the expansion of our mission work. NEEDED: 1,000 churches to give $1,000.00 or more per year.

3. **Home Missions** — An untapped source of power and strength which can undergird every aspect of our Baptist work.

Appendix 52, cont'd

4. **Headquarters** — PNBC members need to support this drive; the State Convention of California and Nevada sets a wonderful example by giving $2,500.00 for our Headquarters for 1972.
5. **The PNBC—ABC Fund of Renewal** — A religious expression of Self-Help of the highest order.
6. **Our Civil Rights Organizations:** SCLC, PUSH, NAACP, OIC, UNCF, Urban League.
7. **The Nannie Helen Burroughs School.**
8. **The Resurrection of Liberian African School:** Recommend $25,000 for Liberian School — Dr. Gardner C. Taylor and Dr. J. H. Beatty have visited this school and approve this drive.
9. Local Bible Schools and Seminaries.
10. Scholarships for Baptist colleges.
11. Boy Scouts and Girl Scouts as church-sponsored institutions.
12. Progressive Sunday School Literature prepared by our National Publishing House.
13. Black writers of religious publications — books, records, tapes, etc.
14. Merger of the two Southern Regions.
15. Cooperation with Southern Baptists and American Baptists.
16. Support Key '73 and realize its significance to Progressive Baptists.
17. Support Baptist World Alliance's 5-year emphasis on World Reconciliation.

I have received a number of endorsements from individuals, churches, educational institutions, newspapers and religious organizations in connection with the recommendation that a national chairman and committee be set up to coordinate the activities relating to the observance of the birthday of Martin Luther King, Jr. Dr. Fanini of Brazil in speaking of Martin Luther King, Jr., remarked: "The perfume of his soul forever will inspire the nations and people of this earth." Stephen Thorngate of the Seventh Day Baptist General Conference commented that: "His idealism and courage and conviction are a credit to your convention and an inspiration to all Baptists." There were others who spoke favorably in endorsing this observance. The following is a list of those who have responded in favor of observing Martin Luther King, Jr. Sunday.

ENDORSEMENTS
OF THE OBSERVANCE OF
MARTIN LUTHER KING, JR. SUNDAY

I. **Churches**

The Mount Moriah Baptist Church
Howard W. Creecy, Dr., Minister
Atlanta, Georgia

Zion Baptist Church
L. Venchael Booth, Minister
Cincinnati, Ohio

II. **Educational Institutions**

Ramapatnam Baptist Theological College and the Andra Christian Theological College
W. G. Carder, Dean
India

III. **Newspapers**

The Philadelphia Tribune
Baptist Progress

IV. **Religious Organizations**

American Baptist Convention
Liberia Baptist Missionary and Educational Convention, Inc.
National Council of Churces
North American Baptist General Conference
Panama Baptist Convention

V. **Personal Endorsements**

Rev. J. A. Boadi
Ghana Baptist Seminary

Appendix 52, cont'd

Dr. Nilson do Amaral Fanini
  President of Brazilian Baptist Convention
Dr. Kenneth R. Kennedy — General Ass'n of General Baptists
Dr. Stephen Thorngate — 7th Day Baptist General Conference
Dr. Carl W. Tiller — Assoc. Sec'y Baptist World Alliance

I represented our Convention at the following meetings:

1. Memphis Tennessee
   January 18-20
   Adjourned Session.

2. Atlanta, Georgia
   Southern Region #1
   February 23, 24
   Special Meeting of the Southern Baptist Convention
   Home Mission Board.

3. Administrative Subcommittee of the Baptist World Alliance
   Washington, D. C.
   March 8, 9.

4. Eastern Regional Convention
   March 21-23.

5. U. S. World Council of Churches (representing Baptist World Alliance)
   April 17, 18.

6. Midwestern Region
   April 19-22
   Detroit, Michigan.

7. Second Baptist — Detroit
   Dr. A. A. Banks' 25th Anniversary
   April 30, 1972

8. Dedicatory Speaker
   Martin Luther King, Jr. Hospital
   Kansas City, Missouri
   May 13, 1972

9. Howard University Chapel — Washington, D. C.
   May 14.

10. Concord Baptist Church of Christ — 125th Anniversary
    May 23rd.

11. Virginia College Commencement — Lynchburg, Va.
    May 29th.

12. Congress of Christian Education
    Antioch — Akron
    June 19-22.

13. Michigan Progressive Baptist Convention — Detroit, Michigan
    July 14th.

14. Baptist World Alliance Execeutive Committee
    Kingston, Jamaica
    July 27-31.
    International Rally Speaker.

15. Progressive Baptist State Convention of California and Nevada
    August 9, 10.

16. Annual Home and Foreign Mission Sunday
    Emmanuel Baptist Church
    Kansas City, Missouri
    August 20, 1972.

Now let us turn our minds and hearts to the consideration of our convention theme: "The Call of God," taken from Isaiah 6:8 which reads as follows:

  Also I heard the voice of the Lord, saying, Whom shall I send, and who will go for us? Then said I, Here am I send me. (KJV)

I would like for you to think in terms of the following subtopics: Called, Cleansed, Challenged, Committed and Commissioned.

When one is called by God there is the possibility of several responses: one may respond affirmatively with immediate action, or one may ignore the call and do nothing or, one may waver and procrastinate. These responses are illustrated throughout Biblical history.

Appendix 52, cont'd

Gideon complained about misfortunes which had befallen the Israelites when God called him. Jeremiah met with hardship in carrying out the work of God and wished to abandon Him. But, he could not abandon the work to which God had called him. Elijah was called while plowing; God calls His servants from every walk of life. God called Moses to the top of the mountain and told him to go down and bring his brother, Aaron, with him; God calls and expects those who are called to become media through which others are called. Those who neglect the call of God must be alerted to it; Jeremiah sounded a clarion to open the ears of the spiritually-minded men lest they forget the call of men and of God. When God calls, he backs up and supports the person that He calls. Moses, tending flocks on Mount Horeb, complained that he couldn't stand up to the Pharoah and God promised, "I will be with you." Jeremiah complained that he was too young when God called him — but God told him, also, that He was with him.

Procrastination, when called, can mean death — spiritual death. The man who told Jesus that he would come when he had buried his father was commanded: "Let the dead bury their dead; but go thou and preach the kingdom of God."

Encounters with God which mark the call of God should not be taken as something which is an ordinary occurrence. Special cases occur when the summons involves a sudden diverting of a life to an entirely new channel. A call is a sense of vocation brought to focus in a decision. It doesn't **have** to be sudden or dramatic. A call is usually the culmination of a growing awareness of what one may and ought to do with his life. Gifts and capacities are given to everyone and the secret of a good life is the use of these capacities and gifts to the highest ends. A man will best realize the powers within him when he is doing work which gives opportunity for these powers to be expressed. A person is happiest when he is doing what he is particularly equipped to do. Guidance counselors in high schools have an important role in that they must be able to intuitively determine what are the capabilities of an individual and help him to determine how he will best use his life. Many people do not even realize that their aptitudes are gifts to be put to use. Aptitudes must be wedded to tasks. Business today has come to realize that a man is most efficient and contented when his work gives him a chance to express what is in him. A well-adjusted life, a life using its endowments for constructive ends, is fulfilling God's intentions and in this manner of sense, this life is answering God's call.

Today, very few of our products are crafted by hand. This was not true years ago when creative work gave a man an opportunity to express himself and he could feel that in it he was fulfilling a purpose: George Eliot's poem, "Stradivarius" reminds us:

> Tis God gives skill
> But not without men's hands; He could not make
> Antonio Stradivari's violins without Antonio.
>
> (George Eliot's "Stradivarius")

But, today man is faced with the extinction of this opportunity to reveal his creativity by the increased use of machines in every facet of creativity. There is very little creativity in the repetition of machinery. And if man's soul is to escape destruction by this lack of opportunity for self-expression, he must realize that he is involved in something greater than the job, something more significant than the physical act required of him. He must understand that the whole mechanical process depends on his fidelity and skill; the product can't be perfected without him.

One must also consider the ends served by a vocation. No man can have a sense of having been called if he is using his talents for evil purposes. A dope peddler or burglar — these people certainly don't have a sense of having been called. The Christian must also consider how to relate his skill or knowledge to the service of God in his environment. He must consciously use his situations and opportunities for the good of others. Then he can truly know the peace of God's call. There are unrealized possibilites awaiting the Christian executive, the Christian doctor, or the Christian teacher. A layman may receive and answer a call just as truly as any minister.

Each individual is spoken to according to the pattern of his life and character of his vocation; Jesus' speech to the fishermen: "Come ye after me and I will make you fishers of men." It is possible for a man facing the opportunity of some honest labor or great profession and ready to give his life to it, to hear, as Isaiah did, a summon and to answer, as Isaiah did: HERE AM I, SEND ME.

After one has been called and made aware of his purpose in God's plan, one must be prepared for the working out of this purpose through spiritual cleansing. One is not safe from the condemnation of God until one's life is evident of spiritual cleansing. Jeremiah warned the people of continuing in their sinful ways and then coming before

Appendix 52, cont'd

the Lord as if they were free of all sin. Confession is spiritual therapy which brings promise of spiritual cleansing and renewal; Saul, recognizing that David had saved his life, confessed that he had sinned and played a fool; and his heart, which was once darkened by jealousy and hatred, was now enlightened. Sins do not just disappear; the sins which so easily beset one, remain always to plague, harass and condemn. Constant cleansing is needed. Isaiah's self-degradation was met by the purging and glowing coal of a seraphim — transforming his will into God's will; Isaiah responded to God: "Here am I; send me." Only the "blood of Jesus Christ cleanseth us all from sin." (I John 1:7)

In living the life of one who has been called lies the challenge of living above the level of humanity's frailties. Abraham was challenged by the altar at Bethel; this was a place where confessions and vows were made and baptism performed. Therefore, the altar reminded him of this and challenged him to live up to these commitments. God is able to meet every challenge thrown at Him; Goliath told the Israelites to choose an opponent for him — God appointed David, the little shepherd boy, who slew him. Joshua challenged men to cease their wavering in serving God; "Choose you this day whom ye will serve . . . but, as for me and my house, we will serve the Lord." The bones of Joseph provided inspiration and challenge to Moses, who carried them with him as the Israelites moved toward the Promised Land. Elijah, also challenged the children of Israel to make a decision: to follow God or Baal; but the people were unresponsive and perished. Christians are called by Christ and challenged to live a life above the level of human comprehension: Paul admonished the Corinthians: "With jealousy and quarrels in your midst are you not worldly, are you not behaving like ordinary men?" . . . In order to claim eternal life, every challenge of God must be met. Jesus challenged the rich man to give up all of his goods for eternal life as well as to fulfill the minimal requirements of the law.

In the final analysis, the life of one who has been called, cleansed and challenged should also be committed from within so that one might be used to maximum capacity by God. It is this commitment from within which determines whether or not we have truly heard the call in our hearts as well as with our ears. This inward commitment is also an indication of whether or not one has been cleansed to the very depths of one's soul; and this inherent commitment will be revealed in the end when the record shows if we have met the challenge issued by the One who made the call.

Solomon lacked inward commitment to God and his kingdom lost its glitter and he became bankrupt. One must turn away from idols if one is to be truly and totally committed to God. A committed response to the Gospel is indicated by one who embraces the Gospel, heart and soul, and finds in it a meaning and purpose to life. One who is committed to the Word of God believes fully. When Mary was informed that she was to bear the Son of God, she said: "Behold the handmaiden of the Lord, but unto me according to Thy Word." God always gives a new heart to those who commit themselves to His kingdom. Saul received a new heart after being anointed by Samuel, who told him that "the Spirit of the Lord would come upon him . . . and he would be turned into a new man." The cross of Christ is a call to discipleship, commitment and action — not an arousement to morbid curiosity. God has committed Himself to us by promising that divine blessings will always attend the labors of consecrated people. In Gethsemane, Jesus poured out His soul in prayer and commitment and God responded. But some heard it only as a loud noise — one must be committed, himself, in order to recognize the true commitment of another. The Upper Room is a place associated with commitment and resolution and such a place strengthens one's spiritual experience.

The name, "Isaiah," means "Jehovah is salvation," which was the message that Isaiah was commissioned to bring to his people in the 6th chapter of Isaiah, which is known as the "Prophet's Commission." Isaiah is caught up in his vision. He has a strong realization that he is being commissioned by God and therefore, he is being shown the secret purposes of God. Throughout this vision, Isaiah is commissioned to bring an uncongenial message, which is laid on him by divine compulsion:

    (a) Isaiah is commissioned to proclaim disaster.
    (b) Isaiah is commissioned to speak a message that will fall on deaf ears.
    (c) Isaiah is commissioned to speak a message that will reveal more clearly the
        disobedience of Judah.

Isaiah laments: "How long, O Lord?" and God shows Isaiah a desolated land where ruthless judgment is visited on those who survive the disaster. No voluntary response to the divine call was given by Isaiah; in the presence of God's judgement, one has no choice but to accept His commission.

This is what the churches of today need to realize: God's commission must be accepted, internalized and executed with all of the power that they can muster.

Appendix 52, cont'd

SOME THOUGHTS ON THE CHURCH

A Great Age for the Church

This is a great age for the Church. Some would want this qualified, to be stated as a great age for the Black Church. The Church I know cannot afford to have a colorline. We may be forced to make our witness in segregated patterns, but the Church Christ gave us has no walls of separation. We have great interpreters today with descriptive eloquence. We have come through periods which necessitate re-discovering our identity. Blackness is not simply an ideology, it is an industry. For many it has become a great economic asset. There are great lessons to be learned from our theologians and our historians. Our cultural heritage has great and tremendous significance. We must avoid with great pain over-romanticizing it. While we are emphasizing the virtues of the Black Church, there is a real danger that we are losing the essence of the real church. There are some danger signs of retrogression as we seek to re-live the experiences of our fathers. One or more generations might very well limp into life and emerge retarded because of our remaining at our "Black Pool of Bethesda" too long. It is exceedingly difficult to enjoy the white man's economics while repecting his stewardship. We relish his wages while rejecting his sacrifices. We claim to excel him in our religion while he excels us in his sense of mission. We find it easy to excel him in religious jubilation, while he far out-distances us in spiritual dedication. It behoves us not to make the same mstake of separation and self-glorification that we claim he has made. Black religious-exclusivism is no more acceptable to God than white exclusivism.

In this great age of man's excitement and depression when he vacillates between the extremes of hope and despair, we need to be sure of some definite word from the Lord. It must not be born out of the smallness of tradition or persecution; it must rather be born out of inspiration and out of faith. Like the prophet Isaiah we must have a vision that "Sees beyond the years." This vision must be of a Saviour whose light pierces all darkness, bridges all gulfs and crosses all waters. We dare not turn the clock back, but we must move forward with the pendulum of time, less we allow ourselves to be left standing at the well of natural water trying to decide who should drink; while Christ offers us a well of water springing up into everlasting life. The real power of our black heritage lies in our invincible faith that "God is no respecter of persons."

All religions are on trial today. The black man's religion with its fervor and zeal; the white man's religion with its stateliness and order. Our Master will measure us all by our fruits. Both of us can reminisce of an "age of power" that seems to have faded into the shadows of our past. The preaching on Main Street has seemingly lost its power and the preaching on Back Street is also failing to draw men to Christ. We can ill afford to make idle claims about our religion without examining what it does to the hearts of men.

Henry Mitchell taught a course at Rochester on "The Black Bible and the Black Imagination." This course was taught to Roman Catholic Priest candidates to aid them in telling the Bible Story in a way that would make it come alive. We are indebted to Emmanuel McCall and his book, **The Black Christian Experience,** for this account and other significant messages of information.

Anyone touched by God can tell a Bible Story and it will live, whether out of a black or white Christian experience. Howard Thurman, a devout black theologian and preacher, has been telling the story, in its richest simplicity, to both black and white audiences for nearly a half of a century, but only those who are willing to think will ever hear it. Perhaps I have unwittingly stumbled upon a great need in the Church today: in all of our religious experiences, we need to THINK.

It is so easy to stir the emotions and never touch the depths of our inner spirit. Our whole Western World tends to be a world of motion, activity and restlessness. In utter desperation, we turn to the East for meditation and transcendentalism. Howerd Thurman tells us in his challenging book, **The Inward Journey,**

It is ever a grace and a benediction to be able to come to a halt, to stop, to pause, to make a rest of motion.

The women of our Convention discovered long ago what we all need to discover the great power of silence. They have read more carefully than we the 46th Psalm: "Be still and know that I am God." Perhaps our ancestors became easy "captives" because they had not learned to be still, to "Steal Away to Jesus". Even now, our secrets and all of our plans for progress are often defeated because they are too readily broadcast.

Appendix 52, cont'd

Ours is an Age of Cooperation and Reconciliation

We are all weighed in the balances and found wanting. The white man's religion failed at the point of reverence for life and brotherhood. It seemingly never climbed the mountains of frustration and segregation. It comforted him in his separation from his brother of another color. The black man's religion failed him because it became a device for survival and never progressed to revival of all those finer instincts which would make for a truly emancipated being. Even to this day, he doubts the intergrity of his white brother's religion. Far too often, the hand of friendship and brotherhood is extended to him and he refuses it for lack of faith.

Arnold Toynbee, the great historian, suggests that our children will "choose their religion for themselves instead of being confined to their inherited beliefs." He also says:

I believe it will be possible one day to have a maximum of religion with a minimum of dogma. That is my hope, not only do I believe that this is possible, but I feel it is necessary for the survival of our species.

We must prepare ourselves for the creation of a religion that will transcend our traditional barriers. This is the age of Communication, Confrontation and Reconciliation. Like Paul, who was then named Saul, our ride to Damascus must be halted until we see the Lord. We must not only see Him, but we must also obey His Command. Perhaps, we too, shall not see until our brother has laid his hands upon us. In this new religious experience, we shall behold how truly wonderful God is.

The true religious experience resolves itself in fellowship, love and brotherhood. We must explore our past, but never worship it. We must enjoy our past, but never sanctify it. The great need of the age is reconciliation. To be reconciled to God one must become reconciled to his brother. The bonds of racism must be broken. The differences in culture, skin color and economic stratification must be overcome and every barrier separating man from man must be broken down.

For a little while we may bolster our ego by bathing in our identity crisis, but we dare not remain submerged in it. We must move ahead to meet the New Age aborning of which the prophet Isaiah spoke with a timeless eloquence:

A voice cries in the wilderness, prepare the way of the Lord,
Make straight in the desert a highway for our God,
Every valley shall be lifted up,
And every mountain and hill be made low;
And uneven ground shall be made level,
And the rough places a plain.
And the glory of the Lord shall be revealed,
And all flesh shall see it together,
For the mouth of the Lord has spoken.

Isaiah 40:3-5

CONCLUSION

It has been a long journey from "Heavenly Houston" to "Enchanting Chicago." We will long remember the great entertainment of the Baptists of Houston under the faithful leadership of Dr. S. M. Weaver, Dr. J. W. Brent and the fine ministers and laymen who supported them. They gave their best and we are grateful. We missed our beloved President who was confined to his sick bed. Little did we dream that he would never preside over us again! He was faithful to the end. He sent a well prepared Annual Message and commissioned me to read it. It was a masterpiece and has now become his last will and testament to our Progressive Family. He left us a great legacy. We shall cherish his contributions and hallow his memory.

As powerful and shocking as death is, our young Convention has already proven it can survive this life defeating blow. In your dedication to a "cause-centered" Convention rather than to a "personality-centered" Convention, you accepted God's providence and moved on. I am most grateful for your acknowledging my right under the constitution to succeed our fallen chieftain. You not only acknowledged this right, but you gave me your warmest blessing and cooperation. Let me acknowledge with the deepest humility that it is an awesome task to lead you so great a people.

It is my prayerful hope that I have not failed you. There were times during this year when I was not certain that I could succeed as your standard bearer. My own little "tug-boat" was hard driven by the raging currents of life's sea. There were waves too great for me to master, but there always loomed before me the vision of the

Appendix 52, cont'd

great "Progressive Ship of State." When the load seemed too heavy and the cross currents too swift — the impossible strength that comes from prayer kept me from going under. Under the spell of faith my anchor held until the storm of disillusionment, heart-break and despair passed over. It was not easy to discover that my own prayerless life was the source of my failure. Throughout this pilgrim journey, it has been necessary to turn again and again to the Home-land of the soul. In this place of refuge I have found anew the true meaning of the Hymn written by a great servant of God:

> From every stormy wind that blows,
> From every swelling tide of woes,
> There is a calm, a sure retreat —
> 'Tis found beneath the mercy seat.
>
> There is a place where Jesus sheds
> The oil of gladness on our heads,
> A place of all on earth most sweet;
> It is the blood bought mercy seat.
>
> There is a scene where spirits blend,
> Where friend holds fellowship with friend;
> Tho' sundered far, by faith they meet
> Around one common mercy seat.
>
> There, there on eagle wings we soar,
> And sin and sense molest no more,
> And heav 'n comes down our souls to greet,
> And glory crowns the mercy seat.

Appendix 53

THE PRESIDENT'S ANNUAL MESSAGE
The Keys To The Kingdom
"And I will give unto thee The Keys of The Kingdom of Heaven
. . ." Mt. 16:19

To our beloved Vice Presidents, our distinguished former Presidents, our Executive Secretary. Officers of all Departments of our Progressive Family, Messengers and Friends here assembled in our 12th Annual Session — greetings in the name of our Lord and Saviour Jesus Christ.

Mississippi: The Magnolia State

From my earliest recollection, Mississippi has been on my tongue. When I grew to the point that I was able to spell, I could spell her name. One of the most intriguing sights that ever struck my vision in my early years was at a railroad crossing — where I read: "Mississippi Law Stop." All the days of my life since, I have felt a sense of caution concerning the issue of life.

This wonderful state, the land of cotton, pulp wood and potatoes, entered the union on December 10, 1817. She became the second state to join the Confederacy in 1861, and was readmitted to the union in 1870. Her scenic beauty is enchanting to the whole world. From the woodall mountain to the Delta plains, from the Natchez trails to the coastal waters — beauty haunts the avid traveler until he lies down to pleasant dreams. Jackson is her capital and is one of the fastest growing cities in the deep south. It is well that we come to our Nation's heart land and renew our faith in the goodness of God. Some of the finest people this side of Heaven had their beginning — in this great state sometimes feared by many, but loved by all who really allow themselves to be drawn into her heart. It was in this state that I saw the light of day and it was here I saw the "Light of Life" — so it I'm extravagant and immodest, it is because I have come home leading one of the greatest Baptist Conventions on the face of the earth.

Let me pause to give thanks for my parents, the Old Hopewell Baptist Church and to Alcorn A & M College and above all to Almighty God who loves me and and leads me.

I shall not call the roll of the great men and women who are natives and residents of this state. I shall however, remind you that some of the greatest preachers, politicians and educators have come from her bosom and what is more — many are still being born. Let me invite you then, during these days, to — let Mississippi come close to your hearts as you learn and work together under the Mississippi sun.

Let us pause now and remember some of our sainted dead who have crossed the River Jordan and await our coming. I shall name only two, but let us remember them all:

> Dr. T. Solomon Boone
> Detroit, Michigan
> Dr. J. H. Lockett
> Atlanta, Georgia

> "On Jordan's stormy banks
> I stand
> And cast a wishful eye
> To Canaan's fair and
> Happy land
> Where my possessions lie."

Let us resolve to live as valiantly as they did and strive to weave a pattern of life which will serve for others as a worthy example.

This year I shall omit my travels and the meetings I have attended. They have not been without meaning and inspiration. To a very great degree, they have been fruitful and rewarding. My efforts here will be to save the time for reflections on where we are and where we must seek to go.

Let me share with you the following recommendations which are submitted with the hope that they will assist us in implementing the great program we envision for our Convention.

Be it Resolved that:

1. The Convention will form an Advisory Committee comprised of former Presidents who will offer suggestions for the good of the Convention.

Appendix 53, cont'd

2. The Convention will appoint a Retirement Promotion Committee whose function will be to encourage pastors to join our Convention's Retirement Plan.

3. The Convention will appoint at each Annual Session, a Program Committee to promote the sharing of ideas, philosophies and programming in keeping with the latest theological trends of today. This Committee will concern itself with the encouragement and support of Christian concerns confronting Black churches today.

4. The Convention will appoint a Stewardship Commission which will plan a 10 (ten) year Stewardship Advance Program aimed at changing the stewardship life of our Convention through her churches. This Commission will concern itself with the utilization of time, talent and treasure. This will include the cultivation of the youth and the preservation of the aged.

5. The Convention will appoint a Regional Promotion Committee — made up of persons representing each region to: (a) recruit new churches in the region
    (b) to encourage monthly giving in the region — thus strengthening our Voluntary Monthly Support Plan.

6. The Convention will encourage, authorize and direct the Executive Secretary' office to do the following:

    (a) keep all resolutions passed during an Annual Session before our member churches through out the year.

    (b) send a monthly reminder to all member churches to send in a contribution to Headquarters between the 1st. and the 15th.

    (c) secure the records of the Convention from any secretary of any department at the close of the Session and in no case any later than 30 days following the Session. If this will not work, then begin the practice of using a tape recorder.

    (d) the Executive Secretary will follow the letter of the constitution in the transaction of financial matters using the proper signatories on all checks and presenting the Convention with a professionally prepared audit by a certified public accountant at each Annual Session.

    (e) set up a Financial Book Keeping System that will harmonize with the Fund of Renewal. Let us strive for the best possible plan of fiscal responsibility and financial control.

7. The Convention consider officially adopting and supporting Hol Reba Bible conference and Nannie Helen Burroughs School as a beginning of establishing Progressive Baptist distinctives through religious education.

8. The Convention will authorize the new Chairman of Life Memberships, Rev. T. Wright Morris, to design and produce a Life Membership Lapel Pin bearing the Progressive symbol.

9. The churches of the Convention will observe Martin Luther King, Jr. Sunday by making use of the materials published by our Progressive Baptist Publishing House and the Scripture Selection — "By Faith — He Still Speaks," published by the American Bible Society.

10. Progressive Churches will emphasize Evangelism through participation in "Key '73'," and the Baptist World Alliance's "Reconciliation through Christ," emphasis: Let us add Soul Winning to our Church Progress.

11. That the Fund of Renewal must be seen as a pressing Stewardship challenge for the whole Progressive Family. Every church, regardless of size, must participate with the understanding that the very future of our Convention will depend upon how well it participates.

12. Regional Conventions will not operate programs independently of the Convention and each Regional Convention will submit its program for approval at the Mid-Winter Board Meeting and make an Annual Report through the Executive Secretary at the Annual Session.

My fellow Progressives these are my recommendations. It is my prayer that they will be adopted and carried out with the highest religious integrity and zeal.

Appendix 53, cont'd

A Special Announcement
American Bible Society Honors Dr. Martin Luther King, Jr.

It was a great moment for me when I was able to get the American Bible Society to publish a Scripture Selection honoring Dr. Martin Luther King, Jr., the greatest Progressive pastor we have ever known. His life of great worth has become a legend in many lands. In all of my travels in lands distant to our shores, there is no instance where his name is not known or revered by men and women of goodwill. Our Progressive Family is blessed beyond measure to claim him as a brother in our "household of faith." He is not only our Moses, he belongs to all who knew him both in the flesh and in the spirit.

We meet each year and observe Martin Luther King, Jr. Memorial Night — and these nights have thus far been the real climax of our Convention. We must go a step further and make this night even more real and meaningful. This is our opportunity to have our youth present excerpts from his sermons and speeches, play recordings of his voice, and give some of the highlights of his life. We are not too far from the day when a generation will come on the scene and not understand why we observe this night. We must keep this Memorial clear, meaningful and imaginative. When we honor his memory, we honor ourselves.

The American Bible Society has honored his memory recently by publishing a Scripture Selection entitled — "By Faith — He Still Speaks." This Selection is available at 2¢ (two cents) a copy and should enjoy wide use and distribution in our Progressive Family. Many will want this Selection for their young people as well as their adults. Please order directly through the New York office. There will be many of our churches who will begin supporting the Bible Cause. Others of us will increase our giving. All of us have grown in our awarness that we have a responsibility to share along with other denominations and provide the Scriptures for those who are needy and cannot afford them. The American Bible Society should be encouraged and congratulated for the recognition and honor she has given Dr. King. The smallest church in our denomination can order this Scripture Selection and our largest churches should make them available to themselves and to other community institutions.

Plan this year to observe Martin Luther King, Jr. Sunday on the third Sunday in January. Plan to make use of this Scripture Selection along with the materials from our Progressive Baptist Publishing House. Order your materials early and plan your program effectively. Our communities will benefit from such efforts and in many instances will be brought to a greater sense of reconciliation.

Dr. Thomas Kilgore, Jr. and Dr. Wyatt T. Walker have consented to serve as National Co-Chairmen and they will have the full support of our Convention. They will have regional chairmen and a complete national organization.

While we run the calculated risk of being accused of capitalizing on the name of Martin Luther King, Jr., we must not think too highly of ourselves that we fail to let the world know that we both honor and cherish his memory. We must be grateful that in the Providence of God, he was one of us and that it is our duty to acknowledge the same. It is to our everlasting credit that our Convention came into being at a time when this great Civil Rights Leader needed a spiritual home. It was our great privilege to provide that home — not only for him, but for all kindred spirits — thus linking ourselves for all times with the forward movement of eternity. Let us proudly exalt his philosophy, his high standard of excellence and his strength to love. Let us firmly embrace his loyalty and love for Christ that we may tell of his greatness to generations following.

Our Convention theme deals with "The Keys to the Kingdom." It is an appropriate theme as well as a great one. This message is an effort to provide for posterity a clear understanding of "why" there is a Progressive National Baptist Convention, Inc. It will in some measure be helpful to some of us who are present in this meeting. Allow me to interpret the theme by using three definitive words: (1) Accountability (2) Compatibility (3) Dependability

I. Accountability

One cannot make use of the Keys to the Kingdom until he first acknowledges that he is not his own. Nothing he possesses is his, but all belongs to God. The great misuse of time, talent and treasure is due largely to a gross misunderstanding of life. Every man must come to the high resolve which has been clearly expressed: "I am a Steward. My life is a trust. I must give an account unto God for my Stewardship."

Appendix 53, cont'd

Somehow the gap between preaching and practice must be closed. There is only one answer to this dilemma and that is remedied by one's accountability. It is far too easy to forget the source of all blessings; we need to remind ourselves as we ponder the words of Chas. Allen — in Psychiatry:

> "Every morning the sun rises to warm the earth. If it failed to shine for just one minute, all life on the earth would die. The rains come to water the earth. There is fertility in the soil, life in the seeds, oxygen in the air. The providence of God is about us in unbelievable abundance every moment. But so often we just take it for granted." (God's Psychiatry, p. 112).

Since all that we have comes from God, it follows that every man is accountable to God for the way he uses his time, talent and treasure.

Progressive Convention an Historic Necessity

The historic necessity of our Progressive National Baptist Convention becomes more significant with each passing year. No matter how slowly we may grow, nor how small we may remain, **we were born out of great historic necessity.** We have the conviction that the time is long past when one leader should hold a post of honor and leadership indefinitely. When we reflect upon this, we are not looking back with enmity, nor are we engaging in stirring up animosity. We are simply acknowledging that the time has come when history demands that we try another way. We believe our system of tenure is best even though we cannot always have a towering international personality as our President. To say this is not to imply that just anybody can be President simply because he wants to serve in this capacity. However, we do suggest that God can use a sincere, dedicated ordinary man to great advantage. To truly be Progressive, we must always subscribe to the lofty Progressive concept with which we began. We must commit both to heart and to practice the significant precepts set forth in Rom. 12:9-21. We must never forget how we were born — nor how we experienced the tragic breakdown of fellowship before declaring that we must be **free or perish.** It was one of our finest hours when we met in our First Annual Session in Philadelphia and heard the commanding voice of Dr. W. H. R. Powell declare:

> "All is well!"

The courage to make a new beginning was an expression of Christian maturity at its highest and best. Neither our past nor our present achievements must allow us to become complacent, nor lifted up in pride. It is not enough for a doctor to open an office and hang out a shingle — he must continue to study and practice medicine at the highest level of his competency — in order to make himself meaningful to his community.

We Must Begin to Compile our History

As we come to our 12th Annual Session, we must consider the importance of compiling our records for those who come after us. From time to time many inquiries are made by other bodies regarding our origin and our purpose. We need to provide an adequate answer that will be both intellectually and spiritually satisfying. It is not too early to begin a compilation of the speeches, blue prints and manifestoes of our former Presidents and leaders. We have had important contributions made by all our former Presidents and these need to be collected and placed in fire proof files in our Headquarter's office to await the day when some concerned scholar will make use of them. In addition to our Presidents, we were blessed in the early days to have had a significant contribution from Dr. W. H. R. Powell, which should become a working theological document for the years to come — stating our Progressive Theological position.

We need to inquire now of the widows of some of our outstanding leaders about books and papers they may wish to share. These could be loaned to some of our Christian Colleges for their use until they are needed by us. Some of the men we can remember who made notable contributions were: Drs. J. Carl Mitchell, J. C. Austin, Sr. H. H. Coleman and T. S. Boone, to mention only a few. We should try to publish selected sermons from all our pastors living and dead. We should look forward to the day when there will be a tape collection of our great preachers and scholars. Our riches are unlimited, but they cannot be enriching unless they are collected and used. Some of the dynamic voices we now hear, will be hushed within a decade or two we shall be left with the stark realization that:

> "Time like an ever rolling stream,
> Bears all its sons away
> They fly, forgotten as a dream
> Dies at the opening day."

Appendix 53, cont'd

We Face a Progress Problem

In the effort to be Progressive, we can easily fall victim to our progress. A significant example is that of the hard work of our Budget Committee. There is a need to work equally as hard contributing money to make the budget valid. It is far easier to plan and adopt a budget than it is to convert pastors to remember to subscribe adequate money for its effectiveness. Some of our leaders once armed with a proposed budget allotment take off spending without any concern about where its coming from.

It has now reached the point that our Budget Committee and our Executive Secretary must work closely together to unify each others' effort to bring about the desired results. Together they can keep the constituency informed as to the level of our operation at a given time. This will make possible greater alertness on the part of the constituency to play a more meaningful role. We must come to the point where we can know what our level of giving must be each month in order to reach our annual goal. It is incumbent upon us to become the real people of God — "forgetting those things which are behind, and reaching forth unto those things which are before — We must press toward the mark for the prize of the high calling of God in Christ Jesus." Phil. 3:13, 14. We can never be any greater than our diligence in God's business. After the financial goal is set, we must strive with a sense of oneness and togetherness to reach it.

Some Blessings of Providence

In the Providence of God, our Convention is not only blessed to have some of the finest men who live, but also some of the finest men who sleep. Our late President, Dr. Earl L. Harrison, had rare vision and keen insight. His leadership genius moved us forward many years, even though he held the office of President for only a few months. He led us into the purchase of a Headquarters Building where we are now housed. We are no longer paying rent, but we are instead paying notes toward the retirement of our debt. This should encourage us, but we should not slacken our pace. Our Executive Secretary, Dr. S. S. Hodges, has moved into his own home and we offer him our congratulations and best wishes. This does not relieve us because he is still entitled to a Housing Allowance. These advances should not make us careless — but rather careful as we carry on.

We Must Make Each Year a Progressive Year

We must make each year "The Progressive Year" of our Lord and thus account for it to the utmost of our ability. While we must at all times be forgiving and must make no strenuous effort to withdraw from other Baptists, we must never deny our unique role as Progressive Baptists. Let women and men, boys and girls be assured with crystal clarity that there is a difference to be found in Progressive Baptists. Our Convention is founded upon the exalted principles of Fellowship, Progress, and Peace. These above all other considerations must hold the supremacy in our working together. There will be times when we shall fail in our conduct and our spirit. This should be the exception and not the rule. We must avoid like a plague immaturity, insincerity and infidelity. Let our conduct always be that of Godly men and women. We must remember that we have a contribution to make that is peculiarly our own.

Key II: Compatibility

Another "Key to the Kingdom" strikes me as being compatibility. Man's relationship to God determines his effectiveness in God's service. Many of us would like to teach, preach, heal and help the down-trodden souls of men. Jesus looks upon us and declares:

> "Unless you remain in me you cannot bear fruit, just as a branch cannot bear fruit unless it remains in the vine . . . whoever remains in me, and I in him, will bear much fruit; for you can do nothing without me." John 15: 4, 5.

We Need an Aroused Curiosity about Christ

There is no possibilty of exploring the inexhaustible riches of Christ without an insatiable appetite for learning. Like the courageous disciple, we must sometimes ask — Master, where dwellest thou? Our generation is witnessing a renewed determination to know Christ in His fulness. Though we see the rise of Charismatic Movements — signifying renewal and revival, the organized church is far too complacent. We need to return to the quest of our Fathers. I can hear a far-off echo in my ears

Appendix 53, cont'd

and it sounds like chanting voices. They seem to express that curiosity the world needs now as they cry:

> I'm seeking the man called Jesus—
> I wonder where is He?
> Go down, go down
> and search among the flowers—
> Perhaps you will find
> Him there!

Too few of us are searching beyond our physical needs — our concern for present existence — food, shelter, clothing — cars and a house to live in — all absorb our day-to-day thinking and living. We have lost our sense of eternity. For too many of us believe that God's Supply House is in Washington, D. C. and that all our help comes from the Treasury House of our Government. The contradiction we face is seen in our dread of higher taxes. Even people in religion seem to be wanting "something for nothing." We have lost our creativity — our ability to make "brick without straw." We need to remember that often when God takes something away from us — He often gives us something better. Likewise, when He says "No" to our foolish request He bids us to look deeper and seek higher things.

When the Progressive National Baptist Convention was born she was not destined to be just another Convention. She was born with an ideal of love, brotherhood and freedom. She was born with a challenging Scripture Lesson and a Song. God gave us the Scripture — Roman 12:9-21 and God gave us a Song. All who seek to lead in this Convention should take time to read the Scripture and sing the Song. It would be well to study the Scripture and practice it. It would be well to sing the Song and explore the depths of its inspiration. These were not the idle wanderings of man — but they are the lofty revelations of God. Take a look at our symbol and study the words. They are fraught with meaning, deep meditation and lofty aspiration. Read the Progressive concept contributed by Dr. Thomas Kilgore — and view its literary excellence and character content. Then meditate upon Dr. T. M. Chamber's fine interpretation of building a "Cause — Centered" Convention rather than a "Personality Centered" Convention. Study the eloquence and brilliance of insight in Dr. Gardner Taylor's warning that our Convention is the "last best hope of Negro Baptists." Study the theological insights of Dr. Searcy and watch the unfolding of his legal and intellectual mind. Set yourself in readiness for great spiritual transfiguration as you sit in your imagination at the feet of Dr. Harrison, the spiritually wise teacher and preacher of great magnitude. It is impossible to pay tribute to all the preachers, prophets and leaders of this great Convention — but it gives me great pride to mention just a few.

There is a need for compatibility in all relations in life and especially in the realm of the spirit. Sin has separated us from God. We are no longer compatible with Him. We have swapped light for darkness. We have chosen strife rather than peace. The Kingdom will come closer to every man when he strives for the Peace of God through faith and surrender. Man can never become compatible with God until he becomes subject to God. When he becomes subject to God, he will live in harmony with God and in harmony with his fellowman.

Our Convention Must Strive After Unity

Our Convention must strive after unity in the midst of diversity. We must never fall apart over the lack of sameness, nor must we become divided over temporary differences. We do not have to be graduates of the same school to respect each other, nor do we have to be followers of the same theological system to be fellow believers in Christ. And, above all else, we must never at the expense of Calvary sanctify any political party because of personal advantage or persuasion. We must love each other so much that we will speak in the most temperate tones when there is the possibility of causing misunderstanding or offense.

One can be as prophetic as God allows him to be without casting insinuations, or stooping to name calling, or resorting to castigations and abuse. Howard Thurman, great theologian and preacher, responded to a simple question that I asked one day which ran: "Dr. Thurman, how did you get to be the man that you are?" He laughed heartily and said, "a strange set of fortuitous circumstances." Somehow, we must realize as we set our Nation's Political house in order, as we institute necessary reforms in the political system, that the words of the Gospel song apply equally to all. We all need — "Just a Closer Walk With God." As preachers and prophets: We must exhort, but always with sobriety; we must condemn, but always with wisdom; we must transform, but always with patience. We must stand resolute as men of

Appendix 53, cont'd

God who firmly believe that our God is able in every circumstance because all things are possible with God including deliverance and salvation for all men.

Our Greatest Challenge Lies Ahead

We are blessed to have made some significant strides forward in denominational acceptance and leadership. God's great providence has smiled upon us and we now have the Presidency of the North American Baptist Fellowship, held by Dr. S. S. Hodges, our Executive Secretary and your President now serves as Vice President of the Baptist World Alliance. We shall not hold these positions again soon and we should be humbly and gratefully proud. In addition to these nominal positions of honor, Dr. Gardner C. Taylor, our great preacher of international fame and one of our former Presidents, heads the powerful commission on Human Rights in the Baptist World Alliance. Our pastors and leaders hold many important positions of leadership and we are justifiably proud.

While we are yet a very young Convention, let me list some of our very important assets:

1. We have a full-time Executive Secretary
2. We have the beginnings of a Headquarters Center in the Nation's Capital
3. We have a profitable Publishing House relationship with one of the Nation's greatest Religious Publishers.
4. We have an outstanding Foreign Mission Bureau engaged in a great healing ministry in Nigeria and significant Mission work in other lands.
5. Our Congress of Christian Education is growing by leaps and bounds and and continues to choose great leadership.
6. Our Women's Department, Laymen, Ushers and Youth are more than challenging in productivity and growth.
7. Our Retirement Plan for Pastors and Christian Workers has relieved us of a great burden of guilt and shame for those who face the sunset of life without hope.
8. Our Fund of Renewal campaign — which is a joint venture between the American Baptist Churches and our Convention has the potential of helping us overcome all the ills of poor Stewardship which now threaten our churches. It has the possibility of advancing the whole Baptist Family through spiritual revitalization and reconciliation. Our success in this joint venture will move the Baptist clock of faith forward, possibly determining our survival and destiny for the next half century. We dare not fail — we must give our best and more for the next five years. Whether the entire Christian Movement will be stronger or weaker is dependent upon us. We must earnestly seek God's guidance and help that we may not fail God nor man.

Our future depends upon our magnanimity, spiritual dedication, and integrity. We can be seriously damaged in any one of our Annual Sessions if we stoop to pettiness and non-essentials. We must avoid yielding to intemperate outbursts, acid criticisms and cultivated bitterness. In the next decade we can emerge as the great people of God and offer some leadership to the entire Christian World. Although we have gained membership in the National Council of Churches, our next step must be the World Council of Churches. We cannot go forward toward this goal until we learn how to support "Causes" in keeping with God's manifold grace. Do we dare drag our feet in support of Causes when the challenge and the call to service is so great? It is well that we recall the words of Jesus and apply them to ourselves while preaching them to others — "We must be about our Father's business." As "time servers" we need to remember that our time is not our own and we must give the best account of it that we possibly can. It takes the same amount of time to go to town to pick up a can of pipe tobacco as it does to go get a bag of flour. We must use our time wisely by investing it fully in Christ's service.

We do not have to be hostile toward any other Baptist group to make progress. We can enjoy the greatest of fellowship with our fellow Baptists in other Conventions and still believe that our way is "the more excellent way." We are here because we believe that tenure of office for Baptist leaders is more Christian, more productive and more satisfying than a life-time, or indefinite tenure. We are here because we believe that Fellowship, Progress and Peace can be achieved better under the Tenure System. Our challenge is to provide this by a more excellent standard of living. If our Convention is going to be just as ordinary in Christian conduct as any other — then we are sailing under a false banner and deserve the greater condemnation. But,

Appendix 53, cont'd

if others find us more warm, honest and congenial and above all else, more sacrifically productive, then we have vindicated our claim.

We must chart new paths, conquer untried ways, rise above the hills of despair and distrust. We must seek the way of prayer, peace and prosperity — keeping in mind that we have a rendezvous with history and with God. Ours is the noble fight to set men free. We must not be afraid to be Progressive. We must not hesitate to honor one another. We must be the generation of noble men "in honor preferring one another." We must not spend our "Tenure-Time" unwisely. Each man who occupies from the humblest office to the highest must occupy it with a sense of urgency. Our fore-fathers were not wrong when they gave a man an opportunity instead of money. A man who does not know what to do with opportunity is not very likely to do anything with money. These heavy "budget-spenders" bear watching and this is especially true when they mix so little of their own with it. Dr. J. J. Koger, our Large Gifts Chairman, will be calling upon us to help liquidate the indebtedness of our Headquarters

We are all "time-servers," and we have no guarantee on how much time we have to serve.

> Tenure—time is serving time—
> Let us work while it is day
> Tenure—time is giving time
> Let us give as well as pray—
> Tenure—time is loving time—
> You can add some spice to life—
> Tenure—time is God's time
> Do not waste it in envy and strife.

Like David we must serve God's purposes in our own time, and die, and be buried beside our ancestors, and suffer decay. (See: Acts 13:36)

Key III: Dependability

There is still another word which might be used to describe one of the Keys to the Kingdom — that word is dependability. Jesus expresses this when He says" "If anyone wants to come with me, he must forget himself, carry his cross, and follow me." Mt. 16:24 How difficult it is to hold out and hold on when the going gets rough. We quit the battle, we desert our friends, we doubt our choice and we deny our Lord. If there is any lesson to be learned from Calvary, it is that our Lord went all the way — He loved us until the end.

Charles Allen reminds us again in his book, **God's Psychiatry,** that "Jesus never promised ease to those who follow Him. Never did He put a carpet on the race track or a bed of roses on the battlefield. He talked about self-denial, about crosses — blood spattered, death dealing crosses. To enter the Kingdom of God may mean decisions that are hard and consecration that leads to persecution. But it can be no other way."

Far too few are dependable in these days. We are too quick in our retreat — we are too desirous of "easy success." The real Key to the Kingdom is dependability, that rugged quality that makes one faithful "unto death."

We Need a World Vision for a World Task

When Jesus gave his disciples the great Commission, He gave it with the understanding that those commissioned would not only go into all the world, but would also be faithful unto death. In the past twelve years, we have seen those who "bloomed out" with Promise, but were of short duration. We have seen those who were confused in their loyalties and were blown by the shifting winds. There is an evident lack of vision. How can we go into all the world when we cannot see beyond the hills? How can we see the world's suffering while we are consumed by our own grief? Somehow we must gain that self-less-ness that Christ possessed that we might follow Him and do His wondrous works. We are now faced with the challenge to build both our Home and Foreign Mission Programs that they will be pleasing in God's sight as well as challenging to the hearts of men. Great effort must be made to train our laymen to work and then give them the "right of way" to serve the present age.

Somehow, we who love the Lord must know that the Kingdom we seek is worthy of all the tribulations that we must bear — worthy of all the sorrows that we must share — because our greatest possession, Jesus Christ, is there. We are comforted on this jounrey because we seek a land in a brighter world than this. We sing with the poet:

Appendix 53, cont'd

There's a land that is fair-er than day, And by faith we can see it a-far; For the Fa-ther waits o-ver the way, To prepare us a dwell-ing place there.

Chorus   In the sweet by and by, We shall meet on that beautiful shore; In the sweet by and by, We shall meet on that beau-ti-ful shore.

We shall sing on that beau-ti-ful shore the me-lo-di-ous song of the blest, And our spir-its shall sor-row no more, Not a sigh for the bless-ings of rest (chorus)

To our boun-ti-ful Fa-ther a-bove, We will of-fer the trib-ute of praise, For the glo-ri-ous gift of His love, And the bless-ings that hal-low our days. (chorus)

Until then we shall keep the faith, fulfilling God's purposes in our own time — Using "The Keys to the Kingdom:" Accountability, Compatibility and Dependability.

Appendix 54

PRESIDENT L. VENCHAEL BOOTH'S THIRD ANNUAL ADDRESS

THE CHURCH REVOLUTIONIZED, OR REVOLUTIONARY?

L. Venchael Booth, President

Do not conform outwardly to the standards of this world, but let God transform you inwardly by a complete change of your mind. Then you will be able to know the will of God—what is good, and is pleasing to him, and is perfect. (Roman 12:2—TEV)

Mr. Vice President, our distinguished former Presidents, Officers of all Departments of our Progressive Family, Messengers and Friends assembled here at our 13th Annual Session; greetings in the Name of our Lord and Saviour Jesus Christ. In this historic hour, I address you with deep and loving gratitude for the honor that has been mine as the fifth president of your great Convention.

Welcome to the Wonderful World of Ohio

A few years ago our State had a strong, dynamic and creative Governor who made the words "wonderful World of Ohio," a household phrase, we need to renew them in our memories and look once more on the beautiful side of life. In a world like this men need to look up and behold the wondrous works of God. We cannot afford to bathe in our troubles forever because we are mortals and are prone to troubles. We must cultivate the better things of life in the interest of our own survival. During this week I wish to invite each of you to see only the beauty of Cleveland and to feel that her beauty transcends any ugly element that may be found in her environs. If you travel by car, take time to view the wonderful world of Ohio. See her farms, quiet villages, small towns and great cities. Stop and rest in her parks, stroll along her lakesides and shop in her great shopping centers. If you have the time, spend a few days relaxing in her luxurious hotels and motels. It is a wonderful world, but you must cast aside your worries and fears and let your soul enjoy it. There is no more wonderful part of the world than Ohio.

13th Annual Session
My Progressive Journey 1961 to Present

It is no secret what God can do with one man when that man is willing to trust in Him. Little did I dream when the Lord moved me to call my brethren across the country to Cincinnati in November 1961, that so many men would answer and that such great events would follow. You will simply have to believe me that when I reminisce, it is not to reflect honor and glory to myself. There is no need for me to be so naive, nor so foolish because Progressive National Baptist Convention did not begin with any one man. It did become necessary for some one man to make the needed sacrifice to bring men of like spirit together. In the bottom of my heart I am most grateful that God allowed me to play a small part. There would have never been a Progressive National Baptist Convention had there not been a Gardner Taylor, Martin Luther King, Jr., Marshall Sheppard and a host of other men whom this nation loved and respected. In the midst of these fine men stood T. M. Chambers, E. L. Harrison and C. V. Johnson.

My Progressive journey began in the Queen City of the Mid-West in 1961 and has continued to this year of our Lord, 1974; and though the Tenure Law of our Convention relieves me of the Presidency in this historic session; it does not mark the end of my journey. It is good for my presidency to end in my adopted home state—among my friends who have watched my growth and have challenged me by their significant contributions. Ohio has some of the finest pastors and leaders that the nation affords. Cleveland stands in the front ranks of providing this worthy leadership.

Cleveland is the home of the Standard Oil Company, founded by John D. Rockefeller in 1870. She has the strategic advantage of being located near the coal fields of Pennsylvania and is accessible by the way of the Great Lakes to the iron mines of Minnesota. Cleveland developed into a major ore port and a center of iron and steel production in the very early days of her history. This great city was laid out in 1796, in what was then the Northwest Territory by Moses

Appendix 54, cont'd

Cleveland, a surveyor and ancestor of President Grover Cleveland. A permanent settlement was established by Lorenzo Carter in 1799, and in 1836 Cleveland was chartered as a city.

The highwater mark of her history came 131 years later when Carl B. Stokes was elected mayor of this great city in 1967, and became the first Negro to be chosen as the chief executive of a major city in the United States. He was elected again in 1969 which let the nation know that the first time he was elected was not an accident. Perhaps, history will record that another highwater mark in Cleveland's great history took place this year when Attorney John H. Bustamante led in establishoing her first Black-Controlled Bank, known as First Bank and Trust of Cleveland. Our Convention is honored to do business with this bank while we are convening here.

Cleveland is the largest metropolis in Ohio and a major Great Lakes Port. Besides iron and steel production, its principal industries are the manufacture of electrical equipment, machine tools, automobile parts and chemicals.

She offers her citizens and visitors many outstanding points of interest: The Cleveland Museum of Art, Western Reserve Historical Society Library and Museum, Zoological Park, The Mall, and Terminal Tower are notable sights. The Cleveland Orchestra is one of the country's leading musical organizations.

It is good to be in Cleveland, it is good to be alive and it is good to be i the 13th Annual Session of our Convention. Let us pray and strive earnestly ' make this the most productive Session that we have ever witnessed.

And Are We Yet Alive

And are we yet alive,
    And see each other's face?
Glory and praise to Jesus give
    For his redeeming grace!
Preserved by power Divine
    To full salvation here,
Again in Jesus' praise we join,
    And in his sight appear.

What troubles have we seen,
    What conflicts have we passed,
Fightings without, and fears within,
    Since we assembled last!
But out of all the Lord
    Hath brought us by his love;
And still he doth his help afford,
    And hides our life above.

Then let us make our boast
    Of his redeeming power,
Which saves us to the uttermost,
    Till we can sin no more:
Let us take up the cross,
    Till we the crown obtain;
And gladly reckon all things loss,
    So we may Jesus gain.

Since we last met, our nation has gone through a period of self-examination and cleansing. The Democratic process proved workable and one president left office with dignity and another was installed with equal dignity. We trust that we can leave it to history to do the judging, lest we fall into condemnation ourselves. Sometime before the culmination of the climax of Watergate and the resignation of the 37th President of the United States, I requested Dr. Thomas Kilgore, Jr., one of our most respected Baptist leaders in the nation today and one whose credentials are impeccable, to edit a book of sermons preached by our great Baptist preachers on the evils and the lessons of Watergate. We hope this volume of sermons will give us a kaleisdescopic view of the prophetic messages that have been delivered from our Black Baptist Pulpits. As a supporter of the former president, Richard M. Nixon, it is understandable that I'm weighed in the balances and found wanting at this point, and consequently have no sermon to contribute. Even now, I plead with you and all others that we unite behind President Gerald R. Ford and try to put Watergate behind us.

Appendix 54, cont'd

As I Leave The Presidency

It has been my privilege to be a vital part of this Convention since her inception. Perhaps in some measure, it has been my privilege to enjoy a relationship and an intimacy with this Convention greater than almost any human spirit can bear. There is a great temptation to feel that one has personal ownership when he has been so closely related to an organization. In a sense this is true, but never in a selfish sense. As the future unfolds, it will be my earnest prayer to divorce myself from our Convention without alienating myself from her great fellowship. It will be my goal to participate whenever possible, in such a manner that my successor will be perfectly free to do as he is led to do without any criticism or interference from me. He will have my prayers and my support because the magnitude of the responsibility is great and the opportunities are even greater.

Our Convention is fortunately in her infancy and has great vigor and vitality. Her best days lie ahead and her future is fraught with great possibilities. In a large sense, our Progressive Convention is in a highly favored position in the Family of Baptists. Our responsibility is so great that we cannot possibly be too dedicated, nor too committed to the cause of Christ and the advancement of His Kingdom here on earth. In the words of one of our former presidents, "the Prince of Preachers," Dr. Gardner C. Taylor, "Our Convention is the last bright hope of our denomination."

We then, must be good stewards of the manifold grace of God. We must continually strive for the mastery of those human defects which plague us all and lead us to engage in rivalries, to seek honor without sacrifice, and to give too little to causes, while lavishing upon ourselves luxuries rather than necessities. Our goal is a lofty one which requires the ultimate in generosity and humility. History has placed on us a great burden. We have been cast in the role of modern pioneers. We have become in a measure pioneers of modern Baptist history. We have the legacy of being the home of "Freedom Fighters," and "Civil Rights Leaders." The greatest leader of all times, Dr. Martin Luther King, Jr., honored us with his membership and his affections. We are the last member of the Baptist Family that he addressed before his martyrdom. It becomes our serious responsibility to not simply remember, but to bring increasing honor to his memory. Recent events in our nation's history bring to light his prophecy and the end is not yet. His views on peace and freedom are bringing new hope to the whole civilized world. We must not only cherish this legacy, but we must also be fair to this legacy. We must give more than lip service to preserving the memory of this great man. We must rise to our opportunity and give generously to help build the Martin Luther King, Jr. Center for Social Change. Progressives have a responsibility to join in wholeheartedly and get the job done. If we had the vision to look down the years and see the legacy we are privileged to leave oncoming generations and the benefits they stand to receive, we would hardly count the cost of such a legacy.

Let us observe Martin Luther King, Jr. Sunday. When we say this, we mean in every church in every city, town, hamlet or village. Let us begin in Sunday School and go right through the day, teaching and preacring about his devotion to Christ, Peace and Non-Violence. In every city, we need to encourage the misguided to throw away their knives, pistols and other weapons capable of human destruction and arm themselves with the Word that will bring life and life more abundantly. We must try to stop filling the jails, workhouses and other institutions of detention with the flower of our manhood. In many states, the best of our manpower is in jail. We must find a better way through preaching, teaching and evangelism to save our men and boys. Every community organization must be utilized, including Sunday School and the Boy Scout program. We who have been turned off in our attitude toward good citizenship must become turned on again. We must become builders rather than destroyers. We can accomplish a great deal for ourselves by remembering Martin Luther King, Jr. and the ideals that he preached and lived.

Our Sainted Dead

It is not possible for me to name all the fine people who have lived and served among us and have now fallen on sleep, but I shall attempt to name a few:

Dr. R. H. Milner, Georgia
Rev. L. Juan Burt, Michigan
Mrs. Alberta W. King, Georgia

Appendix 54, cont'd

It is with deep reverence that we include "Mother King," because of her unique place in history as well as the tragic nature of her death. While she was not a clergyman, she was the daughter, wife and mother of clergymen. We sincerely offer our sympathy and deep compassion to every Progressive Family who has suffered the loss of a loved one since we last met. We are mindful that many families have been touched by grief during the past Conventional year. Let me pause to include a special word of condolence to the Reverend Benjamin W. Robertson and his wife who suffered the loss of a son in a tragic automobile accident. While we have no power to heal the deep hurt that this family has suffered, we can humbly express that we care and we share. The same applies to Dr. G. L. Washington of D. C., and his wife who suffered the loss of a wonderful Christian daughter. The list is longer than any of us would wish it to be, but a loving God knows best.

As we meditate reverently over the passing of the members of our Progressive Family, let us remember the words of that great hymn written by Reverend Robert Lowry.

"Shall we gather at the river,
Where bright angel feet have trod,
With its crystal tide forever
Flowing by the throne of God.

On the margin of the river,
Washing up its silver spray,
We will walk and worship ever,
All the happy, golden day.

Soon we'll reach the shining river,
Soon our pilgrimage will cease,
Soon our happy hearts will quiver
With the melody of peace.

Yes, we'll gather at the river
The beautiful, the beautiful river—
Gather with the saints at the river
That flows by the throne of God.

In the fellowship of faith, let us go on until we reach the shining river where the wicked will cease from troubling and the weary will be at rest.

In the spirit of humility which I would like to achieve, my administration is coming to a close. There remains much to be done. Our thrust for the future must include Stewardship and Evangelism. We have a golden opportunity in the development of our new Home Mission Department. We must not go over board by trying to achieve our objectives too soon. We must of necessity take time, go slow and develop thoroughly. We cannot overtake those who lead us over night. Progressives must select a major objective each year for the years ahead. We cannot put our full force behind several objectives in any one year. Our new Executive Secretary, Dr. Joseph Bass, of the Home Mission Board, is fully able to lead us to new heights in the field of Home Mission. Through his leadership many of our churches will become Monthly Contributors. From my vantage point, there is no other way for churches with small budgets to make the journey and churches with large budgets can hardly do any better. The Voluntary Monthly Support Plan holds great promise for our growth and development if it is ever put into operation. If we do not take stock of ourselves and become consistent and faithful in our stewardship, we shall not only be the laughing stock of our generation, we shall be a great failure in our time. One of the most revolutionary things our Baptist Denomination can do is to start GIVING. So far as I'm concerned a member could appose me and fight my program every day in the week so long as he gives liberally. If he gives liberally, there is hope for the cause, himself and me. On the other hand, a member might praise and love me to death, but if he gives nothing that is worthy he is hardly helpful to me.

Some Literature and Institutions Worthy of Support

Progressives are fortunate to have some worthy institutions to support. In fact there are many reaching out to us with outstretched arms—crying, "help us." We cannot help them all—common sense and practical judgment make this very clear to us. This does not excuse us from helping some of them. Let me mention three that should be given high priority:

Appendix 54, cont'd

1. The Progressive Publishing House represents the foundation of all our work. Unless we build stronger and better Sunday Schools, our work will suffer greatly in the future. We must first buy our literature and then use it effectively—engaging in workshop activities, training Christian teachers at home and sending many workers to our Congress of Christian Education. We must secondly recommend it to others; especially many of our Progressive Churches who are not using this excellent Sunday School Literature.

2. In this same area of literature—high priority should be given our Missionary work. This work cannot go forward without the use of the **Worker**. There was never a piece of literature more exclusively ours than the **Worker**. Some of the finest Christians among us are the writers. This little Christian Periodical was created and developed at the price of blood, sweat, toil and tears. If we have no appreciation for the life and contribution of Nannie Helen Burroughs, then we are dead in trespasses and sin. If we have no zeal for what has gone on before and has been bequeathed to us, then, we are a one generation Convention and will soon disappear from the face of the earth. In fact, if we do not appreciate what God has provided, the sooner we disappear from the face of the earth, the better.

3. The Nannie Burroughs School should head the list of the schools we should determine in our hearts we are going to support. If we cannot support this school we should look to the Lord and be dismissed. This school represents the trend of the future. It is now engaged in the training, nurture and development of growing minds in the delicate, tender and formative period. It is working with young lives when they can be shaped and directed toward high goals. WE need to write our names in history there and let the whole world know—that we honor the **genius** and courage of Black Womanhood. Here is a cause that should challenge every Black Baptist in our Progressive Family.

4. The Morehouse School of Religion, Atlanta, Georgia, offers a great opportunity to our Convention to extend herself for **generations** to come. There is no greater challenge than the challenge of reproduction. If we do not support an institution that produces ministers, we cannot reproduce ourselves and we will die in our generation.

   Here is a school that our Convention can adopt without any fear of having adopted something we cannot defend. If the other denominations can support, expand and develop their schools, for ministers, so can we. This institution represents the interest, dedication and commitment of many of our Baptist Statesmen, but particularly one—Dr. Benjamin E. Mays. If there was ever a man who is a great credit to Baptists, surely it is Dr. Mays. I have, therefore, requested the Committee, chaired by Dr. W. W. Taylor to study the process and the details involved in establishing a relationship that will link Morehouse School of Religion and the Progressive National Baptist Convention together in a meaningful and productive way. When we take this step it does not mean that we will not encourage support for our other fine schools which train ministers, but it does mean that Morehouse School of Religion will become an objective of this Convention. If we do not seize the opportunities that our day affords—we shall be weighed in the balances and found wanting. Generations to come will rise up and condemn us.

Time will not. allow me to mention all of the other fine objectives we have started—but let me say, we must get on with the work and truly be about our Father's business. Pastors are going to have to realize that our churches will die unless we learn to support causes. A man has not lived who only lives well for himself. We deserve no credit for wearing fine clothes and driving high powered cars, nor have we arrived when we live in a great big house. If we do not know how to support causes—we are still ignorant and undeveloped and without a sense of history. Our churches cannot rise above the level to which we ascend and the only description suitable for us is that the blind is leading the blind.

It is almost tragic to see many of our churches satisfied to neglect Foreign Mission, Home Mission and the American Bible Society. We cannot possibly honorthe great commission and have no concern about the spread of the Gospel. It follows when we do not honor the Great Commission, we are a church without

Appendix 54, cont'd

a mission—without a purpose that God can honor with His presence. We really need to stop shouting until we have something to shout about. If you have really not sacrificed, nor given yourself to a worthy cause—you really have nothing to shout about. You know and I know that a mother who has sacrificed herself for her children, her God and the cause of Christ has something to shout about. For her the preacher does not really have to preach—her soul is happy just to be in the House of the Lord. We need to stop missing so much joy in life due to our selfishness and our sin. A church that is alive to Christ can support missions and education, evangelism and stewardship.

No Convention can justify its membership numbering in the thousands when it is low in the support of causes. It would be far better if our Convention numbered fifty thousand and produced a stewardship witness than to number 550 thousand and barely survive. Somewhere along the way Progressives must take a hard look at themselves and raise the question—are we truly Progressives? Do we support causes or do we simply talk about them?

It gives me no particular pleasure to suggest to you that unless we work the Voluntary Monthly Support Plan—our thrust, our claim, our cause is already lost. We cannot build a great Convention unless we remember it every month with support. Our white brothers cannot continue to support us while we waste our substance in "riotous living." The time is out for us to play the role of beggar in religion and, play the role of the prodigal in pleasure. We have been given a start by the American and the Southern Baptist Conventions to help us build a Home Mission Department. We must understand well that they will not be continuing this start. At some point, we must take off and move on our own momentum. We cannot continue the rest of our days beating unfortunate leaders in public office to death and decrying racism—blindness and prejudice. Somewhere along the way we must stop looking at the mote in our brother's eye while overlooking the beam in our eyes. The greatest resolution that can take place in the Black Church is to match her giving with her singing and her preaching.

As I leave the Presidency I'm not bitter—but I'm grateful. There is one thing most of us feel certain about—the motivation for a Progressive National Baptist Convention was right. If things had gone the way some of us felt we had been led—the term of the President would have been four to six years and the method of giving would have been the Voluntary Monthly Support Plan. This would all have been written into the constitution. We would have given the Executive Secretary an indefinite term in which to serve. This latter idea might still come to fruition. In stating this point of view, I do not now suggest a change in the tenure provisions of our constitution. If our Convention is to prosper and grow—no man must stay at the controls too long. It is strongly suggested by many that we do not tamper with tenure for some time to come. It is also felt that we must enforce our constitutional provision with much more diligence. Succeeding presidents must take a stronger hand and not allow the Convention to ever become a Convention where the President is a mere figure head. Let's strengthen the hand of tre President and give him enough money to run his office efficiently and travel with dignity. In this connection, I should like to suggest that the President should have a travel fund and an office fund. They should be separate and distinct. If a man can only serve two years, he should be supported adequately that he might serve well. As one of the founding presidents, I have not made any demands for myself, but I make them now on behalf of him who follows me. As a pastor, I expect my successor to live better than I'm living—because I hope to leave things better in my church than I found them. I'm not bitter—I'm simply grateful. There is one thing that I cannot emphasize too much—Progressive Baptists cannot afford to have a weak President. To be Progressive, we must have a good and efficient Executive Secretary, but we must definitely have a strong President.

Preserving Our Heritage

Our Progressive family is blessed to have a fine crop of young ministers whose potential for leadership cannot be estamiated. They must be cultivated, nurtured and supported in every possible way. No office in the Convention should be off limits to them. There must be no discrimination, nor segregation in the household of faith. We must form partnerships and build fellowships between youth and age. The generation gap can be successfully bridged in the spirit of Christ whose ministry was inclusive of the whole human family. Let us seek out opportunities and dis-

Appendix 54, cont'd

cover ways to help them both in school and in the pastorate. In a large Metropolitan city like Atlanta, there are enough Progressive Churches to give some support to every young Baptist attending Morehouse School of Religion. If there is additional need of help from across the nation, a sister church can be cultivated and the ministry of helping can go forward. Whatever applies to men in the ministry applies also to young women training for Christian service with added concern for their well-being. God will reward our efforts because He never ceases to supply our needs. Every Progressive church should take seriously the words of Jesus:

> "Give to others, and God will give to you; you will receive a full
> measure, a generous helping, poured into your hands—all that you
> can hold. The measure you use for others is the one God will
> use for you." Lk. 6:38 (TEV)

The church must never cease to emphas. e and practice giving and at this point in history it is the most Revolutionary thing the Black Church can do.

Just as we must glorify our youth, we must magnify our aged. The most vital and sure resource of our churches toda: are the elders in our membership. We come again to the old landmark:

> "Honor thy father and thy mother; that thy days may be long
> upon the land which the Lord thy God giveth thee." Exo. 20:12.

Our churches would do well to create new opportunities for her Senior citizens and lead them to become stronger allies in the cause of Christ.

Progressives must not forget her elder statesmen in the ministry. From the beginning of this Convention, we were blessed to have some of the ablest pastors in the Baptist family to join us. They gave up more than any of us who left the old Convention because they had invested nearly a life time there. We should see to it that they are never forsaken nor forgotten. Many preached until Kingdoms were moved and left us churches that are visible empires of greatness. We must help them while they live and honor them when they die. Whatever they left that can be salvaged for good, let us hold on to these riches. Their widows should be always assured that we stand ready to render any service that will be helpful to them.

Let us start a Tape Library and preserve the messages of our great preachers. Some of us now have our misgivings about taping because of what our National Government experienced in the "Watergate Affair," but we need to remember the words of St. Paul:

> "Do not conform outwardly to the standards of this world, but
> let God transform you inwardly by a complete change of your
> mind. Then you will be able to know the will of God—what is
> good, and is pleasing to him, and is perfect." Ro. 12:2 (TEV)

How wonderful it would be to have tapes of the great masters of the pulpit—to name only a few: Drs. H. H. Coleman, J. C. Austin, Sr., E. L. Harrison and T. S. Boone. To these could be added countless others equally as worthy of remembrance. To preserve our heritage of preaching, we must not only tape, we must organize and systematize our taping.

To accomplish the many things we need to be doing, we must get busy and pay off our Headquarters. We cannot build our Convention program without adequate space in which to promote the work. We need to pay off our present Headquarters, and move on to get the kind of facilities we need. Our Executive Secretary, Dr. S. S. Hodges, is a jewel, a God-send to this Convention, but he is having to do too much for one man and still serve the Convention. He needs administrative help so that his absence from the office will not mean that things are not still going forward. Progressives are truly blessed to have Dr. Hodges as our pioneer full-time Executive Secretary.

The Progressive Journey Leads On

As we continue our Progressive Journey we must reckon with the challenges we face—the Red Sea is in front of us and the enemy is close behind us. Though some of us may have forgotten what gave rise to a Progressive Convention, we dare not under estimate those who remember. It ill behooves us to spend our time in divisiveness and dissension. We are still too close to the shores of Egypt. We have not yet crossed the Red Sea. God has blown aside the waters and before us looms the highway, but we must run on swift feet lest the enemy over-takes us. We must master every obstacle that rises before us. As we make hold our claims

Appendix 54, cont'd

as Progressives—we must be very sure that we go forth in the strength and power of Almighty God.

Our immediate challenge includes the Fund of Renewal and our Pastor's Pension Fund. Every pastor must be alerted and every church must be sensitized if we are to reach the goal we cherish. In our struggle to follow the Revolutionary Christ and to make the Kingdoms of this world His blessed Kingdom, we must first give of ourselves. (2 Cor. 8:5). It is imperative that Progressives become imbued with a radical revolutionary spirit of giving. While we reckon with the Black Religion Experience and the Black Revolution that currently seek understanding, we must learn how to give. The Black Theology and Black Power Revolution have made themselves felt and will continue to add new dimensions to our faith, but it will all result in failure and be weighed in the balances and found wanting unless the Black Church mends her ways in the area of the Stewardship of Giving. Somehow the world will never be impressed by a religion that survives on begging—hand-outs and hand-me-downs. Our Convention must address herself to meeting the needs of the whole man. We must not get hung up on definitions and keen interpretation of our superiority in religion nor any other aspect of our identity, lest we fall into the same error of those who created the climate in which we now operate. There is so much work to be done that we dare not spend all our time in debate and definitions. The Black Religious Experience has every opportunity to prove its validity. We shall all be tested and tried and God shall render the final verdict.

In order for the Black Church to be revolutionary she must over come at least three things: Racism, Secularism and Skepticism.

The author, James H. Cone of Black Theology and Black Power writes:

> Revolution is not merely a "change of heart" but a radical black encounter with the structure of white racism, with the full intention of destroying its menacing power. I mean confronting white racists saying: "If it's a fight you want, I am prepared to oblige you."

This is what the Black Revolution means in a practical sense. However, to make such an appraisal of racism is to give it a prominence beyond what it deserves. As terrifying as racism is and—as cruel as its results have been, it must not become the very concern of all our existence. While we must get rid of racism we must also live, love and enjoy our families. We must moreover trust in God who is able to subdue all things unto Himself. God who is no respecter of persons wants His children to "Be still and know that he is God." He will be exalted among the heathen, he will be exalted in the earth. No man must be brazen enough to set himself up as a Savior of the universe. At best man can only see through a glass darkly. God has reserved some things for himself and man must wait for a face to face encounter. During this age when it is popular to glorify the black religious experience we must watch and pray lest we enter into temptation. Until we can develop a religion void of rivalry, jealousy and competition, we must keep seeking for a bright side somewhere. In order for our churches to become revolutionary we must over-come secularism. Much of our religious worship can hardly qualify by the measuring rod that Jesus gave:

> "God is a Spirit: and they that worship him must worship Him in spirit and in truth." (Jn. 4:24)

To keep a church reasonably alive now, we have to yield to the weak flesh and allow the world to walk right in and put on a performance. One does not have to go to the corner bar to find that man has lost his way, he has only to visit some of our churches. Today we have smoking rooms—tomorrow, we shall need drinking rooms and drug rooms. Many have become too nervous to make it through a service that lasts beyond an hour. Our churches must adhere strictly to a limited time schedule—while pleasure is unending. Of course, this kind of talk is obsolete—outmoded and post-dated, but the Black Religious Experience we now try to describe as authentic was born on "Discipline Street". I am not unaware of the faults of the elders, but I would remind you that to them—"God was high and lifted up". When our religion reaches the point at which it has no place for prayer meetings and old-fashioned revivals—then we had better stop the world and try to get off. It is indeed gratifying to read of our gospel of liberation and our churches of liberation, but it is even better to see how our religion has liberated our children and set them free from the ills of this world. We are gripped

Appendix 54, cont'd

in the vice of secularism and men have become noise makers rather than earth shakers. Our lust for power and the riches of this world has left us all, but almost morally and spiritually bankrupt. While we philosophize, men and women are looking for the "Church of What's Happening Now." Sunday after Sunday we go to our churches and nothing of spiritual significance happens.

Finally, we will become Revolutionary again, when we overcome Skpeticism. Our churches are filled with disbelief. A church will check a pastor's background and comb his past with a fine tooth comb and still doubt the veracity of his leadership. We would have far stronger laymen in our churches if they only believed and followed the pastor. Laymen today are not bent on being pastor's helpers as much as they are bent on being pastor's undertakers. We must over-come the fallacy and the false philosophy that the churches are neglecting their lay-power. When the gospel is preached and a man is converted—nobody can stop him from teaching in the Sunday School, working with Boy Scouts and setting the Prayer Meeting on fire. How undeniably false it is for laymen to say, "you won't give us anything to do." The truth of the matter is right before his eyes—the church house needs painting, the lawn needs beautifying and scores of persons need visiting and revitalizing. What some of our laymen are really saying:

> "Put us in a place of honor and place the controls of the church
> in our hands. Let us tell you when to get in and out of the
> pulpit."

Pastors don't have to fear laymen especially when there is love in the church. Perfect love casts out fear today just like it did yesterday. When laymen believe that the preacher has been called and is ordained of God to prach, they will follow and the church will have power once more.

Let's not deceive ourselves—we live in an age where every man wants to be his own leader and few men are willing to humble themselves. When the pulpit is reduced in the Black Church as some believe it has been in the white church, then the whole cause will be lost. There is a need to overcome disbelief and when we do this God will be exalted again. Our churches are being threatened by creeping secularism and the result is, they are becoming like the Sahara Desert. There is a spiritual drought in the land and our souls are dying as surely as the people are dying in the Sahelian region of West Africa. To indeed be Revolutionary, we must overcome racism, secularism and skepticism. The Black Church is in trouble because it is becoming more a form than a force. To put the Black Church in perspective, let me borrow from Otis Moss and use his words, some out of context:

> "The Black Church is often symbol without substance."

There is hope on our Progressive Journey. In every age the church renews herself. Our Progressive Churches can become catalysts in this procss of renewal. We can become leaven in the lump. If we will remember from whence we came, we will re-dedicate ourselves to causes rather than to personalities. We can respect men, while we reverence God. We can support Civil Rights while we labor for soul rights. We can preach a gospel of liberation while we teach the ways of salvation. We can extol the majesty of Blackness while we practice the brotherhood of men. We can eulogize the Black Church while we refuse to criticize the white church. We can be a light in the darkness of this age.

Like the children of Israel, we who are Progressives are on a journey and the God we serve is leading us on. Sin brought us into Egypt, but we are on our way to the promised land. We don't know how long the journey will take and we cannot know what danger lies in our wake, but one thing we do know—God's hand is leading us. As we travel we are not alone because lo' in the distance there is a mighty host marching with banners—and every now and then voices can be heard singing:

God Leads Us Along

In shady, green pastures, so rich and so
    sweet,
God leads his dear children along;
Where the water's cool flow bathes
    the weary one's feet
God leads his dear children along.

Appendix 54, cont'd

Sometimes on the mount where the sun
    shines so bright,
God leads his dear children along;
Sometimes in the valley in the
    darkest of night,
God leads his dear children along.

Tho' sorrows befall us, and Satan oppose
God leads his dear children along;
Through grace we can conquer, defeat
    all our foes,
God leads his dear children along.
Away from the mire, and away from
    the clay,
God leads his dear children along
Aaway up in glory, eternity's day,
God leads his dear children along.

Chorus

Some thro' the waters, some thro the flood,
Some thro' the fire, but all thro'
    the Blood;
Some thro' great sorrow, but God
    gives a song,
In the night season and all the day long.

The Church Revolutionized, or Revolutionary must be ever aware that she cannot run ahead of God. We have made too much of the church in our age and too little of God. We have too much concern about the symbol and too little concern about the substance. We must recall the words of the prophet Zechariah:

"Not by might, nor by power, but by my spirit saith the Lord."

The Revolutionary church must be led by God.

Appendix 55

Remembering The Call

Silver Anniversary Souvenir

"... L. V. Booth envisioned a new mandate of Heaven, a new instrumentality of the Kingdom of Jesus Christ. All honor and credit are due ... [him] for his vision and courage in the face of over-whelming odds for issuing a call to a heartsick, rejected remnant of God's true Israel. ..."

Dr. Gardner C. Taylor

"[Twenty-five] years ago, a few coura-geous men heeded the call of L. Venchael Booth to come to Cin-cinnati, Ohio, to form a new National Bap-tist Convention. Many of us ... loathed the idea, and said so ... here we all are on board, pil-grims seeking a better country."

Dr. Earl L. Harrison

L. VENCHAEL BOOTH, *Founder*

"*Unmistakably, the leading organizer of the Progressive National Baptist Convention, U.S.A., Inc., was Rev. L. Venchael Booth.*" Dr. Leroy Fitts

Organized at Zion Baptist Church, Cincinnati, Ohio, November 14-15, 1961

Edited by William D. Booth   Cincinnati, Ohio – August 4-10, 1986

Appendix 55, cont'd

The Progressive National Baptist Convention and Her Birthplace

L. Venchael Booth

When the Progressive National Baptist Convention comes to Convention Center to hold her Jubilee Session, she will be coming home to where she was born. The Progressive story is a Cincinnati story. In the providence of God, her story will forever be intimately woven into the history of Cincinnati. For many the birth of this Convention was a visible revelation of St. Paul's love message to the Corinthian Church, where he spelled out the significance of Faith, Hope and Love. It is a story of *Faith* that someone could believe that TENURE for the presidency could bring peace among warring Baptists. It is a story of *Hope* for one to feel that it was possible for Baptists to rise above tradition and break new ground. It is a story of *Love* that someone could pay such a great price of self-sacrifice for Baptists whose history is not illuminated with gratitude. There is no simple explanation surrounding the CALL to Baptists to form a new organization. It is difficult in retrospect to believe that one man without a committee and without a powerful inner circle would dare to attempt to form a new organization. It is even harder to believe that one man went forward with the conviction that something had to be done if Baptists were ever to be productive and enjoy Fellowship, Progress and Peace.

The beauty of the struggle is seen in the reluctance with which men embraced the idea. Great leaders from all sections of the country were afraid that the movement would fail. Some openly stated that no one man could pull it off. The roll call of the saints who joined this great cause would make a "Who's Who" that would be inspiring. It is to our everlasting glory that we can claim among our members Martin Luther King, Jr., the great Apostle of Love and Non-Violence, the illustrious Father, "Daddy King" and his mentor, Dr. Benjamin E. Mays, renowned educator and long-time president of Morehead College. There are many others whose contributions have made a real difference in this nation.

Let the record show that the **last** National Baptist Convention that Martin Luther King, Jr. attended was the Progressive National Baptist Convention held in Cincinnati, September, 1967. It was in this session that the Progressive Convention stamped her approval on Dr. King's Vietnam proposals, Dr. Gardner C. Taylor was president and presided over his first session in a Hotel setting. Indeed, this was our Convention's first meeting in a Hotel, but it has never settled for less since.

One of the important things that can be said about the Progressive National Baptist Convention is that she has been a catalyst for change. She has affected other religious bodies in a very significant way. We have seen her open the windows with a freshness that can only accompany the young and growing. In her eleventh year, she contributed a vice president to the Baptist World Alliance. There has not been one from this body since, but we have shared leadership in the world body with distinction.

What lies ahead for the Progressive National Baptist Convention is not easily imagined. One thing is certain, if a real effort is made to live up to her original concept of Fellowship, Progress and Peace, this Convention though modest in size and numbers can make a needful contribution to the Christian world.

Cincinnati will be central in whatever contribution this convention makes; it was here that one of her pastor's dared to "stretch out" on the promises of God presenting himself as a "living sacrifice" in the cause of Christ.

1

Appendix 55, cont'd

THE ORIGIN OF THE PROGRESSIVE NATIONAL BAPTIST CONVENTION

The Progressive National Baptist Convention is largely an outgrowth of dissatisfaction over "TENURE" and the office of Executive Secretary in the National Baptist Convention, Inc. The meeting which culminated in a new organization, was called at Cincinnati, after several previous meetings had been held by outstanding ministers in the National Baptist Convention, Inc. over a period of years.

The first of these meetings was held in St. Louis, Mo., in the Washington Avenue Tabernacle Church of which Dr. John E. Nance is pastor. At this meeting, several prominent ministers met for the purpose of bringing about a solution to the problems that were confronting our Convention at the time. As secretary of this meeting, we pledged ourselves to work within the framework of our Convention without any suggestion of withdrawing ourselves from the Convention. We only expressed ourselves as to how we felt about the existing conditions of the Convention. Expressions were made and published about this meeting which created much dissatisfaction in the Convention's official ranks. Instead of the meeting improving conditions, greater opposition became apparent.

The following meetings of the National Baptist Convention, Inc. were destined to widen the breach. In Denver, Colorado, we spent a whole session seeking to prevent the election of officers by vote of state delegations. The following year in 1957, when we convened at Louisville, Ky., a chair throwing session brought great disgrace to our Baptist Family. The two succeeding sessions marked a repeat in Baptist confusion in both Philadelphia, Pa. and Kansas City. By this time, more than 50% of the convention had pledged itself to support Dr. Gardner C. Taylor, distinguished pastor from Brooklyn, N. Y. as President. Dr. Taylor was defeated after a decision which resulted to the advantage of his opponent, Dr. J. H. Jackson.

The Reverend L. V. Booth of Zion Baptist Church, Cincinnati, Ohio left the convention at Kansas City, determined to call a meeting and allow the opposition to make a clear choice between tyranny and freedom, and confusion and peace. Before many of the messengers had reached their homes, a letter went out calling for all interested in Peace, Fellowship and Progress to attend a meeting in November. This was followed by a second letter in October, urging fellow pastors to come to Cincinnati. His invitation met with opposition from some of the strongest pastors in the nation. Among these were men who were trusted, revered and respected. Very few could see then the wisdom and divine inspiration and unselfishness of his call.

The Cincinnati Meeting drew representatives from 14 States with a total of 33 delegates. After a formal opening, it was decided that Dr. J. Raymond Henderson, of Los Angeles, California would preside over the business session. Dr. Henderson requested that we withdraw from the Sanctuary of Zion Baptist Church to its Chapel where only registered messengers would participate. This request was unanimously accepted. After serious deliberations, two spokesmen were allowed to close the discussion. Dr. Marvin T. Robinson, of Pasadena, California spoke against organizing at this time, and Rev. L. V. Booth of Cincinnati, Ohio spoke for organizing. When the vote was taken by ballot and counted, the group to organize had won by "one" vote. Every member, every church and convention that registered in the Cincinnati Meeting were committed to "Tenure."

The Minutes of this Convention will consist of records ranging from the organizational meeting at Cincinnati, November 14 and 15, 1961, two Regional Meetings, one at Chicago, Ill. and the other at Richmond, Va. through our First Annual Session which convened in Philadelphia, Penna. in 1962.

DR. J. CARL MITCHELL, Secretary

Appendix 55, cont'd

Convention Symbol

Designed by L. Venchael Booth,

Executive Secretary

Convention Song

A PRAYER FELLOWSHIP HYMN

By L. Venchael Booth

Sung at the first Annual Session, Philadelphia, Pa. — 1962
Dedicated to The Progressive National Baptist Convention
To be sung to the tune: "God of Grace and God of Glory," by Harry E. Fosdick

We have come from o'er the nation
Seeking Fellowship and Peace,
We are truly God's creation —
And our love shall e'er increase,
We shall stand firm and united —
As we spread from shore to shore,
As we spread from shore to shore.

We believe God's Holy Spirit
Brought us safely o'er the way,
Thru our God we shall inherit —
Grace and glory day by day,
Gracious God our Holy Father —
Lead us safely, gently on,
Lead us safely, gently on.

Grant us grace amid oppression
When the foe assails our way
Save us from unwise aggression —
May our footsteps never stray,
Make us holy with Thy Spirit —
As we walk this pilgrim's way,
As we walk this pilgrim's way.

Help us yield our great Convention
To Thy Holy Spirit's power,
May no wicked intervention —
Mar the beauty of this hour,
Holy Spirit lead and guide us —
In the path of peace and love,
In the path of peace and love.

3

Appendix 55, cont'd

Convention Scripture

ROMANS, 12 (K.J.V.)

9 *Let* love be without dissimulation (hypocrisy). Abhor that which is evil; cleave to that which is good.
Pa. 34.14; Am. 5.15; 1 Ti. 1.5; Pe. 1.22.

10 *Be* kindly affectioned one to another with brotherly love; in honour preferring one another;
Ph. 2.3; He. 13.1; 1 Pe. 1.22; 2.17

11 Not slothful in business (In diligence not slothful); fervent in spirit; serving the Lord;

12 Rejoicing in hope; patient in tribulation; continuing instant (steadfastly) in prayer;
Ac. 2.42; Ph. 3.1; 1 Th. 5.16; He. 3.6; 10.36; Jam. 1.4.

13 Distributing to the necessity of saints; given to hospitality.
1 Co. 16.1; 2 Co. 9.1,12; He. 13.16; Pe. 4.9.

14 Bless them which persecute you: bless, and curse not.
Ma. 5.33; Ac. 7.60; 1 Co. 4.12; 1 Pe. 3.9.

15 Rejoice with them that do rejoice, and weep with them that weep.

16 *Be* of the same mind one toward another. Mind not (Set not your mind on) high things, but condescend to men (things) of low estate (that are lowly). Be not wise in your own conceits.
Ps. 131.1,2; Is. 5.21; Je. 45.5.

17 Recompense to no man evil for evil. Provide (Take thought for) things honest (honorable) in the sight of all men.
Ch. 14.16; Ma. 5.39; 2 Cor. 8.21; 1 Th. 5.15.

18 If it be possible, as much as lieth in you, live peaceably with all men.
Ch. 14.19; He. 12.14.

19 Dearly beloved, avenge not yourselves, but *rather* give place unto wrath: for it is written, Vengeance *is* mine; I will repay, saith the Lord.
Ver. 17; De. 32.35; Pr. 24.29; He. 10.30.

20 Therefore if thine enemy hunger, feed him; if he thirst, give him drink: for in so doing thou shalt heap coals of fire on his head.
Ex. 23.4,5; Pr. 25.21,22; Ma. 5.44.

21 Be not overcome of evil, but overcome evil with good.

Appendix 55, cont'd

National News Release — September 11, 1961

A Volunteer Committee for the Formation of A New National Baptist Convention announces this week through its Chairman, Rev. L. V. Booth, pastor of Zion Baptist Church, Cincinnati, Ohio that a meeting will be held November 14, 15, 1961 at Zion Baptist Church, 630 Glenwood Ave., Cincinnati 29, Ohio.

The two day session will be devoted to discussion on **How to Build a Democratic Convention Dedicated to Christian Objectives?**

The keynote speaker will be Dr. William H. Borders, pastor of Wheat St. Baptist Church, Atlanta, Ga. Dr. Borders is one of the ten outstanding pastors expelled from the National Baptist Convention, Inc. following its notorious session at Louisville, Ky., in 1957, when President Joseph H. Jackson ruled Tenure unconstitutional. There has been great dissatisfaction since.

All freedom loving, independent and peace loving Baptists are invited. Those who do not wish to form a new Convention are requested not to attend.

Both men and women are invited. Persons who are interested in attending this meeting are urged to write in for reservations to Rev. L. V. Booth at the above address and indicate whether a Hotel or Home is desired. This movement is in no way connected with the past effort of "The Taylor Team." It is an entirely new movement under new leadership. Persons who are concerned with redeeming the Baptist initiative and restoring a democratic Thrust are invited.

Editor's Note: This is the announcement that rocked the nation. Leaders on both sides of the fence were skeptical and afraid of this new venture. It was fought with great vigor by the greatest leaders of our time.

THE CALL LETTER
ZION BAPTIST CHURCH
630 Glenwood Avenue, Cincinnati 29, Ohio
L. Venchael Booth, Minister

September 22, 1961

Dear Brother Pastor:

Our National Baptist Convention has reached an all-time low in fellowship, peace and Christian dignity. We have completely lost our freedom to worship, participate and grow in the kingdom work as it is expressed in the Convention. We can no longer trust the integrity of its leadership.

The time has come for freedom-loving, independent and peace-loving Christians to unite in a fellowship that they can trust. Why are we so afraid of building a new Convention? We act as though it is a terrible sin. Organizations exist to unite persons of similar interest in multiplied strength. There is nothing on earth to keep us from working toward worthy objectives and lofty goals.

It is to this sacred call that you are invited to attend a Special Meeting for the formation of a new Convention on Nov. 14 and 15 at Zion Baptist Church, 630 Glenwood Ave., Cincinnati, Ohio. Kindly respond quickly if possible.

Yours in Christian Fellowship,
L. VENCHAEL BOOTH

Committee for the Formation
of a New National Baptist Convention
Zion Baptist Church
630 Glenwood Avenue, Cincinnati 29, Ohio
L. Venchael Booth, Minister

News Release — October 6, 1961

The Call Meeting of Baptist Leaders across the nation, November 14, 15, at Zion Baptist Church, 630 Glenwood Ave., Cincinnati, Ohio is definitely a

5

Appendix 55, cont'd

meeting to organize a new Convention. Leaders from many states have responded in the affirmative and the way is being cleared for a complete organization of a new National Baptist Convention.

The Chairman, Rev. L. V. Booth announces that every Baptist who is desirous of joining a new Convention is welcome. This includes Baptists from all presently organized Conventions and the many thousands of Baptists who do not belong to any existing Convention. No one will be excluded who represents a Regular Missionary Baptist Church and will commit himself to the building of a new Baptist Convention.

The gross misunderstanding which needs to be cleared up says the Chairman, is that the keynote Speaker, Dr. William Holmes Borders of Wheat Street Baptist Church, Atlanta, Georgia has not been selected to head the organization. He is certainly worthy and if he is considered, his name will be placed in nomination along with 10 or 12 others and will be voted upon by secret balloting.

There is considerable discussion being carried on by prominent leaders led by Dr. J. C. Austin of Chicago to draft Dr. M. L. King, Jr. of Atlanta, Ga. It is not the wishes of the Chairman that any Baptist should feel excluded or left out. The only requisite for any Baptist is to desire a new Convention and come and join others in the building of the same.

ZION BAPTIST CHURCH
630 Glenwood Avenue
Cincinnati 29, Ohio
L. Venchael Booth, Minister

October 9, 1961

Dear Brother Pastor:

Since you have answered the call for a New National Baptist Convention, you have probably encountered many conflicts within and without. The worst is yet to come. Pharoah shall pursue us with full force and try to bring us again into Egypt. It is your duty and mine to trust God enough to continue to go forward. There is no unity possible now in the NBC, Inc. and there can be none until pride is dethroned and humility is enthroned. When this happens every regular Baptist can unite and enjoy peace and progress.

This letter is written to re-affirm that our Meeting on Nov. 14, 15 will be well organized to reach its objective. We are going to organize a new Convention and elect officers to run it in this meeting. To accomplish that you must consider the following:

1. Enlist five pastors other than yourself.
2. Write, or visit the State nearest you and enlist at least 5 pastors who share your conviction.
3. Bring with you 5 persons (pastors and laymen) from your state.
4. Bring a Deacon if possible to help get your Church solidly behind you. Your church is tired of the disgrace that Baptists suffer everywhere.
5. Bring a contribution of $10.00 to $100.00 to get our program started. We are not going to live above our means — nor legislate beyond our possibilities.

Whenever you lose faith in yourself and God, remember all the great leaders of old who had to resist strong, proud majorities. Elijah met the prophets of Baal and prevailed. Gideon took 300 dedicated men and defeated the Midianites. David walked alone with God and defeated the Giant Goliath, and ultimately the Philistine host. With a little faith in God, surely we can build a new Convention to His Name's glory and honor.

Brother Pastor, the only thing we need to fear is lack of faith. With God all things are possible. Let us determine now to trust God rather than man.

Let's build a new Convention dedicated to Peace and Progress.

Your Brother in Christ,
L. VENCHAEL BOOTH

Appendix 55, cont'd

Committee for the Formation
of a New National Baptist Convention
630 Glenwood Avenue
Cincinnati 29, Ohio
L. Venchael Booth, Minister

News Release
October 30, 1961

New National Baptist Convention Meeting

Final plans are now being made for the meeting called for the organization of a New National Baptist Convention by the Volunteer Chairman, Rev. L. V. Booth. The sessions will be held at Zion Baptist Church, 630 Glenwood Ave., Cincinnati, Ohio, November 13, 14, 15, 1961.

A Pre-Convention Musical is planned for Monday Evening, the 13th and will be under the direction of Mr. James V. Roach, Minister of Music in Zion Baptist Church. He will also direct the Music each evening of the session. Other Convention music each day will be under the direction of Mrs. Loretta C. Manggrum Bush, outstanding composer and organist, assisted by Mr. Emmett Anderson, also a composer and organist.

Among the noted speakers to appear are: Mrs. Vivian Carter Mason, Peace Corps, Washington, D. C.; Dr. William H. Borders, Pastor of Wheat Street Baptist Church, Atlanta, Georgia; Dr. C. C. Adams, Corresponding Secretary of the Baptist Foreign Mission Bureau, U. S. A.; and the Reverend Andrew J. Hargrett of Chicago, Ill., representing Education. No speaker's appearance is to be construed as an endorsement of this movement, the chairman explained.

It is expected that there will be an outstanding array of Baptist dignitaries whose sole purpose will be to observe only. The program is being arranged for the enjoyment and inspiration of all who attend. Only registered delegates will participate in business sessions. The public is invited.

ZION BAPTIST CHURCH
630 Glenwood Avenue
Cincinnati 29, Ohio
L. Venchael Booth, Minister

November 8, 1961

Dear Brother Pastor:

We are very happy that you are coming to our National Baptist Meeting on Nov. 14, 15, 1961 at Zion Baptist Church, 630 Glenwood Avenue, Cincinnati, Ohio. Great preparations are being made for your comfort and enjoyment while you are with us. Although this is the most serious meeting ever called by Baptists in this decade, we want it also to be a very pleasant one.

It is not too late for you to tell your friends about this meeting and encourage them to come. They are welcome if they are ready to join in the organization of a new Convention. We do not plan to invite you here to waste time in just re-hashing our troubles. We also do not plan to tolerate persons who are inclined to think our effort is a joke. So please come praying to resist every weakness presented by the "Tempter."

If you requested reservation, your reservation card is enclosed. If you wish to make one after you are here, we hope to give you a choice of a Hotel or a Home. If you wish to make any changes in your reservations after you are here, please feel free to check with our Committee upon your arrival and help will be given you. The room rent will be $2.00 per person per night when two people share a room and $3.00 per night when a single room is occupied by one person.

The response is great and persons are coming from many sections of our great nation. Truly God is smiling upon us as we make this new venture for progress and peace.

We are looking forward to your coming and we are praying for you a safe journey here.

Your Brother in Christ,
L. VENCHAEL BOOTH

7

Appendix 55, cont'd

ORGANIZATIONAL MEETING OF THE
PROGRESSIVE NATIONAL BAPTIST CONVENTION
November 14-15, 1961
Zion Baptist Church, Cincinnati, Ohio
Dr. L. V. Booth, Pastor

REGISTRANT	CHURCH	STATE	ENROLLMENT
1. Binford, Rev. W. H.	Mount Zion Baptist	Mich. City, Ind.	$10.00
2. Booth, Dr. L. V.	Zion Baptist Church	Cincinnati, Ohio	50.00
3. Brent, Rev. A. R.	Shiloh Baptist Church	Plainfield, N. J.	10.00
4. Chambers, Dr. T. M.	Zion Hill Baptist	Los Angeles, Cal.	25.00
		Foreign Mission	10.00
5. Glover, Rev. W. V.	New Virginia Baptist Church	Montgomery, Ala.	10.00
6. Green, Rev. J. F.	Second Baptist	Detroit, Mich.	10.00
7. Henderson, Dr. J. R.	Second Baptist	Los Angeles, Cal.	10.00
8. Hill, Joseph	Tabernacle	Cincinnati, Ohio	5.00
9. Hodges, Dr. S. S.	Pilgrim Baptist	Hamilton, Ohio	10.00
10. Lavigne, Rev. I. B.	First Baptist Church	Farrell, Pa.	10.00
11. Mason, Rev. A. L.	Grace Baptist Church	Columbus, Ohio	10.00
12. McBride, Rev. H. D.	New Temple Baptist Church	Cincinnati, Ohio	10.00
13. Mitchell, Dr. J. C.	Sixteenth Street Baptist Church	Charleston, W. Va.	10.00
14. Parker, Rev. W. W.	Antioch Baptist	Waterloo, Iowa	10.00
15. Patterson, Rev. H. W.	Mount Carmel Baptist Church	Columbus, Ohio	10.00
16. Rawls, Dr. Louis	Tabernacle Baptist Church	Chicago, Ill.	10.00
17. Robertson, Dr. B. W.	Cedar Street Baptist Church	Richmond, Va.	10.00
18. Sorrell, Rev. L. S.	White Stone Baptist Church	Clarksdale, Miss.	10.00
19. Wagner, Rev. C. E.	Zion Baptist Church	Cincinnati, Ohio	10.00
20. Walton, Mrs. Thelma	Antioch Baptist	Cincinnati, Ohio	10.00
21. Williams, Rev. J. A.	Baptist Temple	Pittsburgh, Pa.	10.00
22. Williams, Rev. J. B.	New Zion Baptist	Pittsburgh, Pa.	10.00
23. Williams, Rev. J. F.	Messiah Baptist	Newport News, Va.	10.00

Messengers Registered	23
Churches Registered	22
States Registered	12
Messengers Participating	33
States Represented	14

Registered Delegates and Regular Offering $239.90
Contribution to Foreign Missions 181.36
Receipts from the Churches 300.00

TOTAL $721.26

8

Appendix 55, cont'd

NEW SPLIT THREATENS BAPTISTS;

Like wounded lions licking their wounds after a bitter defeat in the jungle-like politics of the National Baptist Convention, U.S.A., Inc., some losers were roaring in the wilderness last week. While re-elected president Dr. Joseph H. Jackson denied taking a post-election swipe at one of his main opponents, the Rev. M. L. King Jr., invitations to split the group circulated across the nation.

Coming from Cincinnati's Rev. L. Venchael Booth, 42, chairman of a "Volunteer Committee for the Formation of A New National Baptist Convention," the invitations called for a November 14-15 meeting at his Zion Baptist Church on "How to Build a Democratic Convention Dedicated to Christian Objectives."

"This movement is in no way connected with the past effort of "The (Dr. Gardner C.) Taylor team," the Rev. Mr. Booth emphasized. "It is an entirely new movement under new leadership." Listing among 12 objectives for his proposed new convention a limit on presidential tenure protection of voting rights within the group and support for what he called "freedom fighters" in the civil rights struggle, the minister added: "A split is undesirable, but Baptists deserve a choice between freedom and tyranny. We owe the nation much more than lawsuits, stage fights and mob violence. We think it is far more righteous to split than to go to a convention in the fear of returning home in a shroud."

The Rev. Mr. Booth's arguments were backed by Philadelphia's Rev. Marshall L. Shepard Sr. "I can no longer support the convention leadership," he said. "I would be glad to join any group which will give the nation a better image of Baptists."

There was, however, disagreement from at least two other Baptist leaders. The defeated Rev. Gardner C. Taylor declared he would not condone such a split. And the Rev. M. L. King Jr., who nominated Taylor last year in Philadelphia and was rewarded this year with an ouster from his vice-

9

Appendix 55, cont'd

JACKSON DENIES RAPPING DR. KING

presidency of the Sunday School and Baptist Training Union Congress, said: "What ever is wrong with the convention cannot be corrected by a split."

Dr. Jackson, meanwhile, refused comment on the proposed split. Instead he charged his remarks at a post-election news conference were twisted by reporters to make it appear he had accused Dr. King of having "master-minded the invasion of the convention hall" which resulted in the death of Detroit's Rev. Arthur G. Wright.

Dr. Jackson said he described Dr. King as the "mastermind" of the "protest" philosophy on civil rights and contrasted his own philosophy that Negroes must "produce" as well as protest. He said the Rev. Mr. King's philosophy was shared by Taylor followers whom, he charged, were responsible for violence at the convention. "This was no attempt to discredit Dr. King," Dr. Jackson argued. "I did not blame any individual."

However, the Rev. Mr. King remained unconvinced, and disclosed he had received scores of letters saying in effect: "I always thought you were a devil." Revealing that numerous lawyers and religious leaders (including supporters of Dr. Jackson) were pressing him (Dr. King) to seek legal redress, the reluctant minister said: "I believe in non-violence, not only against the body but also against the spirit."

Meanwhile, a group of ministers in New York City issued a formal statement rebuking the Rev. Mr. Jackson for the widely published reports of the attack on King.

Leaders in Baptist affairs include (l.-r.) the Revs. J. H. Jackson, M. L. King Jr., Gardner C. Taylor, Marshall Shepard Sr.

Appendix 55, cont'd

**States Represented in the Organizational
Meeting of the Progressive NBC**

Alabama 1
California 3
Florida 3
Illinois 3
Indiana 1
Iowa 1
Kentucky 1
Michigan 3
Mississippi 1
New Jersey 2
Ohio 8
Pennsylvania 3
Virginia 2
West Virginia 1

TOTAL 33

The Progressive National Baptist Convention, Inc., was organized November 14-15, 1961, in Zion Baptist Church, Cincinnati, Ohio. Since its organization, it has met in the following cities:

Year	City	President	Secretary
1961	Cincinnati, Ohio	Rev. T. M. Chambers, D.D.	Rev. J. Carl Mitchell
1962	Philadelphia, Pa.	Rev. T. M. Chambers, D.D.	Rev. J. Carl Mitchell
1963	Detroit, Mich.	Rev. T. M. Chambers, D.D.	Rev. J. Carl Mitchell
1964	Atlanta, Ga.	Rev. T. M. Chambers, D.D.	Rev. S. S. Hodges
1965	Los Angeles, Cal.	Rev. T. M. Chambers, D.D.	Rev. S. S. Hodges
1966	Memphis, Tenn.	Rev. T. M. Chambers, D.D.	Rev. S. S. Hodges
1967	Cincinnati, Ohio	Rev. G. C. Taylor, D.D.	Rev. S. S. Hodges

LIFE MEMBERS OF THE
PROGRESSIVE NATIONAL BAPTIST CONVENTION, INC.
Michigan
Rev. J. F. Green, Detroit
Ohio
Rev. L. V. Booth, L.H.D., Cincinnati
Rev. S. S. Hodges, D.D., Cleveland
Rev. Lewis M. Durden (Lt. Col. U.S.A. Ret.), Cincinnati

Note: Life memberships may be obtained by paying $150.00 to the Convention Registry at one time.

11

Appendix 55, cont'd

An Ode
To Drs. Booth and Chambers

Zion Baptist Church sits high on a hill,
A beautiful monument to God Pastor Booth did
build,
Within its walls in 1961 on a gray November day,
He called a meeting to make a decision and to
pray.

With his own resources he ventured forth,
He sent out letters, South, East, West and North,
He wanted men and women of stamina and with-
out fear,
He had faith in God to steer him clear.

He said farewell in Kansas City,
The picture painted there was a masterpiece of
shame and pity,
Ten stalwart men had long since been released,
In Kansas City a Christian Convention had to be
policed!

Unfortunately a few felt Dr. King was not good
enough,
He, who's life is always at stake, who's going is
rough,
As long as the pages of history unfurl,
Martin Luther King will be the Negro's freedom
PEARL.

There is the Philadelphia Story,
But let us just tell the story of Jesus and Glory,
We put our arms around C. C. Adams a missionary
veteran of many sands,
Who for years have guided missions in many for-
eign lands.

A few brave souls answered Pastor Booth out there
on a limb,
He made the appeal, "Shall we sink or shall we
swim?"
Unanimously they voted to swim not to float,
And for a new captain and a new boat!

Wise Dr. Booth was not looking for fame,
Nor for popularity or a big name,
He wanted dignity and Christian grace,
He wanted to lift his denomination's face.

They elected a man with Abe Lincoln's gait,
Tall and lanky but destined by fate,
A man acquainted with Convention ills and cures,
Ability to make a Convention "Christ-like" and
secure.

President Chambers does not advocate under-
ground detours,
His head is not inflated and his mind is mature,
He is not a Solomon and he is not a Saul,
But he will put the Convention on the "ball."

He has a unique style of preaching,
He uses rich similes, suitable and far reaching,
In the Spirit's mood he'll give that electrifying
Chamber's moan in a soft key,
In a pensive mood he'll say, "Well bless my bones
and body."

He is honest, outspoken and qualified,
He'll listen to reason, he wants the Convention
to rise,
The other good brothers all fall in line,
The year will come when it will be their time.

Versatile Dr. Booth is a proficient helper,
He is not a Judas or a Convention "leper",
The Auxiliaries and Regional Meetings had to be
organized,
He is not backslapper always using the pro-
noun "I".

One by one the brothers see our freedom light,
We're not looking for trouble, we're not looking
for strife,
We ask His blessing on every sister and brother,
We're out for Kingdom Building, the world's for
the other.

God has blessed us to be about 700 churches
strong,
We are striving for RIGHT - God steer us from
all WRONG,
We are the PROGRESSIVE NATIONAL BAPTIST
CONVENTION, practicing TENURE,
We do not advocate an office for a lifetime ad-
venture.

High upon that Cincinnati hill,
The Convention's birthplace - not down in a rill,
God heard our prayers that gray November day--
To God be all Glory, - We're well on our way.

—by Esther L. Fishburn
Columbus, Ohio

Appendix 55, cont'd

BETWEEN THE LINES

Of Baptists . . . and Baptists

By GORDON B. HANCOCK

As much as the writer, an old line Baptist, regrets the latest schism in the ranks of the Negro Baptists of this country, he must in charity hail the new body with the earnest hope that it may find what it so much seeks and desires: brotherly peace and accord.

The Philadelphia convention was a tragedy. It brought to the writer's mind what happened in Chicago in 1915 where the Negro National Baptist Convention had its first split. He had just been elected statistician the year before in Philadelphia and went to Chicago prepared to make what was perhaps the only well-wrought statistical report to come before the Negro Baptists of this country in convention assembled.

Subsequent statistical reports have been largely estimates and not authentic studies based upon minutes of associations and state conventions here and there about the nation. My state, South Carolina, went out in toto with the Boyd Convention which turned out to be the lesser of the two.

I followed the brethren to Kansas City and Atlanta and then talked over the matter with Henry Allen Boyd in an attempt to bring the two wings together again. But Boyd was cool to the idea and I made my departure and remained persona non grata to both conventions and this "cured" me of conventions.

The tragedy that was enacted at Chicago was recently reenacted in Philadelphia and this brought into being the Progressive National Convention. And there is ample room for such convention providing it was a progressive program. Baptists, like Methodists, have a right to split if they deem it wise and honorable. Negro Methodists are split four ways and now Negro Baptists are split three ways; they have another split coming to them if they are to keep pace with the Methodist brethren.

When we consider what the split Methodists are doing and what the split Baptists are not doing there is room for soul-searching among Negro Baptists of this country, Split or unsplit. Vast sums of money have been raised through many years but Negro Baptists do not have one college or university built by money taken at the National Baptist Convention. Methodists have several fine colleges to show for their splitting.

In the first place, Negro Baptists have held too many annual meetings. Some enterprising Negro scholar could come up with a fine thesis on "Millions Negro Baptists Have Invested in The Railroads of the Nation."

The monies taken in by these annual conventions is but a small part of the take by the railroads which have reaped an abundant financial harvest from Negro Baptists of the country. It has taken millions and millions to transport thousands and thousands annually to diverse parts of this country through the many years of Baptist conventioning by Negro Baptists.

The meetings of the National Methodists make more sense and it is fervently to be hoped that the new convention will take a leaf from the program of their Methodist brethren.

Then there is the momentous matter of the Baptists denomination serving as feeder for other denominations and cults. Here is another study which is long overdue. If we sift the Father Divine movement and the Daddy Grace organization and the Holiness faith, we find that these all are fed by Negro Baptists. That is to say, if we would subtract from these bodies the Negro Baptists which they have recruited, they would speedily go out of business.

Some way must be found to hold those baptized into the Baptist denomination, for the Holiness church is recruiting them from one level and the Episcopal and Presbyterian churches are at work on still another level.

If the new convention will address itself to some of these problems, it will more than justify itself. There is a field for a convention that really has a progressive program. But there is little room for an organization which *imitates* and *duplicates* the shortcomings of the *old* conventions.

The fight against life-time *tenure* of convention presidents is a justifiable fight. The very idea that when a Baptist accedes to office it is for life, is archaic and should be banned everywhere. While it is to be regretted that this whole matter of tenure could not have been fought out within the older convention, there is reassurance in the fact that there is a "breaking point."

Hail, Progressive Baptists!

Appendix 55, cont'd

REMEMBERING THE CALL

"We are National Baptists, not better than the other National Baptists, but Progressive National Baptists. We are Baptists with a vision of a brighter horizon, and of a new world of Christian fellowship. We are restless dreamers, seekers of a Promised Land, men and woman who grew impatient with the unbroken and unbreakable reign of the Pharoahs. We were weary with the terror of hired overseers; we were tired if the whiplash of teat sucklings. We are escapees from the intolerance of political lords, and violence against the Kingdom of God,"[1] so penned Earl L Harrison, that statesman now sainted, more than a decade ago in his first annual address. These are they that gather in the city of their founding and their founder to celebrate their 25th Anniversary. What a prime opportunity to reminisce and reassess their origin and their orders. Such an undertaking would surely find Progressive Baptists *"Remembering the Call."*

There comes to mind as the call is remembered, the *"spirit filled pastor"*[2] who issued the call. *"Unmistakably, the leading founder of the Progressive National Baptist Convention, U.S.A., Inc., [is] Rev. L. Venchael Booth"*[3] so concluded the historian Dr. Leroy Fitts. Booth's foray into hitherto uncharted terrain was no picnic. *"Both took care to separate this call from the defunct 'Taylor Movement.' Their call received various responses, ranging from condemnation to approval. Most pastors who responded called for restraint, while acknowledging the existence of serious problems. Neither Taylor nor the Reverend M. L. King, Jr., favored Booth's suggestion; both again called for unity. Despite all the words of caution, however, Booth proceeded., and with only a handful of ministers, the Progressive Baptist Convention emerged in November 14, 1961 in Cincinnati."*[4] In his incomparable and inimitable way, Dr. Gardner C. Taylor nearly two decades ago in the same city in which the 25th Anniversary is being celebrated, Cincinnati, said it best, *". . . L. V. Booth envisioned a new mandate of Heaven, a new instrumentality of the Kingdom of Jesus Christ. All honor and credit are due [him] . . . for his vision and courage in the face of overwhelming odds for issuing a call to a heartsick, rejected remnant of God's true Israel who were deprived of a true denominational home in which their worthiest Baptist instincts of freedom could be exercised and honored."*[5] Clearly, L. Venchael Booth was the *"earthly instrument"* in Kilgore's words for *"the call . . . from a higher source."*[6] As a consequence, what he wrote and writes, thought and thinks, did and does should be of inestimable interest to the PNBC.

Remembering the Call, then means, that the Convention will return to the summons once delivered for consideration, for contemplation, and for commitment anew to the God-given triune concept conveyed through the earthly instrumentality, the Founder of the Progressive National Baptist Convention, L. Venchael Booth. That triune concept embraces a Scripture, a Symbol, and a Song. Resident in this trinitarian configuration is at once the root and the roadmap for this great Convention.

THE SCRIPTURE

Paul's epistle to the Romans, chapter 12, and verses 9-12, was laid by the Spirit upon the heart of the Founder. The same Spirit that prompted the call pointed to the Word of knowledge. In the heart of those verses one will find a sober, prayerful and humble relationship suggested as one works with his fellowman. It is implicit throughout these verses that a real effort will be made to lead a godly life – not resorting to pretension, nor a presumptuous attitude toward one's fellowman. The very spirit of *"in honor preferring one another,"* is a lofty step forward and is far above what is commonly practiced by religionists today. The idea, *"let love be without dissimulation,"* or *"not slothful in business, fervent in spirit, serving the Lord,"* is most challenging. No matter how talented one may be, the text offers that inclusive caution that none can afford to ignore *"be not wise in your own conceits, providing things honest in the sight of all men."* How pregnant this entire passage is with righteousness. To conclude it all is the Knock-out blow to all our selfishness and pride, *"Be not overcome with evil, but overcome evil with good."*

Over the twenty-five year stretch many an occasion was presented to draw upon this text to prepare poignant theological treatises, to spawn creative litanies, to develop refreshing retreat resources, to provide themes for oratorical contests, and to offer plots for plays. Yet, the sad chronicle of our Convention is that we've sidetracked and sidelined this Word especially given to us. Had the Convention nurtured its soul with the food of this Word, incalculable contributions would abound to us and the world. Instead, our myopic memory has stymied and stunted our growth.

14

Appendix 55, cont'd

THE SYMBOL

A symbol is a mark or sign with special meaning. A symbol is not required to carry the cross of every connotation, but special meaning as the Oxford American Dictionary notes. The creation of the PNBC symbol with the words – Fellowship, Progress, and Peace was complete in and of itself. While it may not have captured all of the themes in the Convention's text, it was not intended to. Indeed an effort to cram all of the themes of the text in the symbol would make of it something grotesque.

In 1977 the word *"Service"* was added. What would keep someone from recommending in the future that *"Love"* be added as well. The adequacy of Fellowship, Progress, and Peace stems from its capacity to capture the original intent of the Convention's beginnings. In that letter of September 22, 1961, the intent was illuminated. *"our National Baptist Convention has reached an all-time low in fellowship, peace, and Christian dignity. We have completely lost our freedom to worship, participate, and grow in kingdom work..."* Explicitly the first two themes were stated, fellowship and peace. However, implicitly the theme of progress is hinted at in the loss of *"our freedom to worship, participate, and grow in kingdom work."* Plus, it was an infringement upon historical integrity to alter the symbol. Likewise, biblically to add service was not critical for service flows out of fellowship, makes possible genuine progress, and insures the presence of peace. Our symbol is our seal and as such should engrave upon the minds and hearts of observers not all that we are, but rather convey an accurate extract of our essence graphically.

THE SONG

Like the National Anthem or an Alma Mater, the Convention Song, *"A Prayer Fellowship Hymn"*, deserves to stand as given. To commission a new Convention Song, not born out of the agony of the Convention's conception, is an act of irreverence for our past. It's paradoxical that the roots we can recover we attempt to replace and the roots replaced we attempt to recover.

That *"Prayer Fellowship Hymn"* sung at the First Annual Session, Philadelphia, Pa., 1962, ought to open every session of the Convention. These lyrics, born out of the bosom of a brooding spirit longing for a new day, comprise meaningful and descriptive words regarding our experience and why we have come together. This hymn is not great because the writer wrote it, but it is great because it is a God revealed hymn. Other original hymns have their place in lifting up special themes and underscoring special events, but not as usurpers of that originating melody and message which grew out of the primal impulse behind our being.

Let me conclude it all with this word uttered by L. Venchael Booth, in the 1973 Presidential Address in his home state and who by his life and labors for this Convention has a right to be heard above the other voices who weren't given the vision to which he'll not be disobedient:

> **When the Progressive National Baptist Convention was born she was not destined to be just another Convention. She was born with an ideal of love, brotherhood and freedom. She was born with a challenging Scripture Lesson and a Song. God gave us the Scripture – Romans 12:9-21 and gave us a Song. All who seek to lead this Convention should take time to read the Scripture and sing the Song. It would be well to study the Scripture and practice it. It would be well to sing the Song and explore the depths of its inspiration. These were not the idle wanderings of man – but they are the lofty revelations of God. Take a look at our symbol and study the words. They are fraught with meaning, deep meditation and lofty aspiration.[7]**

Rev. William D. Booth
Author, The Progressive Story

[1] Earl L. Harrison, "President's Address," **Minutes of the Tenth Annual Session** (Sept., 1971), p. 84.
[2] Thomas Kilgore, "The Call - The Journey - The Future", (President's Address), **Minutes of the Seventeenth Annual Session** (Sept., 1973), p. 141.
[3] A History of Black Baptists, (Nashville: Broadman Press, 1985), p. 104.
[4] Edward Wheeler, "Beyond One Man: A General Survey of Black Baptist History", **Review and Expositor** (Summer, 1973), Vol. LXX, No. 3, p. 317.
[5] Gardner C. Taylor, "The President's Message", **Minutes of the Sixth Annual Session**, p. 42 (September, 1967).
[6] Thomas Kilgore, "The Call - The Journey - The Future" (President's Message), **Minutes of the Seventeenth Annual Session**, p. 140.
[7] L. Venchael Booth, "President's Address," **Minutes of the Twelfth Annual Session** (Sept., 1973), p. 78.

Appendix 55, cont'd

SUBJECT INDEX

Appendix 55, cont'd

A TRIBUTE
TO BROTHER BOOTH

By President T. M. Chambers

One cannot expect to get away to a successful start without recognition of and the spirit of appreciation for his vices and other co-workers. **Much respect is due Bro. L. V. Booth, whose influence and determination brought together those who launched upon this endeavor.** I have traveled with him in Europe and the Holy Land, and have seen the fruits of his leadership in the erection of one of the most spaciuos, beautiful and modern departmental Church plants to be found in our Nation.

Captain Naaman of Syria made the blunder of minimizing the ability and divine authority of Elisha because he was not as famous as Elijah. The king tore his clothes. Naaman was wroth and went away in a rage, but Elisha said, "If he'll condescend, or come down, he shall know that there is a prophet in Israel."

Chicago, Illinois 1962

Appendix 56

A Challenging Beginning
By L. Venchael Booth, Founder

The *Wall Street Journal* carried an advertisement several months ago which provides the introduction to this article assigned to me for the 25th anniversary. The Journal was advertising a copy machine. The article read: "All great revolutions have been-started by a single piece of paper." It stated further: "Over 750 years ago, the Magna Carta gave the English individual liberties. Over 200 years ago, the Declaration of Independence gave Americans the right of life, liberty, and the pursuit of happiness. Over 100 years ago, the Emancipation Proclamation gave slaves their freedom." (The *Wall Street Journal,* Wednesday, March 12, 1986.)

Twenty-five years ago, God gave me the inspiration to write a call letter to Baptists to form a new convention based on tenure for the presidency which was later to be named the Progressive National Baptist Convention, Inc. It began with a single piece of paper destined to change the lives of thousands. Today this convention is comprised of many who have only a vague idea of how it was started and why, because they are far removed from the struggle that brought it into being.

The inspiration to call Baptists to organize a new convention grew out of several years of agony. As a young pastor, I grew very weary of sitting up all night on trains year after year discussing the same subject, the presidency of the convention. It became a never ending subject, and it revolved around the one personality whose genius was so great that no one could defeat him. In addition to all of this, I participated in several events which suggested the growing separation and alienation of great souls who dearly loved the National Baptist Convention, USA, Inc. As the strain grew, it galvanized its position and convictions thus, making them grow more and more incompatible with reality. Beginning in 1955 in Memphis, Tenn. and continuing through 1961, my soul was fed a steady diet

Appendix 56, cont'd

leading to the conviction that a convention based on tenure for the presidency was our only hope for peace.

One needs to delve into history to adequately understand that the time was ripe for a new convention based on tenure. One needs to read "The Progressive Story," a well authenticated document by William D. Booth. This book is written from published materials and sources carefully chosen. It is a book of unvarnished truth, and the only history of our convention based on published facts. The unpleasant details are not treated in this statement. It suffices here to recall the "lifting of tenure for study in Memphis," the disruptions of sessions in Denver, the open fracas in Louisville, and the accidental death of a prominent messenger in Kansas City, Mo. All suggest the widening breach in the fellowship over one single issue, the presidency.

There was also some controversy over the civil rights movement. It was felt that many men of stature had no voice, and the civil rights leaders had very little support. Most importantly, the fellowship that we once held so dear had disintegrated.

In retrospect, we were wrong to blame one man as we have been so prone to do. Instead, we should have blamed the system that created the opportunity for a one-man, powerful rule. It could make a world of difference when one finds room in his heart for that kind of understanding.

The call to organize a new convention was not a mere whim, or a fluke, or a fantasy. It was a real, sincerely prayed-about effort. The cost was well counted. The convener had to give up a popular lectureship in the women's convention, a very prestigious assistantship in the pastors' division of the Sunday school congress, and a proud position as corresponding secretary of the stewardship division of the convention.

Then too, it involved estrangement from one he admired greatly, and to whose church he once belonged. He could never forget that his first trip to a national convention was in the

Appendix 56, cont'd

company of this great preacher and towering leader. He also had to remember that this pastor had preached his installment sermon for his first outstanding pastorate. The man he had to oppose was not a stranger, but a very dear friend.

It was a great and blessed revelation when I realized that I was not really opposing a man, but a system. History will vindicate Dr. Joseph Harrison Jackson as a man who was true to the tradition of the fathers. Most of his contemporaries wanted money, power and position. Dr. Jackson had the will and the talent to make these a reality.

The combination of idealism, youth and inexperience served as a catalyst for me to become a "willing sacrificial lamb" for what I believed to be the Baptist cause. Like Esther of the Hebrew people, I stepped out, stuck my neck out, with the resolution to save the Baptists even if "I perish."

It is amazing what idealism mixed with inexperience can lead a man to do. Little did I realize that a new movement with a new name does not create a new people. Instead, it brings together people with potentialities to become a new people. They never become a new people unless they become willing to work hard and unselfishly.

Back in those days I was certain that I had a rendezvous with history. From my divinely constructed platform, painted with prayer and varnished with the Holy Spirit, I sought to begin a movement that would end greed and rivalry forever. It was not too long before I had to come to grips with the fact that few would even recognize my effort, and those who benefited the most would be reluctant to give credit and acclaim to my initiative and suffering. For this I do not cry because, whatever a man does honestly and sincerely for God does not go unrewarded.

The call to organize was issued with the best of intentions. No energy, no sacrifice, no talent was spared in trying to build a Progressive National Baptist Convention. I lost many old friends, and my new friends were few and far between if one tried to count them. People remained the same. I lost the favored

Appendix 56, cont'd

positions I held in the old convention and was greeted with suspicion and suspect in the new. Just the same I took an old canvas bag (once owned by the late Dr. W. H. Williams, illustrious pastor of Antioch Baptist Church) and filled it with mimeographed materials and traveled wherever I could to promote what I believed to be a just Baptist cause.

God gave me something to give the new convention. He gave me a selection of Scripture, a symbol and a song. The Scripture is not read too often, the symbol is changed to give it a stronger meaning, and the song is not sung.

The convention finds it necessary to move from voluntary giving to compulsory contributions. There seems to be less emphasis on the old type of fellowship we, envisioned: the concern for the small and growing churches, and the uplifting of the spirit of the downtrodden. There is little mention these days of our being a cause-centered convention. We do not despair over the progress we are making. Thank God nothing is written in concrete. Our convention is still very young. It has plenty of time for the selfish, ambitious and greedy to pass off the scene and still be made whole.

We are indebted to many saints who were precious while they lived and are even more precious while they sleep. Our first president, Dr. Timothy M. Chambers, emphasized a cause-centered convention. Our other presidents emphasized the same. All emphasized fellowship above power and numbers. Not one has been against freedom, though some seem to forget it at times.

We all feel that if we are to grow, our various departments must have breathing space. Too much streamlining and control often cannot get the desired results. We have too short a tenure, and we seem to try to do too much in one session. Many are drifting away, and some are simply drifting.

In retrospect the call had its agony, but it was the most exciting period of my ministerial career. This humble servant had a number of years when he lived and breathed excitement.

Appendix 56, cont'd

The birth of PNBC was a time of excitement and expectation. It was cause-centered. We rallied under the banner of fellowship, progress and peace. Later, we discovered that service would give more glory to our effort.

As we celebrate the 25th anniversary of our convention, let us take fresh courage and believe in our sacred destiny. We have a charge to keep. We have a journey to make. We must not simply try to make history. Let us so live, love and serve God that our history will be transformed into His-story.

Appendix 57

MY PROGRESSIVE JOURNEY
1961 - 2001
by L. Venchael Booth

INTRODUCTION

It is not too often that one who is in the inception of a movement lives to view it's growth and progress for nearly 40 years. In the light of this fact, it is almost a responsibility, if not a duty to give some kind of testimony. There is little reason to believe that there are many still around who care about the motivation that caused a small band of pilgrims to set out on such a perilous journey in 1961. Despite this lack of concern, there is a real need to recall and remember those who gave up so much to follow through on their dream. They all need to be called by name and their name should be accompanied by a photograph, but this is not now a possibility. They should be enshrined in a HALL OF FAME, but this will be left to future generations. This small booklet will be devoted in trying to recapture something of their goals and aspirations. Our attempt here will be to stimulate interest and debate for a very talented and blessed generation.

From 1953 in Miami, Florida to 1961 in Kansas City, MO., there was manifested a spirit of 'win and rule,' no matter who was hurt in the process. In 1952, an idealistic group thought they had put TENURE in the Constitution of the National Baptist Convention USA, Inc. at its annual session meeting in Chicago, Illinois. There were great leaders like Dr. J. Raymond Henderson and Dr. Lester Kendall Jackson who became spokesmen and advocates of this as a guiding principle to decrease corruption and abuse of power. They were sure of this until the new president, Dr. Joseph Harrison Jackson had his clause 'lifted' for studying a meeting in Memphis, Tenn., by a Committee heavily tilted in his favor. This persisted until it was ruled unconstitutional in meeting Louisville, KY in 1957. The fat was

Appendix 57, cont'd

in the fire and progressive pastors began to plan how to overcome one of the smartest technicalities ever faced by Black Baptists. Opposition and disruption reached its boiling point by 1961 in Kansas City, Mo. When a prominent pastor from Detroit was pushed from the platform in a scuffle and died.

PNBC WAS NO ACCIDENT

Your writer innocently entered this struggle in 1947 when he was under the influence of his pastor, Dr. William Holmes Borders, who had ordained him in 1941. Dr. Borders became a volunteer to champion the candidacy of Dr. E. W. Perry who was Vice President at Large, and in line to succeed Dr. David V. Jemison, noted leader from Alabama. Dr. J.H. Jackson, a rising star made the decision to oppose Dr. Perry for his post. The campaign that followed demonstrated that Dr. Jackson would become a strong contender finally eclipsing Dr. Perry in becoming president of the Convention in 1953. The successor chain was broken and the way was paved for Dr. Jackson to serve for life once the 'tenure barrier' was removed. Dr. Jemison retired from the Presidency due to the loss of his vision and many saw in the election of Dr. Jackson, "a new day," born. The symbol of a broom was used to indicate that a clean sweep would be made with his friends rewarded and his enemies punished. At that time I was Corresponding Secretary of Stewardship, and was just getting started when I was removed from office. This bit of history is given simply to indicate that my appearance on the scene as a critic and opponent was no mere accident. For your further information, I served as a lecturer in the Women's Department under Ms. Nannie Hellen Burroughs for 16 years and served as Assistant to Dr. Roy Love in the Pastor's Division of the Sunday School Congress. When the die was cast in 1947 and Dr. Jackson started his rise to power, Dr. Gardner C. Taylor (my esteemed friend) was supporting him in a significant way. He was a winner and I was a loser. As the years rolled by and dissident Baptists in the Convention needed a leader, he was

Appendix 57, cont'd

chosen as the challenger and our paths were destined to merge in the new Convention.

ANSWERING THE CALL TO LEAD

Following the Kansas City debacle, the Spirit of the Lord led me to enter the Baptist arena as a leader of a new Convention. Without the endorsement of anyone, I returned to Cincinnati to my church and began writing letters to the Baptists to join me in forming a new Convention. The meeting was called for November 15 and 16 in Cincinnati at the Zion Baptist Church. Leaders of distinction doubted the feasibility of such a move. Their doubt could not overcome my determination. It was not sheer folly or a desire for power that propelled me to move ahead, but a belief in a cause. This undertaking was the death of my popularity and peace among Baptists. Those who joined me did not seem too sure of the move and those who refused seemed certain that it would not prevail. There were those who felt that if certain personalities would come aboard that the ship might sail. We all need to know that Dr. T. M. Chambers, first president of the Progressive National Baptist Convention never wavered and brought a sweetness and wisdom to the office that was greatly needed. We who follow are forever in his debt. His long years as a pastor and evangelist attracted many who came with us. His sacrificial contribution personally and professionally cannot be estimated. We were also fortunate to have Dr. Gardner C. Taylor, to become his first vice president because he brought influence and prestige to the office and gave us a "running start." Dr. Louis Rawls, an astute businessman and soul filled preacher became our first treasure. When Dr. E. L. Harrison joined us, we started climbing "Jacob's Ladder." In the short time he served, he wrote a large page in our history. Because of him, we got our first full time Executive Secretary, and laid the foundation for a permanent headquarters. In fact, he preceded all our efforts when his patience and genius helped to build the Million-Dollar Administration Building under the

Appendix 57, cont'd

leadership of Dr. Aurelia Richey Downey. Dr. W. H. R. Powell, Dr. C. C. Adams, and Dr. Marshall Shepard, Sr., among a host of other fine men helped to make the Convention a meaningful effort. At no time has this writer claimed, or sought all the credit. He has opposed the re-writing of history even to the point of trying to write him out.

Let it be said loud and clear that this Convention is not a Civil Rights Movement. It was not organized as a Civil Rights Movement. It was organized to institute once and forever TENURE in a Black Baptist Convention. We welcomed our Civil Rights Leaders because many of us were their friends and were involved in the movement. This convention was organized to remove the 'imperial majesty' of the presidency and to lead our people to become "Christ-centered and Cause-centered." We are far from succeeding because we have seen a succession of presidents who appeared to be power-centered and self-centered. We have had the feeling at times that a real effort was being made to "return to Egypt." These are evident in stretch limousines and other trappings of materialism.

There also seems to be little interest in small churches, and a program that will lift the moral standards of the people. The effort to try to hold the Convention in August strikes me as not being certain of our mission. The combining of the Congress with the Convention strikes me as giving Christian Education a minor emphasis. There is no doubt in my mind that it has affected the growth of this wonderful Convention.

CHANGES TOO RAPIDLY MADE

If I were to critique the Convention and its operations after nearly forty years, I would consider the following concerns:
+ there have been too many changes without prayerful consideration;
+ among these are the addition of "service" to the symbol;
+ the change of meeting from September to August;
+ combining the Congress with the Convention;

Appendix 57, cont'd

✝ making all Department Heads "vice presidents";
✝ too little time for the Women to do a meaningful program and;
✝ the congress has too little time to do its work effectively.

One gets the impression that everything is a 'rush' from beginning to end. The exhaustion leads to frustration and to disinterest. Our children seem not to be chaperoned or supervised. There are still too many of us who seem to be taking a vacation rather than becoming involved in a spiritual experience. There is too little evidence of putting our best foot forward and making an impact on the city in which we convene. We do not seem to be aware that we are being observed by saints and sinners. We do not seem to give serious consideration for what our people are given worthy of being taken home and shared. Having attended business or secular Conventions there is often seen more consecration and dedication than in our Convention. There is sometime a ruthlessness and arrogance displayed that is unbecoming to Christians. One of the great shortcomings is in the area of worship and fellowship. For years we have displayed a partisanship that is wholly unbecoming to a Christian body. Since 1972 when a messenger from the White House was not received by this body until now, there has been no effort at balance. We seem to forget that God is neither Republican nor Democrat.

There is too little "light" coming from the Lighthouse. In other words, we do not hear from our national office with any regularity. Our constituency is very poorly informed about our objectives and plans. Our "Progressive Distinctives" have been sorely neglected or entirely forgotten. We care so little about history until the beginning of the history we have is totally left out of the picture.

Our Progressive National Baptist Convention is destined to very slow growth. We have no passion to reach the masses. We need to remember that greatness comes through service. We can all be great, if we all learn to serve.

Appendix 57, cont'd

This brings us to our failure to observe, or keep alive Martin Luther King, Jr., Sunday. It was set for the Third Sunday in January at which time we were to devote time to his teaching of Love and Non-Violence, from the Sunday School to the Morning Worship. We did not embrace this recommendation given in 1972 in Memphis, Tenn., and we have not even made the effort. By this time when our nation has become so violent that our schools are no longer safe, we could be leading the way. Earlier, we had designated Friday Night of our convention as Martin Luther King, Jr. Memorial Night, and this was changed to Civil Rights Night thus losing a great spiritual thrust for non-violence.

LEADERS OPPOSED MY PRESIDENCY

As you read these observations of our Convention from my viewpoint, let me assure you that they are not given out of any sense of bitterness. After calling the organizational meeting of the Convention, I have had many honors. Almost from the beginning, I have willingly taken whatever I have had to take. First, I refused to be the organizing President and deferred to Dr. T. M. Chambers. By 1963, I was offered the opportunity to become a part-time Executive Secretary, so the office of the Vice Presidency would go unopposed to Dr. Gardner C. Taylor, our "Prince of Preachers, " and pastor of the largest Baptist Church in the denomination. Then, I was asked to choose between my church and becoming full-time Executive Secretary in 1969. I was given a retirement banquet because many thought that I had gone from the leadership scene forever. The whole Convention was surprised when I came back on the scene to offer myself as a candidate for the first vice president. Some of the leaders begged me not to run suggesting that I may avoid making myself a martyr. In order to enforce this, the nominating committee refused to carry me on the slate that was to elect Dr. Earl L. Harrison as president.

From the floor and excelled my opponents by a 2-1 margin.

Appendix 57, cont'd

In short, I was nominated by the women and a fine group of pastors who felt that I deserved the post. Thus, I became the first and last president to be elected in a contest. From then, until now, it has been a game of 'musical chairs' affair in the Convention. My presidency was assaulted by great men as often as they could. It was rugged, but satisfying. Dr. Harrison passed before his term ended and I succeeded him in office for a year and was elected on my own in Chicago in 1972. As always, I gave my best and thus served this Convention in an official capacity for at least 13 years. From 1961 to 1974, I was actively engaged in building our Convention. When I stepped down in Cleveland in 1974, the politicians seemingly said good riddance, we are through with him now. Then began the changes because as one leader said: How can you have enough vision to plan for a Convention for forty years? Well, I'm not certain, but I believe that too many changes have lessened our growth. Change is good if it makes for strong spiritual growth. There is a penalty to be paid if we leave our people too far behind. As of now, we have no new churches built by us, nor do we have any students testifying that we made a difference in their lives.

INFLUENCED BY GREAT LEADERS

Before Ms. Nannie Helen Burroughs died, she was able to testify that she had given 60 years to building the Women's Auxiliary to the National Baptist convention, USA, Inc. I'm truly glad that she touched my life. In fact, I would not take anything for having lived to know many of the great Baptists of generations past, such as, Dr. William H. Jernagin, Dr. Benjamin E. Mays and Dr. Howard W. Thurman, to name just a few. There were a host of others equally as worthy and I hope that generations of Baptists following will know that they have a great legacy in the leadership of the past. In fact, every existing National Baptist Convention has something very worthy and commendable about

No one has had a greater opportunity to be duly aligned with either the American or Southern Baptist convention than I

Appendix 57, cont'd

have, but by choice I gave my life for what at times seems to be a losing cause. With singleness of heart, I have served the Progressive National Baptist Convention. In the same like manner, I served the National Baptist Convention, USA, Inc. in the early days of my ministry. I don't have anything to show for it, but I have not lost anything as well. My journey with the Baptist Family has led me from the local church to the Baptist World Alliance where it was my privilege to serve as one of her 12 Vice Presidents from 1970, Tokyo, Japan to Stockholm Sweden, 1980. It has been a great privilege to serve with world leaders and to engage in conversations with them.

In my pilgrimage, I have failed miserable at times. There have been those times when I thought my wisdom and knowledge had accomplished things for me. God knocked me to my knees and brought me to see that it was never my greatness that accomplished anything, but it was always His grace.

This testimony will not make me popular or more greatly loved, but it serves to give me peace and satisfaction that I tried to pass on to a promising generation something of my view of the past. As for the convention and my expressions regarding her shortcomings, I will be the first to confess that I could very well be sincerely wrong. So, don't take my word as the Bible, but take the Bible and measure my word.

PNBC HAS WROUGHT WELL

We have come a long way in our Progressive Convention and many wonderful things have been accomplished. It is quite possible that we could have done no better. My observations have not been intended to imply that we have not done great things. What I have set forth here may be no more than nostalgia for the past. The truth of the matter is, we must at times take time to examine the past, present and future. What we have tried to suggest here that the machinery of the convention should not absorb us so much that we cannot do the work of the Convention. Our convention should inspire us to do greater

Appendix 57, cont'd

kingdom building. This will lead us to 'winning souls,' strengthening discipleship and transforming lives. We cannot afford to attend a Convention and leave more disillusioned than we come.

Up to now the impression conveyed is that each administration is trying to make history without regard to the history that has been made. We seem to lack the ability to build on the foundation that another has laid. We seem to think that the General Secretary is the President's Assistant. Instead of the Secretary coordinating programs and continuing business procedures, he is busy carrying out the president's orders. The president should stand tall as the leader in inspiring efforts rather than becoming bogged down in carrying the efforts. There needs to be a clearer delineation of duties in the executive branches.

There is almost no use of past presidents. Each should be helpful because of his experience and expertise. There should be a 'past-president's hour,' at each session for people to get the richness of a Convention practicing tenure.

We live and die complaining because we have not learned that there is great strength in sharing honors as well as duties.

PRESIDENT CHAMBERS LEADERSHIP

To provide an overview of the Progressive National Baptist Convention, Inc., an effort will be made to extract a few notes from printed materials during the early years of the convention.

Here is an excerpt from the first annual message delivered by Dr. T. M. Chambers in 1962:

> Secondly, the Transition from monopoly and life-time office-holding as convention presidents to TENURE, thereby providing opportunities for progressive and capable leaders to aspire, and taking politic out of religion to put religion into politics.

> The Convention is not lacking in able scholars and interpreters. One of the past such person was Dr. W. H. R. Powell who wrote regarding MOTIVATION. In the act

Appendix 57, cont'd

of withdrawing from any Christian fellowship of which
they have been long time members, to which they have
given their allegiance, prayers, goodwill and support;
whose fellowship and brotherhood have been deeply
meaningful to them over a long period, for the purpose
of creating a new and independent body that, in the very
nature of things, cannot help but be parallel in its aims
and in many respects a duplication of much that already
exists, men of honor and high Christian integrity realize,
that they have embarked upon a course of serious and
far-reaching consequences; that their persuasions and
motives toward such an act should be impersonal,
Christian and of such solid worth that men of good
judgment can approve and the Holy Spirit endorse; and
that, concomitantly they owe it to themselves, to their
brethren, to the world, to their Saviour, to set forth the
motivations for their action in such a way, that sane men
and women can understand their compulsion and history
their valor. See. Minutes, 1962, p. 29

In the first annual session of the convention which met in
Philadelphia, Pa. In 1962, Dr. T. M. Chambers, initiated steps in
the organizing and projecting of an auxiliary body, properly
designated as the progressive National Baptist Sunday School
and Baptist Training Union Congress. The general officers were
elected and instructed to take all necessary steps to assure said
Congress would hold its first sitting, June 18-23, 1963. The first
congress was held at Metropolitan Baptist Church, Dr. E. C.
Smith, host pastor. Thus, the first congress was held in this
great city, our nation's capital.

In the second annual session, Dr. E. I. Harrison warned,
"Salaries and honorariums must become an open matter of the
Convention." We need a yearly budget to undergird the work of
the convention. Legislate wisely against office seekers. Replace
self-centered men with center men. We must hasten to get an
Executive Secretary and a National Headquarters, preferably in
Washington, D.C. We must publish a monthly paper and

Appendix 57, cont'd

establish a bookstore. A representative from each state should be elected to the Nominating Committee.

(*Which Way Ahead In Convention Structure*) Detroit, 1963)

COMMENTS FROM LEADERS

The first Annual Session in Philadelphia, PA was addressed by one of the greatest of our Baptist Educators. The record reads: Rev. L. V. Booth, Vice President, with choice diction and flowing language, presented to the Convention one whom he had held in high esteem for 25 years. Dr. Benjamin E. Mays, President of Morehouse College.

Dr. Mays' Issues are a challenge to Progressive Baptists to Support Education. Dr. Mays of Morehouse College spoke on "The New Look in Christian education." The great educator and World Citizen declared. The program of the National Convention, Inc. has not justified a membership of four or five millions. This convention (the Progressive National Baptist Convention) has a chance to do what no other convention has done. With tenure, no man can perpetuate himself in office. Therefore, the convention is free to concentrate on objectives. Dr. Mays with ringing challenge declared. During his twenty-two years at Morehouse College, the college has received only $2,000 from the National Baptist Convention." In stern declaration he went further and said to the delegates, "Objectives (of this convention) should be the support of colleges and seminaries and recruitment of young ministers. We are 10% of the population but only 3-1/2% of the college population and even less in the seminaries." He challenged this convention to grow strong enough to support Baptist Colleges in a substantial way. He reminded us in his singular way. "The private college has produced most of our great leaders." As long as this Convention exists, it shall owe President Mays a debt of gratitude for his challenge, character, and courage. He paid us a great tribute by visiting us in our first annual session.

Dr. T. M. Chambers, our founding president, should never

Appendix 57, cont'd

be forgotten for his great sacrifice and contribution. Among
many creative and wise statements, he reminded us:

> We are diving in a world and at a time when too many
> people, even Christian people want palms without victory;
> possessions without toil, thrones without valor; honor
> without worthiness; salvation without repentance; crowns
> without crosses; and kingdoms without warfare.

*Dr. Benjamin E. Mays, President of Morehouse College in
Atlanta, GA*

Dr. Mays said he was disturbed about the future of the Negro
Baptist Ministry. Seminary graduates have to roam around for
several years before being placed in the pastorate of a church.
Negro Baptists in Theological Seminaries with college degrees
number only about 125. There are about 20,000 Baptist
churches. There are more Baptist Ministers going out, by death
and retirement than there are trained ministers coming in. He
predicted that the time is fast approaching when churches will
call only trained ministers with college and seminary degrees.
He predicted that unless we produce a sufficient number of
trained ministers, Baptist numbers will decrease and Negro
Baptist churches will call white pastors. Baptist Pastor and
churches must recruit and support young ministerial students.
Dr. Mays appealed to Pastors and laymen present to contribute
toward the building of a dormitory for Baptist students at the
I.T.C. Seminary in Atlanta, GA. This was a most challenging
speech. See: Minutes, 1963.

Dr. W.H.R. Powell distinguished educator and pastor
compiled, along with others, the motivation for starting the
Progressive Convention. Those that believe themselves to be

- ✝ Of Christian maturity, free from the spirit of fanaticism
  and above emotional extravagance;
- ✝ free from the spirit of fanaticism;
- ✝ above emotional extravagance, opponents of schism, and
  capable of forming an intelligent concept of Christian

Appendix 57, cont'd

procedure, the promoters of the Progressive Baptist
Convention of America; Incorporated;

Opposing by declaration in their unvarnished conviction that
all such incidents as occurred at:

✝ Denver 1956;
✝ Louisville, 1957;
✝ Philadelphia 1960; and
✝ Kansas City 1961

All are indefensible; an embarrassment to Baptist churches,
an offense to sober intelligence, an enduring impediment to
Christian witness, and constitute a situation which reasonable
men should not be expected to tolerate any longer. Nor violate
their conscience by support of such. The organization now
taking shape is not a division for division's sake. However, an
honest protest of honest men and women directed against a
situation they believe has grown intolerable and for which there
does not appear, at present, any other solution.

WILL PNBC BE A LEADER IN THE 21st CENTURY?

In the early 60's when PNBC was organized, one of the clarion
voices hailed her birth as 'the last bright hope of the Baptists'.
As controversial as it was to declare 'freedom from tyranny,'
there was an air of excitement and enthusiasm. Some of the
tallest timber in the Baptist family answered the call to battle.
This organization, with one of her main objectives to establish
'tenure' for the office of president, sought to break the chains of
bondage that had long been a stumbling block to Baptists. This
objective was buttressed by her support of the Civil Rights
Movement, her pledge to support Baptist Colleges; her advocacy
of equality for women distinguished her outstandingly.

From 1961 to 1975, the skies were blue and the sun was
bright. Some able, well-intentioned leaders conceived the idea

Appendix 57, cont'd

that we could serve our young people more effectively and make possible greater attendance of our school teachers if we would unite the Congress of Christian Education with the so-called "parent body." They also felt that the symbol of the convention church emblazoned her goals as "Progress, Fellowship and Peace," would be strengthened by the word, "service." They are innocent in realizing that this would be a "slap on the face" of the leading founder. They were also in such a hurry to put the changes into action that they dishonored the "little founder" by changing the convention scheduled to meet in Cincinnati, his home town, on the convention's tenth anniversary. It was held in Atlanta instead. The founder had long witnessed the "righteous brutality" of Baptists. He swallowed hard and remained loyal to the convention, but openly critical. There is a loneliness that goes with trying to be a "trailblazer or a reformer" in the Baptist family.

One of the most brilliant things we have revealed to the nation is our genius to re-write our history. There is a certain shame we seem to have in recognizing our convention had been born of life, courage, and faith. We are reluctant to acknowledge that a poor little Baptist pastor had to be willing to give up popularity, and approval and walk a lonely road to his death. Since the convention has lately been streamlined to do all of her national and international business in one week, this writer has felt like John on the Isle of Patmos. Outstanding Progressive Spokesmen have attributed the organizing of the convention to great personalities who were far removed from the scene. They have even said that she was organized to promote the Civil Rights Movement. The valiant efforts of men of stature have gone unnoticed. The first President and sacrificial pastor, Dr. G.K. Offutt is hardly remembered. He had started a growing Congress of Christian Education, which like all Nation Congresses would have served as a 'feeder' to the convention. There are thousands of loyal Baptists who are eager to learn and as much eager to grow.

When some of our great leaders who are still alive hear his

Appendix 57, cont'd

message, they will simply dismiss it as being written by a "sore-head." Quite the contrary, it is written with "malice toward none, but with charity toward all." Our convention unknowingly suffers from "big-I-tess." We have no testimony from small churches saying we have helped them. We have no testimony from the beginning preachers saying, "we helped them get off to a good start." We have no testimony from pastors saying, "we helped them locate and build churches." We have no testimony from young people saying, "we helped them get through college." We could go on and on. Now it is probably true that we have done all of this, but we are so crunched for time that nobody has time to testify.

As we face the 21st Century, we might help ourselves if we raise some of the following questions:

- ✝ Do our women have enough time and freedom to build a program that will nurture our children, young people, and senior citizens?
- ✝ Have we really reached more teachers, school children, and laborers in general by meeting the first week in August?
- ✝ Are we being thoughtful of our elders, many of whom are 'heart victims', by meeting in the hottest month of the year?
- ✝ Have we improved morale by having 'ONE PRESIDENT' and making all other heads vice presidents?
- ✝ Is our concept of making a general secretary an assistant to the president raising our level of integrity?
- ✝ Do we have ministries to locate and build new churches?
- ✝ Do we have a 5-year plan to multiply our outreach to the rural south and other deprived areas?
- ✝ Do we have the courage to conduct music workshops to inspire better Christian music?
- ✝ Do we have ministries to serve senior citizens, alcoholics, drug addicts, prisoners and abused women and children?
- ✝ Are we offering 'spiritual retreats' and helping in general our 'burned out', our 'leaders'?

Appendix 57, cont'd

✝ Do we have seminar scholarships to help deprived pastors gain greater momentum for service?

If we do not have these ministries, let us not despair, but start working to offer greater service.

Our mandate is "to decrease that others might increase." There is no quarrel with men enjoying their achievements, receiving due honor and all other consideration due them. They must be careful not to forget the least among them, while in the process. It is great for the president and his entourage to ride in a 'stretched-limousine,' but he must have a genuine concern for those delegates who can hardly ride a city transit bus.

We must express our appreciation to the president, who gives service for four years, but it must never appear to be staged, and small givers are made too small to give. We once declared that we left "Egypt," then why not let a president who is able to give his appreciation offering to some worthy cause. We remember our sainted Dr. Martin Luther King, Jr. who gave his Nobel Peace Prize money to the SCLC. Today his oldest son heads that organization.

This founder is not bitter, nor envious of those who lead today, nor those who led in yesteryears. Honors will fade and money will be spent, but a dedicated life will live on and on. He is not hurt that changes have been made, to his judgment, which have been detrimental to our progress. The One I met many years ago is a great healer of broken hearts. He is grateful there is still a Progressive National Baptist Convention. He is even more grateful to have lived long enough to see it for almost forty years. Whatever I have suffered, I can still say, "The Lord is good and His mercy endureth forever."

Thank you "Progressive Baptists," for all the honors bestowed upon me. I have not deserved them, but I am truly grateful. All you have neglected doing can never compare with what you done. It has been a long day, but a good day. Soon, I must bid you farewell. I'm working and waiting now for the last commendation, "Well done, thou good and faithful servant."

Appendix 57, cont'd

PNBC NEEDS TO UNDERGO A RADICAL REVOLUTION

PNBC needs to go backwards to go forward. She needs:

✝ a leader who is courageous enough to risk changes;
✝ to separate the convention from the congress;
✝ to stop meeting in August in the hottest month of the year;
✝ a goal for new building and merging old churches,
✝ to communicate her program rather than display personalities;
✝ to report accurate statistics regarding her numbers;
✝ to do advance planning, looking five, ten or more years ahead;
✝ to meet the challenge of new movements like the Full gospel Churches;
✝ to put quality into her programs rather than quantity;
✝ to use her 'woman power,' rather than try to diminish it;
✝ to think 'nationally,' in order to be effective globally;
✝ to take a new look at her inherited institutions and plan a program to secure them
✝ a strategy to add new churches annually rather than to continue losing those whom cannot comply with our annual percentage giving.
✝ to raise the question, What are we giving to our churches?
✝ to re-examine her beginning when the emphasis had been on a Christ centered/Cause-centered Convention.
✝ to remember her past leaders and publish historical information regarding the contributions by them.

The suggestions laid out in this booklet are not made to be smart, nor because the writer is bitter; rather because he believes that they might lay the foundation for debate and progress.

Remember that nobody was with him when he 'made the call' for a new convention and it is reasonable to assume that he is a 'lonely voice' today.

Appendix 57, cont'd

SOME DEDICATED VOICES IN PNBC

If our future leaders are to catch the vision of how PNBC was started they must be made acquainted with the vision and thoughts of leaders who laid PNBC's foundation.

The first Recording Secretary, Dr. J. Carl Mitchell from Huntington, W. Va.:

The progressive National Baptist Convention is largely an outgrowth of dissatisfaction over 'tenure' and the office of executive secretary in the National Baptist Convention, Inc. The meeting, which culminated in a new organization, was called at Cincinnati, after outstanding ministers had held in several previous meetings in the National Baptist Convention, Inc., over a period of years.

The Rev. L. V. Booth of Zion Baptist Church, Cincinnati, Oh., left the convention at Kansas City to call a meeting and allow the opposition to make a clear choice. Those included making a clear choice between tyranny and freedom, and confusion and peace. Before many of the messengers had reached their homes, a letter went out calling for all interested in Peace, Fellowship, and Progress to attend a meeting in November. This was followed by a second letter in October, urging fellow pastors to come to Cincinnati. His invitation met with opposition from some of the strongest pastors in the nation. Among these were men who were trusted, revered, and respected. At that time very few could see the wisdom and divine inspiration and unselfishness of his call. (See minutes of the Convention, 1962)

Dr. E. C. Smith, pastor of Metropolitan Baptist Church in Washington, D.C.:

"This convention is the salvation of many moving down the drain to destruction." In his sermon, he used as his subject, "Using What's Left." Dr. Smith reminded us, 'there is always something left. Noah's ark is an example. It takes a real man to

Appendix 57, cont'd

wait until the smoke has cleared from the battlefield and use what is left. Some people cannot play in the Minor League after they have played in the Major League. God requires that we use what is left." (See 1962 Minutes, p. 21)

Dr. J. C. Austin, pastor of Pilgrim Baptist Church in Chicago, Ill., championed the cause of Foreign Mission:

Dr. Austin lifted us for a few minutes by interpreting the word 'with.' In his own inimitable way, he asked that we 'feed them' and not 'eat them.' His reference was to our fellow Africans. (See Minutes, 1962, p. 22)

Dr Louis Rawls, first convention treasurer and pastor of Tabernacle Baptist Church in Chicago, Ill.:

His sermon topic titled, *The Need for Prophetic Preaching as We Close the Twentieth Century,* using as his text, Jer. 1:5. Dr Rawls stressed the need for prophetic preaching in this day, the need for love, and the need for unity. He warned "We must not look to the Pope for inspiration and direction, nor seek to be priest, but we must be prophets. The prophet must believe in and preach the virgin birth of Jesus, his life, death, resurrection and promised return."

Dr. T. M. Chambers, first president and pastor of Zion Hill Baptist Church in Los Angeles, Cal.:

His first annual address emphasized *Nothing Little.* The transition from monopoly and life-time office-holding as convention presidents to tenure, thereby providing opportunities for progressive and capable leaders to aspire and taking politics out of religion to put religion in politics.

"Despise not the day of little things." The word 'little' is often used by some persons as a term of indignity and reproach with reference to some individual or group, with a purpose of minimizing and organization in the stimulation of the public. If the cause is righteous, David says, "little that a righteous man hath is better than the riches of many wicked." I would

Appendix 57, cont'd

rather be with a little concern doing big things, than to be with a big concern doing little things." (See 1962 Minutes, p. 47)

Dr. Gardner C. Taylor, pastor of Concord Baptist Church of Christ in Brooklyn, N.Y:

Dr. Taylor remarked that he saw many of his friends and had come to support Dr. Chambers and the Convention. He characterized the Progressive Baptist Convention as a 'rising sun'. He advised, "You cannot put new wine in old bottles. The Lord's Supper was started in a narrow room on a dead end street. The Roman Government was against Jesus. The Jewish Church was against Jesus. He was facing treachery from his own friends. Everyone needs the courage to be brave. God can fix anything regardless how bad it is." Dr. Taylor's presence and message brought new life to the convention (See 1962 Minutes, p. 39)

President T. M. Chambers advocated fiscal integrity:

The President showed and explained new vouchers that he had made, which must be filled out and signed by the proper officers before a check can be issued. All four officers—president, secretary, treasurer, and auditor—must sing and in the order given. (See 1963 Minutes, p. 27)

PAST LEADERS ADVOCATED A "CONGRESS OF CHRISTIAN EDUCATION"

In an address on "The Methodology of Christian Education," Dr. L. K. Jackson, pastor of St. Paul Baptist Church, Gary, IN, stated that he made a sacrifice to be here, because of his interest in the Congress Methodology means 'the way we are to do things'. There is a necessity of destroying some of our methods of thinking. We have thought too much of "I," "Me", and "Myself." The Negro race is the most anti-social group in the world.

Appendix 57, cont'd

First president of the congress, Dr. G. K. Offutt, in his annual address:

Our congress represents the leadership of many of our Baptist Churches across the nation. We have come to this glorious hour to launch, as it were, upon the turbulent sea of the twentieth century, our craft of Christian leadership. May our craft prove seaworthy and sail far and wide. May the inhabitants of ports at home and abroad rejoice greatly when they behold her mast on the horizon, realizing that in her bosom she carries good things—good things for the nourishment and development of the best in man.

Dr. E. L. Harrison, pastor of Shiloh Baptist Church in Washington, D.C., and a former president:

We Must Free Our Women From the Constitutional Control of the Convention:

Why should our women be hog-tied to the men's control? Let us control them by love and not by law. Already, they are our superiors in business. Women own 85 percent of the wealth of the nation; they direct the spending of the other 15 percent. They are ahead of us in the field of education. They do 90 percent of the teaching in our public schools. They have more college and university degrees. They are the budgetarians in our homes. Why then can't they be trusted to run their own convention? Why should we be afraid of our women? They are 3/4 of our supporting congregations. Nevertheless, without them we could not exist. "Let her alone." He said this of the term "Parent Body."

It is this "parent body" concept that continues to divide us. Some self-conceited, power loving, naturally gifted, self-seeking, politically minded man get hold of the helm of these conventions, and makes himself 'daddy' and dictator over the Lord's heritage; and there will always be those who will resent such a concept.

We must make our convention cause-centered. I am not opposed to salaries, legitimate expense accounts, or gifts of

Appendix 57, cont'd

appreciation, but outlets for graft and windfalls must be closed now, at the beginning. Offices in a convention are not positions of honor as much as they are positions to be honored. Men should not seek office in the convention to earn a living, but to serve a cause.

Dr. Gardner C. Taylor, in his first annual address:

"The growth of our convention is evidence of God being in it. We are God's remnant—a convenant people with God. We are the largest givers to education of any National Negro Baptist Convention. He reviewed the work of the department of the convention. Leading Civil Rights workers as Dr. Martin Luther King, Jr., Abernathy, and Shuttlesworth who were members of this household of faith. The world is waiting for the redemption of the sons of God." (See 1966 Minutes, p. 58)

Dr. Martin Luther King Jr., in his first visit to the convention:

Dr. King apologized for being late, because he is a member of the Progressive National Baptist Convention. He was happy to see the church concerned about civil rights. He congratulated president Chambers and President Taylor and all the cabinet for what have been accomplished here this week. Out of the 51 board members of the Southern Christian Leadership Conference, there were 47 preachers. A staff of 200 workers at $25 each per weak. He spoke from the subject, "The Greatest Dilemma Facing America Today."

We have guided missiles and misguided men. Racial injustice is still the black man's burden and the white man's shame. There is nothing wrong with the Negro family that a little more in the pocket of the Negro male cannot cure. (See 1966 Minutes, p. 62)

Dr. Howard W. Thurman, noted Theologian, Scholar and Preacher:

In his Civil Rights Emancipation Address, delivered from Ps. 39:14, he acknowledged some of his former students who were

Appendix 57, cont'd

present and paid a tribute to Dr. S. A. Owens who traveled at his expense from Memphis, TN., to Roanoke, VA., to preach his ordination sermon. Dr. Thurman had recently retired as Dean of March Chapel at Boston University, where he served for 12 years.

He gave a poem on dedication to the truth. He has written a book titled The Luminous Darkness. It grew out of an experience he once had; (1) The experience of segregation; (2) The experience of hate; (3) The experience of love.

Segregation undermines a man's dignity. The segregated is frozen in his place but the segregator has freedom of movement. Under slavery, a slave has no legal rights or recognition before the law, not even legal marriage. Hate feeds on itself and destroys every thing it touches. It knows nothing about justification.

The love ethic that is the core of the gospel, can become a technique. The technique may be used without the user loving. Where is the church? If love and brother-hood were practiced by professing Christians, people would rush to the church to find out what the Christian had to make him behave as they do. (See 1965 Minutes, p. 65)

Dr. T. R Washington, pastor of Second Baptist Church in Philadelphia, Pa.:

The sacrifices made for the Holy cause of progressive will not go unrewarded. The valued time, talents, and money contributed by the great men of our convention will be seen and heard all over this nation—for it is a sacred and hallowed privilege to be a member of such a communion. (See 1965 Minutes, p. 22)

Dr. Thomas Kilgore. Jr., pastor of Second Baptist Church in Los Angeles, Ca.:

Someone has said wisely that when God has a job to be done he always gives the contract to one of faith. The progressive concept is, basically, an idea and movement of faith. The progressive concept is of fellowship, progress, and peace. We

Appendix 57, cont'd

will keep these before us and go forward. We welcome all Baptists who want to travel this road of valid responsibility. (See 1965 Minutes, p. 5)

We will close this section with a statement from one of the finest interpreters our convention has ever had, or probably ever will have. We have not included as many as we might have, but we hope it will cause you who read this paper to 'dig a little deeper'. Our convention needs recorded minutes for future historians to study.

Now, we give you our beloved leader and celebrated preacher of the Gospel of Jesus Christ.

Dr. Gardner C. Taylor from Brooklyn, NY.:

"I do not know how to assess the contribution and consecration of L. V. Booth to our progressive Baptist work. I have found him thorough and thoughtful, filled with vision and vigor. Indeed, I count the friendship that has grown between us as one of the rich rewards of my tenure. He has put aside personal preference and opportunity more than once, as you know, in order to serve our convention. I pray and hope that the convention will remain aware of his spirit of devotion to our cause."

Appendix 58

Baptists and the Philadelphia-Dilemma
L. V. Booth
September 1960

The 80th Annual Session of the National Baptist Convention, Inc. closed with two pastors claiming to be president. One claimed the election by "voice vote," or acclamation. The other claimed it by a process of organized voting, or by tabulation. One claimed the office because he felt that the people did not have the right to express their choice, the other claimed it because the people had persuaded him to serve.

Once in Israel two women claimed the same child. The child could not express a choice of mothers. It was only a baby. It could not speak for itself. Solomon wisely suggested that the baby be cut in half and the real mother offered to give it up rather than have her baby mutilated. The real mother passed the test (I Kings 3:24-26). Early in our Baptist confusion, Dr. Taylor offered to step aside and give the Convention another opportunity to make a clear expression of her choice if Dr. Jackson would do likewise. He has not concurred in this very Christian and sound suggestion. It is more than a wise and peaceful suggestion which can save the dignity and purpose of our great Convention. It further protects the integrity of the people who compromise our Convention. It was also a fair, Christian and mature suggestion.

Whatever happened in Philadelphia cannot reflect more shame upon us than to persist in deepening the confusion. If we were emotional then, why not act like sober-minded Christians now. If we were unbrotherly then, why not redress ourselves to the questions and be brotherly now?

Why is President Jackson unwilling to submit to a voters' test? Why was he afraid in Philadelphia and thus threw his own Convention into bedlam by denying the people the right to vote? The true Philadelphia Story had to be understood only at this point. When President Jackson refused to allow the people to express themselves (both his supporters and opponents) he lost control of the Convention. On the other hand—why is President Gardner Taylor willing to step aside and accept the people's verdict and relieve the harmful tensions which weaken and divide?

Must we ask God who is President of our National Baptist Convention? Surely God has given us enough judgment to decide for ourselves. It seems that the President Taylor's attitude is fair, sane and sensible. If he is not president now it stands to reason that he deserves to be.

It is quite a paradox that at a time when Negroes are being evicted from their homes, whipped, and brutally beaten and some have even died for the right to vote—that a question of voting should be troubling the National Baptist Convention which should be in the vanguard of the struggle for freedom and civil rights. It is even more of a paradox that we should be blessed with some of the most distinguished members of the Freedom Fighters of our nation and still be struggling over the right to vote. How long shall we be kept waiting for righteous rule in our National Baptist Convention? Surely the nation can ill afford to have one of her largest Negro bodies conducting itself so poorly.

Appendix 59

Dr. L. Venchael Booth, President
Progressive National Baptist Convention
630 Glenwood Avenue
Cincinnati, Ohio 45229

Dear Dr. Booth:

May I extend my sincere congratulations for your having
been elected President of the Progressive National Baptist
Convention. Your devotion to the Convention and the inspired part you played in organizing the group certainly
deserves the recognition that has come your way.

I look forward to working with you during the following
year both at the Baptist convention level and through the
Baptist World Alliance.

I especially appreciate the privilege of being with you
for your closing session in Chicago. I wish I could have
attended more of the meeting, but previous commitments made
this impossible.

With every good wish for a highly successful tenure of office
and a prayer that God will continue to bless and use you, I am

                              Sincerely,

                              Owen Cooper

OC:br

Appendix 60

THE KING CENTER

March 19, 1997

The Reverend L.V. Booth
Olivet Baptist Church
6838 Montgomery Rd.
Cincinnati, Ohio 45236

Dear Reverend Booth,

On behalf of the King family and the King Center family, please accept our warmest greetings and congratulations to you on this joyous celebration of your 60 years as a Christian minister.

We commend you for your dedicated service to your congregation at Olivet Baptist Church. Yet, your ministry has long been far larger than any single church. As a friend and devoted supporter of Martin Luther King, Jr. and as an energetic civil rights and religious leader in your own right, you have been in the forefront of the struggle for interracial justice, progress and reconciliation in our nation.

We deeply appreciate your friendship and your unflagging loyalty to the King Center and the King family, which has been a source of comfort and inspiration to us throughout the years. You have given generously to our efforts to carry forward Dr. King's unfinished work as an active member of our Board, and as a friend, advisor and confidant.

We have been profoundly inspired by your abiding faith and commitment to nonviolence and the teachings of Jesus Christ. With gratitude, respect and a deep appreciation for your contributions, we proudly join with the many who have gathered together to honor you in this tribute in saying we salute you, we thank you for all that you have done and we love you.

Sincerely,

Coretta Scott King

Coretta Scott King   Dexter Scott King

THE MARTIN LUTHER KING, JR. CENTER FOR NONVIOLENT SOCIAL CHANGE, INC.
449 AUBURN AVE., NE ATLANTA, GA 30312-1590 (404) 526-8900 FAX: (404) 526-8901

Appendix 61

CENTRAL BAPTIST CHURCH

2842 WASHINGTON AVENUE

ST. LOUIS 3, MISSOURI

THOMAS ELLIOTT HUNTLEY, D.D., Pastor
4959 Cote Brilliante Avenue

WILLIAM N. CLAIBORNE, Director Christian Education
MRS. FRANKIE W. ANDERSON, Church Visitor

Novemvember 11,1961

MISS HAZEL L. HOPSON, Secretary
ELLIS S. OUTLAW, Church Clerk

Dr.L.V.Booth;
Zion Bapt.Church,
Cinnati,Ohio,

My dear Friend Booth:

I have planned to write you for some time but just never got around to
to it,hoing that you and all the family are well,as we redong nicely.

As regards your call meeting for next week,I am hopeful that you will
not get too out upon your adventure justyet,although you mayhve have many
sympathizers there for.I too,am in deep sympathy withthe adherents of
such movement but I do not think that the time is propitous as yet for
such a movement;it lo oks too much like it might be playing right into
the hands of the opposite group,bring to pass that they failed to get done
in Kansas City etc.I have just about finished writing my Second Epistle
To The National Baptist Convention U.S.A,Inc. I hoped to be able to get
a copy to you before your meeting but it would have rushed me too much.I
hope to get you one of the first copies as so as it isoff press.Dr.Mays
has seen a part of the script already.I want you to see itbefore any thing
too remote on your part;and then makeyou decision.Remember again,that your
movement may have the sympathy of several but I think think tht it will
meet the sentiment of the Baptist and Christian World at large,just now.
Since we have se n eye to eye upon so many issues thus far and still
do upon many,I wish you would go slow at this time until you readmy
Epistle. In the meantime since the meetingis call,just have agood"old
fashion prayer meeting"with the boys who may atend and give them some good
good wholesome advice as you can for his time.
    I hope you will accept this in the sirit of the wter.I am,
        THOMAS ELLIOTT HUNTLEY.

Appendix 62

CHURCH PHONE JA 2-6958   *"Her Influence Blesses th. Earth"*   RESIDENCE PHONE JA 2-5447

The Sixteenth Street Baptist Church
And Community Center

CORNER NINTH AVENUE AT ELM STREET
HUNTINGTON, WEST VIRGINIA

Dr. J. Carl Mitchell, Minister

July 4, 1962

Rev. L. Venchael Booth
630 Glenwood Avenue
Cincinnati 29, Ohio

Dear Rev. Booth:

It is a pleasure to submit to you statements concerning the three
meetings held in Cincinnati, Chicago and Richmond, Virginia.

Our first meeting was held in Cincinnati, at which time we raised
from all sources $721.26. At the close of the meeting, after expenses
were paid, we turned over $378.60 to the treasurer. Representation
from churches is not available at this moment. This total included
monies raised for the Foreign Mission Bureau. I think you have a
similar record of this meeting.

At our Chicago meeting, 37 churches were represented with the sum of
$727.00. This did not include public offerings.

At our Regional Meeting in Richmond, Virginia, 46 churches reported a
sum of $746.00. This in itself is a great improvement over the other
meetings in that this only represented, for the most part, churches
in Region No. 2 and a few other churches from other sections of the
country. Our total receipts for the Richmond meeting was $938.37.

I trust that this will help you in your pamphlet of progress for the
Progressive Convention. If this is not sufficient, I'll be glad to
list the churches represented.

Yours truly,

Rev. J. Carl Mitchell

Appendix 63

REFLECTIONS AND PROJECTIONS OF THE
MID-WEST REGION OF THE PROGRESSIVE
NATIONAL BAPTIST CONVENTION, INC.

The Mid-West Region has undertaken to do what the Progressive National Baptist Convention must find it possible to do in the very near future. This is especially necessary while many of the founders are still present and have papers that can provide verification and documentation. If we fail to do this it will make possible many inaccuracies and could undermine our credibility. Already there are publications which have reported our origin inaccurately. We need to make our history as accurate as possible. Every organization owes it to her followers to acquaint them thoroughly with her origin, purpose, and thrust. It is with great reluctance that this task is being undertaken because anything said by this writer could be felt to be biased. Despite this, what must be done, must be done.

The reader will understand if this foreword is offered in a larger context than our region, because this is a real opportunity to present some of the amazing developments of our young Convention. You will also understand if the writer is not concise because he has lived through so much of these eventful years. For the same reason, you will forgive the writer if he tells his story in a frank and personal way.

The Progressive National Baptist Convention is not an accident of history. It is totally wrapped up in God's purpose. It was not born in me, nor with me. I was called out, chosen and commissioned to do what needed to be done at that particular time in history. It is for this reason I have nothing to boast about, or glory in, save in the grace of God who not only works wonders, but does the impossible. The Progressive Convention is not a one man creation. There is no way one man so weak, so vulnerable, so full of inconsistencies, could do such a noble work as to build a Convention. So, whatever has happened in the Progressive National Baptist Convention was not of man's doing, but was man plus God with man as the instrument.

The Apostle Paul explains what I am trying to say:

> *But God hath chosen the foolish things of the world to confound the wise; and God hath chosen the weak things of the world to confound the things which are mighty. And the base things of the world and things which are despised hath God chosen, yea, and the things that are: That no flesh should glory in his presence.*

> *I Cor. 1:27-29.*

The Progressive Convention grew out of a desire for unity. The Power Struggle in the Incorporated Convention was not only great, but bitter. So after many years of attending Conventions which for me began in Dallas, Texas in 1944, and continued through to

Appendix 63, cont'd

Kansas City in 1961, it became a clear conviction to me that God
had something better for his people to do. So, in 1957, in
Louisville, Kentucky, I believe, that a light broke from heaven in my
heart. It was there I offered the suggestion that if we wanted a convention that honored "tenure," we would have to organize one. My
voice was so small that it was not even heard, nor was it heard in
meetings following. It was following Philadelphia and Kansas City that
it dawned on me that God had called me to offer my life as a living
sacrifice to lift the Baptist Cause. My conviction became so strong that
it never wavered from then until now.

It was my great privilege for twelve years or more to serve the
Convention in some area of leadership. During that period it was my
privilege to serve twice as a First Vice President, three years as a part-
time Executive Secretary and three years as President. From this great
Convention, I also served as a Vice President of the Baptist World Alliance.

In the period mentioned above our Mid-West Region either supported or
led in the following developments:

* A convention structure was created
* Regional Conventions were organized
* A Publishing Board was selected
* Our first Convention Minutes were compiled
* Our Convention Song was composed
* We joined the National Council of Churches
* We began a working relationship with the American and
  Southern Baptist Conventions
* We began supporting Nannie H. Burroughs School
* Led a mission to Haiti
* Established Martin Luther King, Jr. Civil Rights Night
* Established Martin Luther King, Jr. Sunday
* Advocated preservation of Martin Luther King, Jr.'s
  Birthplace
* Established the "Martin Luther King, Jr. Civil Rights Award"
* Initiated support of Morehouse College School of Religion
* Launched the Fund of Renewal
* Edited and Created the Progressive Baptist Hymnal
* Led our Convention to meet in Hotels
* Created the Voluntary Monthly Support Plan
* Developed a Convention organ, the *Baptist Progress*
* Negotiated a Retirement Fund for Clergy and
  Christian Workers
* Established a Convention Headquarters in Washington, D. C.
* Negotiated support for a full-time Home Mission Secretary
* Entered into fellowship with the Baptist World Alliance

Appendix 63, cont'd

As I recall the progress of our Convention and its many initiatives, it gives great pause for thanksgiving. I was there, but these were the creations of all the people. They represent the will, unity and visions of a great people . . . . . the people comprising our Progressive Family. My recalling these developments are not intended to glorify myself or any other person. They are reflected upon to glorify God. Indeed, they are the wondrous works of God. The story could have been so very different. We should all proudly declare:

> *"The Lord hath done great things for us;*
> *whereof we are glad."*   *Psalm 126:3*

Our Progressive Family is comprised of great men and women who are strongly dedicated. They come from small churches as well as large ones. They are spirit-filled as well as educated. They are devout as well as determined. They are love-inspired as well as aggressive. They are cause-centered as well as Christ-centered.

All who have led our Convention have come on the scene at the time they were most needed. Each has made an important and unique contribution. Each has added to the growth and dynamics of this God-guided movement. We must face the future with humility, sincerity. and fidelity.

Our Mid-West Region must continue to grow in fellowship, faith and love.

L. Venchael Booth
Founder and Former President

Progressive National Baptist Convention, Inc.

Appendix 64

National Prayer "Minute"
Suggested to All Baptists in the U. S. A.
On September 3, 1961

The member Churches of the National Baptist Convention, Inc. are asked to spend "One Minute" in prayer for the unity of our Convention.

Each pastor is asked to lead his congregation in a minute of prayer on Sunday, September 3, 1961 during the Morning Worship hour at a time when most of the members are present for the largest participation possible.

The following prayer is suggested that it might be reproduced in the bulletins of churches who will participate:

> O God our Heavenly Father, whose Son Jesus Christ is our Lord and Saviour, hear us we pray: Thou who hast led us to believe in the doctrine of One Lord, One Faith and One Baptism; lead us now to believe in a spirit of one-ness in our great National Convention. Help us to surrender pride, selfishness and ambition until we find unity in Thee. In Jesus' name we pray. Amen.

The National Prayer Minute is suggested by: L. Venchael Booth, Editor of the *Nation's Prayer Call*, published at: 630 Glenwood Avenue, Cincinnati 29, Ohio.

Appendix 65

*Scene at the Organization of Progressive National Baptist
Convention at Zion, November 14-15, 1961.*
*Left to right: Rev. L. V. Booth, First Vice President, Progressive
National Baptist Convention; President Chambers, right, shaking
hands with Rev. W. H. Benford.*

February 4, 1975

Dr. L. Venchael Booth
Zion Baptist Church
630 Glenwood Avenue
Cincinnati, Ohio 45229

Dear Dr. Booth:

Thanks for your kind letter of November 8th.

I agree with you that all of us ought to try and take some time to put down on paper some of the ideas that come to us through study, meditation, inspiration, and revelation. But all of us are the victims of a kind of busy-ness which must be dismissed if we can ever embrace the moments of creative production. As I see it, the writing is a part of our total responsibility.

I am always glad to hear from you. My family joins me in love to you and family.

Yours truly,

J. H. Jackson

nm

Bibliography

Books

Baldwin, Lewis V. *There Is a Balm in Gilead*. Minneapolis: Fortress Press, 1991.

Booth, L. Venchael. "Baptists and the Philadelphia Dilemma," *The Progressive Story: New Baptist Roots*, William D. Booth. St. Paul, Minnesota: Baum Press, 1981.

Booth, L. Venchael. "A High Call to Greatness," *The Progressive Story: New Baptist Roots*, William D. Booth. St. Paul, Minnesota: Baum Press, 1981.

Booth, L. Venchael, "Will Baptists Vote Against Integration?" *The Progressive Story: New Baptist Roots*, William D. Booth. St Paul, Minnesota: Baum Press, 1981.

Booth, L. Venchael, "21 Reasons Why Every Freedom Loving Baptist Should Vote for Retention of Tenure in our Constitution," *The Progressive Story: New Baptist Roots*, William D. Booth. St. Paul, Minnesota: Baum Press, 1981.

Booth, William D. *The Progressive Story: New Baptist Roots*. St. Paul, Minnesota: Baum Press, 1980.

Brackney, William H. *Historical Dictionary of the Baptists*. Lanham, Maryland: 1999.

Branch, Taylor *Pillar and Fire: America in the King Years 1963-65*. New York: Simon and Schuster, 1998.

Bruce, M. C. "National Baptist," Dictionary of Baptists in American, ed. by Bill J. Leonard. Downers Grove, IL: InterVarsity Press, 1994.

Fairclough, Adam. *Martin Luther King, Jr.* Athens, Georgia: The University of Georgia Press, 1995.

Fitts, Leroy. *A History of Black Baptists*. Nashville, Tennessee: Broadman Press, 1985.

Fitts, Leroy. "Progressive National Baptist Convention of America," *Encyclopedia of African American Religions*. ed. by Larry G. Murphy, J. Gordon Melton, and Gary L. Ward. New York: Garland Publishing, Inc., 1993.

Freeman, Edward A. "Negro Conventions (U.S.A.)," *Baptist Relations with Other Christians.* ed. James Leo Garrett. Valley Forge, Pennsylvania: Judson Press, 1974.

Garrow, David J. *Bearing the Cross: Martin Luther King, Jr., and the Southern Christian Leadership Conference.* New York: William Morrow and Company, Inc., 1986.

Gaver, Jessyca Russell. *"You Shall Know The Truth": The Baptist Story.* New York: Lancer Books, 1973.

Jackson, J. H. *A Story of Christian Activism: The History of the National Baptist Convention, U. S.A., Inc.* Nashville: Townsend Press, 1980.

Jackson, L. K. "Seven Reasons Why Young, Trained, Christian Ministers Should Resist The Efforts of The 'Lift-Tricksters'," *The Progressive Story: New Baptist Roots*, William D. Booth. St. Paul, MN: Baum Press, 1981.

Jordan, Anne Devereaux. and Stifle, J. M. *The Baptists.* New York: Hippocrene Books, 1990.

Kilgore, Jr., Thomas with Kilgore, Jini. *A Servant's Journey: The Life and Work of Thomas Kilgore.* Valley Forge, Pennsylvania: Judson Press, 1998.

Leonard, Bill J. Leonard, ed. *Dictionary of Baptists in America.* Downers Grove, Illinois: InterVarsity Press, 1994.

Lincoln, C. Eric and Mamiya, Lawrence H. "The Black Baptists: The First Black Churches in America," *Baptists in the Balance: The Tension between Freedom and Responsibility.* ed. by Everette C. Goodwin. Valley Forge, Pennsylvania: Judson Press, 1997.

Lincoln, C. Eric Lincoln and Mamiya, Lawrence H. *The Black Church in the African American Experience.* Durham & London: Duke University Press, 1990.

Lippy, Charles H. and Williams, Peter W. Williams, eds. *Encyclopedia of the American Religious Experience: Studies of Traditions and Movement.* Vol.1. New York: Charles Scribner's Sons, 1988.

Mead, Frank S. and Hill, Samuel S. *Handbook of Denominations in the United States.* rev. Nashville: Abingdon Press, 1995.

Miller, William Robert. *Martin Luther King, Jr.: His life, Martyrdom and Meaning for the World.* New New York: Weybright and Talley, 1968.

Melton, J. Gordon. *The Encyclopedia of American Religions.* 3rd ed. Detroit, Michigan: Gale Research Inc., 1989.

Newsome, Clarence G., ed. *Directory of African American Religious Bodies: A Compendium by The Howard University School of Divinity.* 2nd ed. Washington, DC: Howard University Press, 1995.

Peterson, Eugene. *The Old Testament Wisdom Book in Contemporary English.* Colorado Springs, Col.: NavPress Publishing Group, 1996.

Reid, Daniel G., ed. *Dictionary of Christianity in America*. Downers Grove, Illinois: InterVarsity Press, 1990.

Taylor, Gardner C. *The Words of Gardner Taylor*. compiled by Edward L. Taylor. Vol. 1. Valley Forge, Pennsylvania: Judson Press, 1999.

Wardin, Albert W., ed. *Baptists Around The World: A Comprehensive Handbook*. Nashville: Broadman & Holman Publishers, 1995.

Journals/Proceedings/Pamphlets

Adams, Charles G. "Progressive National Baptist Convention, Inc.: A People of Faith and Action," PNBC publication, updated 1997.

Booth, William D. "Dr. L. Venchael Booth and the Origin of the Progressive National Baptist Convention, Inc." *American Baptist Quarterly*. XX (March, 2001): 1.

Gilbreath, Edward. "Redeeming Fire." *Christianity Today* 6 December 1999, pp. 39-47.

Gilbreath, Edward. "The Pulpit King: The Passion and Eloquence of Gardner Taylor, a Legend among Preachers." *Christianity Today*. 11 December 1995, pp. 26-28.

Mitchell, J. Carl. "The Origin of the Progressive National Baptist Convention." *Minutes of the First Annual Session of the Progressive National Baptist Convention, Inc., 4-9 September 1962*, p. 5.

Ohlmann, Eric H. "American Baptist Churches," *American Baptist Quarterly*. XIX (September 2000), pp. 197-207.

Pitts, Tyrone S. "Annual Report of the General Secretary," *Minutes of the 39th Annual Session of the Progressive National Baptist Convention, Inc.* 7-11 August, p. 3.

Powell, W. H. R. "Towards The Creation of a New Convention Being a Declaration of the Organization, Principles and Aims of the Progressive Convention of America, Incorporated." *Minutes of the First Annual Session of the PNBC, Inc., 4-9 September 1961*, pp. 29-31.

Roberts, J. Deotis. "Ecumenical Concerns Among National Baptists." *Journal of Ecumenical Studies* (Spring 1980).

Smith, Wallace Charles. "Progressive National Baptist Convention: The Roots of the Black Church." *American Baptist Quarterly*. XIX (September 2000), pp. 249-255.

Taylor, Gardner C. "Acting President Taylor's First Annual Address." *Minutes of the Fifth Annual Session of the Progressive National Baptist Convention, Inc.* 6-11 September 1966, p. 67.

Taylor, Gardner C. "The President's Message," *Minutes of the Sixth Annual Session of the Progressive National Baptist Convention, Inc.* 1967, p. 42.

Wheeler, Edward. "Beyond One Man: A General Survey of Black Baptist History." *Review and Expositor* LXXX, (Summer, 1973): 3.

Newspaper/Magazine Articles

Anderson, Trezzvant W. "King Won't Fight Firing by Jackson." *The Pittsburgh Courier*, 23 September 1961, p. 2, Sec. 2.

Bacoats, J. A. "Plea To Avert Split In Nat'l Baptist Convention." *Journal and Guide*, 14 October 1961, p. 9.

Hancock, Gordon B. Behind the Headlines: "Baptists Produce First Rate College Presidents." *Journal and Guide*. 14 October 1961, pp. 8, 9.

Graham, Alfredo. "Election Satisfies Taylor." *The Pittsburgh Courier*, 23 September 1961.

Oestreicher, David J. "Tragedy Stuns U. S. Baptists." *Journal and Guide*, 9 September 1961, pp. 1, 2.

Robinson, Rev. Marvin. "Explains Why Many Baptists Ignored Newly Formed Group." *Cleveland Call And Post*, 25 November 1961.

"Another State Joins." *The Afro-American*, 2 March 1963, p. 19.

"Chicagoan Elected At Baptist Parley." *New York Times*, 9 September 1961.

"Convention Victory for Jackson and Call to Close Ranks." *The Kansas City Star*, 8 September 1961.

"In Business." *The New York Courier*, 16 March 1963, p. 2.

"King Asks Retraction." *The Afro-American*, 23 September 1961, p. 7.

"Minister Dies After Floor Row: Dr. Taylor Loses In Bid For Presidency Of National Body." *Journal and Guide*, 16 September 1961, pp. 1, 2.

"New Split Threatens Baptists; Jackson Denies Rapping Dr. King." *JET*, 28 September 1961, p. 18.

Letters

(In the order they appear in the manuscript.)

Letter from J. Carl Mitchell to L. V. Booth July 4, 1962.

Letter from Cornell E. Talley, (Mimeographed) to L. V. Booth, October 23, 1959.

Letter from M. L. King, Sr., to L. V. Booth, August 9, 1960.

Letter from Gardner C. Taylor to L. V. Booth, October 10, 1960.

Letter from Gardner C. Taylor to L. V. Booth, December 12, 1960.

Letter from Gardner C. Taylor to L. V. Booth, August 9, 1961.

Letter from J. H. Jackson to L. V. Booth, February 4, 1975.

Letter from L. V. Booth to Theodore F. Adams, October 19, 1957.

Letter from L. V. Booth to Benjamin E. Mays, October 19, 1957.

Letter from L. V. Booth to W. H. Jernagin, October 19, 1957.

Letter from L. V. Booth to Mordecai Y. Johnson, October 19, 1957.

Letter from Benjamin E. Mays to L. V. Booth, October 21, 1957.

Letter from W. H. Jernagin to L. V. Booth, October 24, 1957.

Letter from Theodore F. Adams to L. V. Booth, October 30, 1957.

Letter from Mordecai Y. Johnson to L. V. Booth, November 7, 1957.

Letter from L. V. Booth to Gardner C. Taylor, November 21, 1961.

Letter from Uvee Mdodana-Arbouin to L. V. Booth, November 21, 1961.

Letter from Marvin T. Robinson to L. V. Booth, October 11, 1961.

Letter from A. Ross Brent to L. V. Booth, November 3, 1961.

Letter from Gardner C. Taylor to L. V. Booth, July 8, 1963.

Letter from Gardner C. Taylor to L. V. Booth, September 9, 1963.

Letter from Gardner C. Taylor to L. V. Booth, September 13, 1963

Letter from Gardner C. Taylor to L. V. Booth, December 27, 1963.

Letter from Gardner C. Taylor to L. V. Booth, January 6, 1964.

Letter from Gardner C. Taylor to L. V. Booth, April 8, 1964.

Letter from Earl L. Harrison to L. V. Booth, September 19, 1970

Letter from Earl L. Harrison to L. V. Booth, August 12, 1972

Letter from Owen Cooper to L. V. Booth September 12, 1972.

Letter from C. T. Murray to L. V. Booth, October 23, 1961.

Letter from Coretta Scott King to L. V. Booth, April 26, 2001.

Letter from Coretta Scott King to L. V. Booth, March 19, 1997.

Letter from Coretta Scott King to L. V. Booth, October 5, 1976.

Letter from J. C. Austin to L. V. Booth, October 10, 1961.

Letter to L. V. Booth from E. L. Harrison, September 19, 1961.

Letter to L. V. Booth from Rev. Herbert H. Eaton, September 18, 1961.

Letter to L. V. Booth from Dr. D. E. King, October 12, 1961.

Letter to L. V. Booth from Dr. Thomas Kilgore, October 30, 1961.

Letter from L. K. Jackson to L. V. Booth, September 15, 1961.

Letter from Thomas E. Huntley to L. V. Booth, November 11, 1961.

Letter from J. Pius Barbour to L. V. Booth, September 15, 1961.

Letter from Benjamin E. Mays to L. V. Booth, September 21, 1961.

Letter from J. C. Austin to L. V. Booth, September 26, 1961.

Letter from C. C. Adams to L. V. Booth, September 28, 1961.

Letter from C. C. Adams to L. V. Booth, October 11, 1961.

Telegram from C. C. Adams to L. V. Booth, October 20, 1961.

Letter from W. J. Davis to L. V. Booth, October 18, 1961.

Minutes

National Baptist Convention, USA, Inc. *Minutes of the 75th Annual Session.* Memphis, Tennessee., 1955, pp. 11, 63.

Progressive National Baptist Convention, Inc. *Minutes of the First Annual Session.* Philadelphia, Pennsylvania, 1962, p. 39.

Progressive National Baptist Convention, Inc. *Minutes of the Second Annual Session.* Detroit, Michigan, 1963, p. 61.

Progressive National Baptist Convention, Inc. *Minutes of the Third Annual Session.* Atlanta, Georgia, 1964, pp. 71-80.

Progressive National Baptist Convention, Inc. *Minutes of the Fourth Annual Session.* Los Angeles, California, 1965, pp. 75-77, 90-93.

Progressive National Baptist Convention, Inc. Minutes of the Fifth Annual Session. Memphis, Tennessee, 1966, 71-72.

Progressive National Baptist Convention, Inc. *Minutes of the Sixth Annual Session.* Cincinnati, Ohio, 1967, pp. 31, 45-46.

Progressive National Baptist Convention, Inc. *Minutes of the Seventh Annual Session.* Washington, D.C. And Vicinity, 1968, pp.43-44.

Progressive National Baptist Convention, Inc. *Minutes of the Eleventh Annual Session.* Chicago, Illinois, 1972, pp. 65-74.

Progressive National Baptist Convention, Inc. *Minutes of the Twelfth Annual Session.* Jackson, Mississippi, 1973, pp. 73-81.

Progressive National Baptist Convention, Inc. *Minutes of the Thirteenth Annual Session.* Cleveland, Ohio, 1974, pp.85-94.

Progressive National Baptist Convention, Inc. *Minutes of the 39th Annual Session.* Louisville, Kentucky [Annual Report of the General Secretary], p. 3.

Interviews/Tapes

Barbour, J. Pius. Pastor of the Calvary Baptist Church, Chester, Pennsylvania. Interview, 11 April 1969.

King, Jr., Martin Luther, President of SCLC, Taped November 29, 1964, Zion Baptist Church's 122nd Anniversary, Cincinnati, Ohio.

Index

* * *

The Reverend Dr. Lavaughn Venchael Booth

The Rev. Dr. Lavaughn Venchael Booth

Dr. Booth was born in Covington County, Mississippi, where he was restricted and circumscribed, but never defeated. His deep abiding faith in God, lead him to fulfill his dream. He emerged and made his way to Alcorn College to earn an A.B. degree, from Howard University he earned a B.D. degree, from the University of Chicago he earned an M.A. degree. He received honorary Doctorates from Wilberforce University, Central State University, the University of Cincinnati, Morehouse College, and Temple Bible College.

Dr. Booth's ministry has spanned over sixty years, His spirit of excellence has earned him numerous honors, including Citizen of the Day Citation, Cincinnati Man of the Year, Distinguished Service Award, Certificate of Merit from the NAACP, and he was featured as one of the 100 most influential Black Men in *Ebony* Magazine.

Because of his pioneering spirit he has scaled many heights. He was the founder of the Progressive National Baptist Convention and Vice President of the Baptist World Alliance. He devoted 21 years as a member of the Board of Trustees of the University of Cincinnati. He pastored Zion Baptist Church for 31 years. While there he built a new Church, a Nursing Home and 339 Units of Low Income Housing. He founded Olivet Baptist Church and served as pastor for 13 years.

Dr. L. V. Booth is a Pastor, Builder, Author, Poet, and Community Leader. He has fellowshipped with dignitaries all over the nation and the world, but still remains humble enough to reach out and champion the cause of the poor, the hurting, the lonely and the brokenhearted. He is a dynamic man, called of God, who has touched many lives. He claims no honor for himself; but sincerely believes:

To God Be the Glory!